M000310240

THE GARDEN OF
THE SOUL

THE GARDEN OF THE SOUL

A MANUAL
OF SPIRITUAL EXERCISES
AND INSTRUCTIONS

for Christians who, living
in the world, aspire
to devotion

BY
BISHOP
CHALLONER

Whereto are added
the Public and private Devotions
now in most frequent use.

THE NEWMAN PRESS
WESTMINSTER, MARYLAND

Nihil obstat.

GEORGIUS CAN. SMITH, S. TH. D., PH. D.,

Censor Deputatus

IMPRIMATUR

E. MORROGH BERNARD

Vic. Gen.

Westmonasterii, die 19 Februarii 1945

PRINTED IN BELGIUM

264.02.
C435q

4755

PUBLISHERS' NOTE

THE first edition of *The Garden of the Soul*, by Bishop Challoner, was published in 1740, and it was reprinted without alteration in 1741. Bishop Challoner was born in Sussex in 1691, the son of a wine cooper, and was educated (for he was received into the Catholic Church with his mother) at the College of English exiles of Douay. After twenty-six years there as student, minor professor, and finally director of studies, he returned in 1730, a priest and a D.D., to the England of the Penal Laws. By personal service and by his writings he encouraged and fortified the secret and saddened but eager Catholicity of his countrymen. After eleven years he was made coadjutor, and after another seventeen succeeded to the charge of the London Vicariate.

In the midst of harassings that often quickened into downright persecution, he carried on his work of organisation, of spiritual ministration, of care for the poor, and of writing. His saintly life came to its end in 1781, six months after the furious Gordon Riots, during which, an aged and infirm man, he had seen the flames of the burning Catholic churches and heard the roar of the mob that was seeking after him.

The present edition of Challoner's justly popular devotional work reproduces the text of the 1741 impression almost in its entirety. In a few instances the spelling and punctuation have been altered to conform with modern usage. The book has also been amplified by the inclusion of those Church services at which the faithful commonly assist.

CONTENTS

Contents

Contents

Contents

THE
Garden of the Soul

CHRISTIAN DOCTRINE

or, a

Summary of Christian Faith and
Morality

SECTION I
WHAT EVERY CHRISTIAN MUST BELIEVE

1. EVERY Christian must believe that there is one God, and no more than one God : that this God is a pure Spirit, the Lord and maker of heaven and earth, who has neither beginning nor end, but is always the same ; is every where present, knows and sees all things, can do all things whatever he pleases, and is infinite in all perfections.

2. Every Christian is bound to believe, that in this *one God* there are *three several persons,* perfectly equal, and of the same substance : The *Father,* who proceeds from no one ; the *Son,* who is born of the Father before all ages ; and the *Holy Ghost,* who proceeds

eternally from the *Father* and the *Son*. And
that these three persons have all the same
age, the same power, the same wisdom, and
are all three one and the same Lord, one and
the same God.

3. We must all believe, that this God created
the *angels* to be with him for ever, and that
one part of them fell from God by sin, and
became *devils*. That God also created *Adam*
and *Eve*, the first parents of all mankind, and
placed them in the earthly *paradise ;* from
whence they were *justly* banished for the sin
they committed in eating of the *fruit* of the
forbidden tree : and that by this transgres-
sion of *Adam* we are all born in sin, and
must have been lost for ever, if God had not
sent us a *Saviour.*

4. We are bound to believe in this Saviour
of all mankind, *Jesus Christ*, the Son of God,
true God, and true man ; *perfect God* from
all eternity, equal to his Father in all things ;
and *perfect man*, from the time of his coming
down from heaven for us, having a body and
soul like us.

5. We must believe, that this *Jesus Christ*
our Saviour, who had long been foretold by
the prophets, was at God's appointed time
conceived in the womb of the Virgin *Mary*
by the power of the Holy Ghost, without
having any man for his father, and was born
of her, she still remaining a pure virgin.
That during the time of his mortal life,
he founded the Christian religion by his

heavenly doctrine and wonderful miracles, and then offered himself a sacrifice for the sins of the whole world, by dying upon a cross, to purchase mercy, grace and salvation for us. And that neither mercy, nor grace, nor salvation, either can, or ever could, since *Adam's* fall, be obtained any otherwise, than through this death and Passion of the Son of God.

6. We must believe, that Jesus Christ, after he had been dead and buried for part of three days, rose again on the third day from death to life, never to die any more; and that, for the space of forty days, he was pleased at different times to manifest himself to his disciples, and then ascended into heaven in their sight; where as man he continually intercedes for us. From thence he sent down the Holy Ghost upon his disciples, to abide with them for ever, as he had promised, and to guide them and their successors into all truth.

7. We must believe the *Catholic* or universal *Church* of Christ, of which he is the perpetual head, and his spirit the perpetual director ; which is founded upon a rock, and is ever victorious over all the powers of death and hell. This church is always *one*, by all its members professing one faith, in *one* communion, under *one* chief pastor succeeding St. *Peter*, to whom Christ committed his whole flock, St. *John* xxi. 15, 16, 17. This same church is always *holy*, by teaching a

holy doctrine, by inviting all to a *holy* life, and by the eminent *holiness* of many of her children. She is *Catholic* or universal, by subsisting in all ages, by teaching *all* nations, and maintaining *all* truths ; she is *apostolical*, by deriving her *doctrine*, her *communion*, her *orders*, and her *mission*, by an uninterrupted succession, from the *apostles* of Christ.

8. With this *Catholic* Church the scriptures both of the Old and New Testament were deposited by the apostles : she is, in her pastors, the guardian and interpreter of them, and the judge of all controversies relating to them. These scriptures, thus interpreted, together with the traditions of the apostles, are to be received and admitted by all Christians for the rule of their faith and practice.

9. We must believe that Jesus Christ has instituted in his church seven sacraments, or mysterious *signs* and instrumental *causes* of divine *grace* in our souls. *Baptism*, by way of a *new birth*, by which we are made children of God, and washed from sin. *Confirmation*, by which we receive the *Holy Ghost* by the imposition of the hands of the successors of the apostles, *Acts* viii. The *Blessed Eucharist*, which feeds and nourishes our souls with *the body and blood* of Christ, really present under the forms of bread and wine, or under either of them. *Penance*, by which penitent sinners are *absolved* from their sins, by virtue of the commission given by Christ to his ministers,

St. *John* xx and St. *Matt.* xviii. *Extreme Unction*, which wipes away the relics of sin, and arms the soul with the grace of God in the time of *sickness*, St. *James* v. *Holy Orders*, by which the ministers of God are *consecrated*. And *Matrimony*, which, as a sacred sign of the indissoluble union of Christ and his church, unites the married couple in a holy band, and imparts a grace to them suitable to that state, *Eph.* v.

10. We must believe, that *Jesus Christ* has also instituted the great *Eucharistic Sacrifice* of his body and blood, in remembrance of his death and Passion. In this sacrifice he is mystically immolated every day upon our altars, being himself both priest and victim. This sacrifice is the principal worship of the new law, in which, and by which, we unite ourselves to Jesus Christ, and with him, and through him, we *adore* God in spirit and truth, give him *thanks* for all his blessings, obtain his *grace* for ourselves and the whole world, and *pardon* for all our sins, and those of the living and the dead.

11. We must believe that there is, in the Catholic or universal Church of God, a *communion of saints*, by means of which we communicate with all *holy ones*, and in all *holy things*. We communicate with the saints in heaven, as our fellow-members under the same head Christ Jesus ; we give thanks to God for his gifts to them, and we beg a share in their prayers. We communicate with all

the saints upon earth, in the same sacraments and sacrifice, and in a holy union of faith and charity. And we communicate with the faithful (who have departed this life in a more imperfect state, and who, by the law of God's justice, are for a while in a place of suffering) by offering prayers and alms and sacrifice to God for them.

12. We must believe also the necessity of divine *grace*, without which we cannot make so much as one step towards heaven. And that all our good, and all our merits, are the gifts of God. That Christ died for all men. That God is not the author of sin ; and that his grace does not take away our free-will.

13. We must believe that Jesus Christ will come from heaven at the last day to judge us all. That all the dead, both good and bad, shall arise from their graves at the sound of the last trumpet, and shall be judged by him according to their works. That the good shall go to heaven with him, body and soul, to be happy for all eternity, in the enjoyment of the sovereign good; and that the wicked shall be condemned, both body and soul, to the torments of hell, which are most grievous and everlasting.

SECTION II

WHAT EVERY CHRISTIAN MUST DO

to obtain life everlasting

If thou wilt enter into life, keep the commandments.—St. Matt. xix.

1. EVERY Christian, in order to obtain life everlasting, must *worship* God as his first beginning and last end. This *worship* is to be performed first by *faith*, which makes both the understanding and the will humbly adore and embrace all those truths which God has taught, however obscure and incomprehensible they may be to our weakness. *Secondly*, by *hope*, which honours the infinite power, goodness, and mercy of God, and the truth of his promises, and upon these grounds raises the soul to an assured expectation of mercy, grace and salvation, through the merits of Jesus Christ. *Thirdly*, by *charity*, which teaches us to love God with our whole hearts, for his own sake, and our neighbours as ourselves, for God's sake. *Fourthly*, by the virtue of *religion*, the chief acts of which are *adoration*, *praise*, *thanksgiving*, *oblation* of ourselves to God, *sacrifice* and *prayer*, which ought to be the daily employments of a Christian soul.

2. We must fly all idolatry, all false religion and superstition, under which name are comprehended all manner of *divinations*, or pretensions to fortune-telling; all witch-craft, charms, spells, observations of *omens*, *dreams*, &c. All these things are heathenish, and contrary to the worship of the true and living God, and to that dependence a Christian soul ought to have on him.

3. We must reverence the name of God and his truth, by a religious observance of all lawful oaths and vows, and by carefully avoiding all false, rash, unjust or blasphemous oaths and curses.

4. We must dedicate some notable part of our time to his divine service; and more especially consecrate to him those days that he has ordered to be sanctified, or kept holy.

5. Under God we must love, reverence, and obey our parents, and other lawful superiors, spiritual and temporal, and observe the laws of the church and state. As also we must have a due care of our children, and of others that are under our charge, both as to their soul and body.

6. We must abstain from all injuries to our neighbour's person, by murder, or any other violence; and from all hatred, envy, and desire for revenge. As also from spiritual murder, which is committed by drawing him into sin, by words, actions, or ill example.

7. We must abstain from adultery, and from all uncleanness of thoughts, words, and actions.

8. We must not steal, cheat, or any other way wrong our neighbour in his goods and possessions ; we must give every one his own, pay our debts, and make restitution for all unjust damages which we have caused.

9. We must not wrong our neighbour in his character or good nature, by detraction or rash judgment ; or in his honour, by reproaches and affronts ; or rob him of the peace of his mind, by scoffs and contempt ; or of his friends, by carrying stories backwards and forwards. In all which cases, whosoever wrongs his neighbour, is obliged to make restitution or satisfaction.

10. As we are commanded to abstain from all deeds of lust and injustice, so we are also strictly obliged to restrain all desires in these kinds, and to resist the irregular motions of concupiscence. So far the ten commandments, which are a short abridgment of the whole eternal and natural law, which admits of no dispensation.

SECTION III

GOSPEL LESSONS
to be pondered by every Christian soul

1. ENTER ye by the narrow gate, for wide is the gate, and broad is the way, that leads to destruction, and many there are that go in thereat : how narrow is the gate and straight the way that leadeth to life, and few there are that find it. *Matt.* vii. 13, 14.

2. Many are called but few are chosen. *Matt.* xx. 16, xxii. 14.

3. Not everyone that saith to me, Lord, Lord, shall enter into the kingdom of heaven. But he that doth the will of my Father that is in heaven. *Matt.* vii. 21.

4. What doth it profit a man, if he gain the whole world, and lose his own soul ? Or what shall a man give in exchange for his soul ? *Matt.* xvi. 26.

5. One thing is necessary. *Luke* x. 42.

6. He that loveth father and mother more than me, is not worthy of me ; and he that loveth son or daughter more than me, is not worthy of me. And he that taketh not his cross, and followeth me, is not worthy of me. *Matt.* x. 37, 38.

7. He that shall deny me before men, I will also deny him before my Father that is in heaven. *Matt.* x. 33.

8. Whosoever shall be ashamed of me, and of my words, in this adulterous and sinful generation, of him also shall the Son of Man be ashamed, when he shall come in the glory of his Father with the holy angels. *Mark* viii. 38.

9. Fear not them that kill the body, but are not able to kill the soul ; but rather fear him that can destroy both soul and body in hell. *Matt.* x. 28.

10. He that loveth his life shall lose it, and he that hateth his life in this world, shall keep it unto life eternal. *John* xii. 25.

11. If any man will come after me, let him deny himself, and take up his cross, and follow me. *Matt.* xvi. 24.

12. Every one of you that doth not renounce all that he possesseth, cannot be my disciple. *Luke* xiv. 33.

13. If any man come to me, and hate not his father and mother, and wife and children, and brethren and sisters, yea, and his own life also, he cannot be my disciple. And whosoever doth not bear his cross, and come after me, cannot be my disciple. *Luke* xiv. 26, 27.

14. The friendship of this world is enmity with God. Whosoever therefore will be a friend of this world, is made the enemy of God. *James* iv. 4.

15. Love not the world, nor the things that are in the world. If any man love the world, the love of the Father is not in him.

For all that is in the world, is the lust of the flesh, and the lust of the eyes, and the pride of life, which is not of the Father, but is of the world. And the world passeth away, and the lust thereof; but he that doth the will of God abideth for ever. 1 *John* ii. 15, 16, 17.

16. Except you be converted, and become as little children, you shall not enter into the kingdom of heaven. *Matt.* xviii. 4.

17 Blessed are the poor in spirit, for theirs is the kingdom of heaven. Blessed are the meek, for they shall possess the land. Blessed are they that mourn, for they shall be comforted. *Matt.* v. 3, 4, 5.

18. Woe to you that are rich, because you have your consolation.—Woe to you that laugh now, for you shall mourn and weep. *Luke* vi. 24, 25.

19. Come to me all you that labour, and are heavy laden, and I will refresh you. Take my yoke upon you, and learn of me, because I am meek and humble of heart, and you shall find rest to your souls. For my yoke is sweet, and my burthen light. *Matt.* xi. 28, 29, 30.

20. Whosoever exalteth himself shall be humbled; and he that humbleth himself, shall be exalted. *Matt.* xxiii. 12.

21. God resisteth the proud, and to the humble he giveth grace. *Peter* v. 5.

22. Take heed that you do not your justice before men, that you may be seen by them ;

otherwise you shall have no reward of your Father who is in heaven. *Matt. vi.* 1.

23. No man can serve two masters. —You cannot serve God and mammon. *Matt. vi.* 24.

24. Lay not up for yourselves treasures upon earth, where moth and rust doth corrupt, and where thieves break through and steal. But lay up for yourselves treasures in heaven, etc. *Matt. vi.* 19, 20.

25. Seek first the kingdom of God, and his justice, and all these things shall be added unto you. *Matt. vi.* 33.

26. If you live according to the flesh, you shall die; but if by the spirit you mortify the deeds of the flesh, you shall live. *Rom. viii.* 13.

27. Neither fornicators, nor idolators, nor adulterers, nor effeminate, nor abusers of themselves with mankind; nor thieves, nor covetous, nor drunkards, nor revilers, nor extortioners, shall inherit the kingdom of God. 1 *Cor. vi.* 9, 10.

28. If any man defile the temple of God, him shall God destroy; for the temple of God is holy, which *temple* you are. 1 *Cor. iii.* 17.

29. Whosoever looketh on a woman to lust after her, hath committed adultery with her already in his heart. *Matt. vi.* 28.

30. If thy right eye be a scandal [a stumbling-block] to thee, pluck it out, and cast it from thee.—And if thy right-hand be a

scandal to thee, cut it off, and cast it from thee ; for it is better for thee that one of thy members should perish, than that thy whole body should go to hell. *Matt.* v. 29, 30.

31. If you forgive not men their trespasses ; neither will your Father forgive your trespasses. *Matt.* vi. 15.

32. Love your enemies ; do good to them that hate you, and pray for them that persecute you and calumniate you ; that you may be children of your Father that is in heaven. *Matt.* v. 44, 45.

33. A new commandment I give unto you, that you love one another, as I have loved you. *John* xiii. 34.

34. Though I speak with the tongues of men and of angels, and have not charity, I am become as sounding brass, or a tinkling cymbal : and though I have prophecy, and understand all mysteries, and all knowledge, and though I have all faith, so that I could remove mountains, and have not charity, I am nothing : and though I should bestow all my goods to feed the poor, and though I should give my body to be burned, and have not charity, it profiteth me nothing. 1 *Cor.* xiii. 1, 2, 3.

35. Render to no man evil for evil. If it be possible, as much as lieth in you, have peace with all men. Not revenging yourselves, &c. Be not overcome by evil, but overcome evil with good. *Rom.* xii. 17, 18, 19, 21.

36. Let not the sun go down upon your anger. *Eph.* iv. 26.

37. Through many tribulations we must enter into the kingdom of heaven. *Acts* xiv. 21.

38. All that will live godlily in Christ Jesus, shall suffer persecution. 2 *Tim.* iii. 12.

39. In your patience you shall possess your souls. *Luke* xxi. 19.

40. Whatsoever you would that men should do to you, do you even so to them. *Matt.* vii. 12.

41. Take heed to yourselves, lest at any time your hearts be over-charged with surfeiting and drunkenness, and cares of this life, and so that day come upon you unawares. *Luke* xxi. 34.

42. Be you perfect, even as your heavenly Father is perfect. *Matt.* v. 48.

43. Ask, and it shall be given you; seek, and you shall find; knock, and it shall be opened unto you. *Matt.* vii. 7. Whatsoever you shall ask the Father in my name, he will give it you. *John* xvi. 23.

44. Let him that thinketh he standeth, take heed lest he fall. 1 *Cor.* x 12.

45. Watch; for you know not at what hour your Lord will come.—Be ready, for the Son of Man will come at the hour that you know not. *Matt.* xxiv. 44.

46. Watch and pray, that ye enter not into temptation. *Matt.* xxvi. 41

47. Whether ye eat or drink, or whatever

else you do, do all to the glory of God.
1 *Cor.* x. 31.

48. We brought nothing into this world, and 'tis certain we can carry nothing out. Having therefore food and raiment, let us be content therewith. But they that will be rich, fall into temptation, and the snare of the devil, and many useless and hurtful desires, which drown men in destruction and perdition. For the love of money is the root of all evil. 1 *Tim.* vi, 7, 8, 9, 10.

49. Every tree that bringeth not forth good fruit, shall be cut down, and cast into the fire. *Matt.* vii. 19.

50. Except you do penance, you shall all perish. *Luke* xiii. 3, 5.

51. He that shall persevere to the end, the same shall be saved. *Matt.* xxiv. 13.

52. Be faithful unto death, and I will give thee the crown of life. *Apoc.* ii 10.

53. It is a dreadful thing to fall into the hands of the living God. *Heb.* x. 31.

54. Behold I come quickly, and my reward is with me, to give every man according to his works. *Apoc.* xxii. 12.

MORNING DEVOTIONS

WE *must get up before the sun to bless thee (O God) and adore thee at the break of day.* Wisd. xvi. 28.

O God, my God, to thee I watch from the morning light. Ps. lxii. 2.

At your first waking in the morning make the sign of the cross, saying, *In the name of the Father, and of the Son, and of the Holy Ghost.* Amen. *Blessed be the holy and undivided Trinity, now and for ever.* Amen. Then adore God, and make an offering of your whole being to him for that day and for ever. Take great care not to let the devil run away with your first thoughts : for very much depends upon giving them to God, who is your first beginning and last end, and therefore expects from you the first fruits of the day. And as he has with an incomparable love watched over you all the night whilst you were asleep, it would be very ungrateful not to open the eyes of your soul, to look up towards him, and give yourself to him, as soon as you awake.

Take care also to rise early that you may gather the manna of heaven ; of which you will have little or no share, if you begin the day by indulging sloth and sensuality in bed, instead of employing that first and most precious time in conversation with God.

Whilst you are dressing and washing yourself, entertain some pious thoughts, and by devout aspirations beg of God to clothe your soul with heavenly virtues, and to wash you clean from all stains of sin. Then kneel down in your oratory, or by your bed-side : make the sign of the cross in memory of Christ crucified ; and place yourself in the presence of the Divine Majesty, by a lively faith that he sees and beholds you, and is in the very centre of your soul. Bow yourself down to adore him, beg pardon for your unworthiness and sins, and crave his grace, that you may behave yourself as you ought in his presence. Then say

The Lord's Prayer

OUR Father who art in heaven, hallowed be thy name : thy kingdom come : thy will be done, on earth as it is in heaven. Give us this day our daily bread : and forgive us our trespasses as we forgive them that trespass against us : and lead us not into temptation : but deliver us from evil. *Amen.*

The Hail Mary

HAIL *Mary*, full of grace, the Lord is with thee: blessed art thou among women, and blessed is the fruit of thy womb, JESUS. Holy *Mary*, Mother of God, pray

for us sinners, now and at the hour of our
death. Amen.

The Apostles' Creed

I BELIEVE in God the Father Almighty,
Creator of heaven and earth. And in
Jesus Christ his only Son our Lord : who
was conceived by the Holy Ghost, born of
the Virgin *Mary ;* suffered under *Pontius
Pilate*, was crucified, dead, and buried ; he
descended into hell, the third day he rose
again from the dead ; he ascended into
heaven, sitteth at the right hand of God the
Father Almighty ; from thence he shall come
to judge the living and the dead. I believe in
the Holy Ghost ; the holy Catholic Church ;
the communion of saints ; the forgiveness of
sins ; the resurrection of the body ; and life
everlasting. *Amen.*

The Confiteor

I CONFESS to Almighty God ; to blessed
Mary ever Virgin, to blessed *Michael* the
Archangel, to blessed *John* the Baptist, to
the holy apostles *Peter* and *Paul*, and to all
the saints, that I have sinned exceedingly
in thought, word, and deed, through my
fault, through my fault, through my most
grievous fault : therefore I beseech the
blessed *Mary* ever Virgin : blessed *Michael*
the Archangel, blessed *John* the Baptist,
the holy apostles *Peter* and *Paul*, and all the
saints, to pray to the Lord our God for me.

May the Almighty God have mercy on me, and forgive me my sins, and bring me to everlasting life. *Amen.*

May the almighty and merciful Lord give me pardon, absolution, and remission of all my sins. *Amen.*

ACTS OF
FAITH, HOPE AND CHARITY

proper for the Morning, or Any Other Time of Day

OF FAITH

O MY God, I believe with a most firm faith all those things which thou hast revealed, and which thy holy church proposes to my belief. I believe in one true and living God, my first beginning and last end ; and that in this one God there are three distinct persons, Father, Son, and Holy Ghost. I believe in Jesus Christ the Son of God, true God and true Man, who was born of the Virgin Mary, and died upon the cross to deliver us all from sin and hell. I bow down my understanding and my will to adore these, and all other thy sacred truths, how incomprehensible soever to my weakness. I embrace them all, and adhere to them with all my soul, because they have been revealed by thee, the sovereign truth, who neither canst deceive nor be deceived. I believe in all things according as the holy

Catholic Church believes. In this faith I now live ; in the same, by thy grace, I resolve to die. Be thou pleased daily to increase and strengthen this my faith.

OF HOPE

O MY God, nothing is hard or impossible to thee, because thy power is infinite ; and there is nothing that thou art not willing to do in favour of us poor mortals, because thy mercy and goodness for us are infinite. Thou has made us to thy own image and likeness, and thou lovest the work of thy hands ; thou hast redeemed us by the precious blood of thy only Son ; and for his sake thou art ever opening thy hand to pour out thy graces upon us ; never forsaking us, if we forsake not thee ; and still calling upon unhappy sinners that have forsaken thee, to return to thee : thou hast promised mercy to such as sincerely seek it ; grace to such as heartily pray for it ; and eternal salvation through Jesus Christ to such as persevere to the end in thy fear and love. Upon these strong grounds I build all my hopes ; and relying upon the assistance of thy grace, and the merits of my Saviour Jesus Christ, I trust to find mercy in the forgiveness of my sins, and so to pass the remainder of this mortal life in thy divine service, that I may come hereafter to enjoy thee in a happy eternity. In thee, O Lord, is my hope, O let me never be confounded.

OF CHARITY

O MY God, thou commandest me to love
thee with my whole heart, with my
whole soul, with all my mind, and with all
my strength ; and it is my sincere desire so to
love thee. O come and take possession of my
whole heart and soul, and teach me this
heavenly art of love. Let this sacred fire ever
burn upon the altar of my heart : let nothing
be able to extinguish it. O let nothing in life
or death ever separate me from thy love.
Thou art the supreme good ; the fountain of
all good ; and thou art infinitely good to me.
Thou art the sovereign beauty, the sovereign
bounty, and the sovereign truth, the immen-
se and incomprehensible ocean of all perfection. Thou art my creator, my redeemer, the
best of friends, and my perpetual benefactor.
Thou art my sweet repose, my true and only
joy, and eternal felicity. Thou art my constant lover, the father and spouse of my soul.
Thou art my God and my all. Oh ! when shall
I be so happy as to see thee, to love thee, to
enjoy thee for ever ?

I desire with my whole heart, that the whole
universe may glorify thee ; that thou mayest
be known, worthily praised and served by all
nations ; that thy love may subdue all
hearts ; and that all thy creatures may fulfil
thy will in all things. Oh ! when will sin have
an end ? When will thy kingdom perfectly
come ? When wilt thou reign all in all ? In

the meantime I offer thee my whole self without reserve, and I desire to be for ever a servant of thy love ; and to invite as many as I can to love thee, whom I desire to love in thee, and for thee. I rejoice with my whole soul, that thou art in thyself eternally and infinitely happy ; and that nothing can be added to thy greatness and glory. O grant that we may all be eternal witnesses of this glory, and eternally rejoice therein, through Jesus Christ thy Son. *Amen.*

ANGELUS DOMINI

1. THE angel of the Lord declared unto Mary, and she conceived of the Holy Ghost. *Hail* Mary, &c.

2. Behold the handmaid of the Lord, may it be done unto me according to thy word. *Hail* Mary, &c.

3. And the word was made flesh, and dwelt among us. *Hail* Mary, &c.

V. Pray for us, O Holy Mother of God.

R. That we may be worthy of the promises of Christ.

Let us pray.

Pour forth, we beseech thee, O Lord, thy grace into our hearts, that we to whom the incarnation of Christ thy Son was made known by the message of an angel, may by his Passion and cross be brought to the glory of his resurrection, through the same Christ our Lord. *Amen.*

EVENING PRAYERS

Let us pray.

O GOD, whose property is always to have mercy and to spare, receive our petition ; that we and all thy servants, who are bound by the chain of sins, may by the compassion of thy goodness mercifully be absolved.

HEAR, we beseech thee, O Lord, the prayers of the suppliant, and pardon the sins of them that confess to thee, that in thy bounty thou mayest both give us pardon and peace.

OUT of thy clemency, O Lord, shew thy unspeakable mercy to us, that so thou may'st both acquit us of our sins, and deliver us from the punishments we deserve for them.

O GOD, who by sin art offended, and by penance pacified, mercifully regard the prayers of thy people making supplication to thee, and turn away the scourges of thy anger, which we deserve for our sins.

O ALMIGHTY and eternal God, have mercy on thy servant *N.* our chief bishop, and direct him, according to thy clemency, into the way of everlasting salvation ; that by thy grace he may desire those things that are agreeable to thee, and perform them with all his strength.

O GOD, from whom are holy desires, right counsels, and just works, give to thy servants that peace which the world cannot give; that both our hearts may be disposed to keep thy commandments, and the fear of enemies being removed, the times by thy protection may be peaceable.

INFLAME, O Lord, our hearts and members with the fire of thy holy Spirit, that we may serve thee with a chaste body, and please thee with a clean heart.

O GOD, the creator and redeemer of all the faithful, give to the souls of thy servants departed the remission of all their sins, that through pious supplications they may obtain the pardon which they have always desired.

FORWARD, we beseech thee, O Lord, our actions by thy holy inspirations, and carry them on by thy gracious assistance; that every prayer and work of ours may begin always from thee, and by thee be happily ended.

O ALMIGHTY and eternal God, who hast dominion over the living and the dead, and art merciful to all whom thou foreknowest shall be thine by faith and good works; we humbly beseech thee, that they, for whom we have determined to offer up our prayers, whether this present world still detain them in the flesh, or the world to come hath already received them out of their bodies, may by the clemency of thy goodness, all thy saints interceding for them, obtain pardon and full remission of all their sins, through our Lord Jesus Christ, thy Son, who liveth and reigneth one God, with thee and the Holy Ghost, world without end. *Amen.*

V. O Lord, hear my prayer.
R. And let my cry come unto thee.
V. May the almighty and most merciful Lord graciously hear us. *R. Amen.*
V. And may the souls of the faithful, through the mercy of God, rest in peace.
R. Amen.

AN EXAMINATION OF CONSCIENCE

For Every Night

First, PLACE *yourself in the presence of God ; humbly adore him, and give him thanks for all his blessings, especially those bestowed on you this day.*

O ALMIGHTY and eternal God, whose majesty filleth heaven and earth, I firmly believe that thou art here ; that thy adorable eye is upon me ; that thou seest and knowest all things ; and that thou art most intimately present in the very centre of my soul. I desire to bow down all the powers of my soul to adore thee ; I desire to join my voice with all the angels and saints, to praise thee, and glorify thee now and for ever. I give thee thanks, from the bottom of my heart, for all thy mercies and blessings bestowed upon me, and upon thy whole Church; and particularly for those I have received from thee this day, in thy watching over me, and preserving me from so many evils, and favouring me with so many graces and inspirations, &c. O let me never more be ungrateful to so constant and so liberal a benefactor! And now dear Lord, add this one blessing to the rest; that I may clearly discover the sins that I have committed this day, by thought, word, or deed; or by any omission of any branch of my duty, to thee, to my neighbour, or to myself: that no part of my guilt may be hidden from my own eyes; but that I may see my sins in their true colours, and may detest them as they ought to be detested.

THEN examine yourself, how you have passed the day; how you have performed your prayers, and other spiritual exercises; in what manner you have acquitted yourself of the duties of your calling; what care you have taken to perform well your ordinary actions of the day; what company you have been in, and what your conversation has been; and in particular, how you have behaved yourself with regard to your customary failings, and your predominant passions.

Having diligently examined your conscience, and discovered the faults you have been guilty of, endeavour to be heartily sorry, and humbly beg pardon of the divine majesty for them, saying for this purpose the Psalm *Miserere, Have mercy on me, O God,* etc., p. 107.

Then make a firm purpose of amendment for the future, and especially resolve to be more watchful over yourself the following day ; to be more diligent in flying the occasions of your sins ; and to take such and such precautions with regard to the fault you are most subject to.

OTHER EVENING PRAYERS

Let us pray.

VISIT, we beseech thee, O Lord, this habitation, and drive far from it all snares of the enemy : let thy holy angels dwell therein, to preserve us in peace ; and thy blessing be upon us for ever, through Christ our Lord. *Amen.*

Look down, we beseech thee, O Lord, upon this thy family, for which our Lord Jesus Christ did not hesitate to be delivered into the hands of sinners, and to undergo the torment of the cross ; who liveth and reigneth with thee, in the unity of the Holy Ghost, God, world without end. *Amen.*

SALVE REGINA

HAIL to the queen who reigns above,
Mother of clemency and love :
Hail thou our hope, life, sweetness ; we,
Eve's banish'd children, cry to thee.

We from this wretched vale of tears,
Send sighs and groans unto thine ears ;
Oh ! then, sweet advocate, bestow
A pitying look on us below.

After this exile, let us see
Our blessed *Jesus*, born of thee :
O merciful, O pious maid,
O gracious *Mary*, lend thine aid.

V. Pray for us, O holy mother of God.
R. That we may be made worthy of the
promises of Christ.

Let us pray.

O ALMIGHTY and eternal God, who
didst prepare the body and soul of the
glorious *Mary*, mother and virgin, that by
the co-operation of the Holy Ghost she
might become a worthy dwelling for thy
Son : grant, that as we rejoice in her commemoration, so, by her pious intercession,
we may be delivered both from present evils
and everlasting death, through the same
Jesus Christ our Lord. *Amen.*
Defend, we beseech thee, O Lord, by the
intercession of blessed *Mary*, ever virgin,

this thy family from all adversity; and as with our whole heart we lie prostrate before thee, mercifully protect us from the snares of our enemies, through Christ our Lord. *Amen.*

O angel of God, who art my guardian, watch over me this night, whom the divine goodness has committed to thy charge; direct me, keep me and defend me from all evil spirits, and all misfortunes.

Into thy hands, O Lord, I commend my spirit : Lord Jesus, receive my soul.

In Thee, O Lord, is my hope; O let me never be confounded.

May the blessing of almighty God, Father, Son, and Holy Ghost, descend upon us, and remain always with us. *Amen.* ✠

INSTRUCTIONS
FOR HEARING MASS

1. FROM the beginning of the world the servants of God were always accustomed to offer sacrifice to him ; by way of acknowledging his sovereignty, and paying their homage to him. And in all ancient religions, true or false, this worship of sacrifice was always looked upon as a most solemn act of religion, due to the Deity which they worshipped.

2. In the law of nature, and in the law of Moses, there was a great variety of sacrifices ; some bloody (in which the victim was slain), others unbloody ; some were called holocausts, or whole burnt offerings, in which the whole host, or victim, was consumed by fire upon God's Altar, for his honour and glory ; others were called sin offerings, which were offered for sins ; others were offerings of thanksgiving, others, in fine, were pacific, or peace offerings, which were offered for obtaining favours of God ; the word peace in the Scripture style signifying all manner of good and prosperity.

3. All these sacrifices of the law of Nature, and of the law of *Moses*, were of themselves but *weak and needy elements*, and only figures of a sacrifice to come, *viz.* that of

Jesus Christ ; in consideration of which sacrifice only, and of the *faith* of the offerers, by which they believed in this redeemer to come, those ancient sacrifices were then accepted by the divine majesty, when they were accompanied with the inward sacrifice of the heart : but not for any intrinsic worth or dignity of the things offered ; for no other blood but the blood of Christ could wash away our sins. Hence in the 39th Psalm, spoken in the person of Christ to his Father, we read, *Sacrifice and oblation thou didst not desire, but thou hast fitted a body for me.* (So St. Paul reads it, *Heb.* x. 5.) *Burnt-offering and sin-offering thou didst not require, then said I, Behold I come.* To give us to understand, that by reason of the insufficiency of the sacrifices of the old law, Christ himself would come to be our sacrifice, and would offer up his own body and blood for us.

4. Accordingly our Saviour Jesus Christ, at the time appointed by his Father, having taken flesh for us, was pleased to offer himself a sacrifice for us all, dying upon the cross for the sins of the whole world. By this one offering we were completely redeemed, inasmuch as our ransom was paid, and all mercy, grace, and salvation were purchased for us. Neither can there now be any need of his dying any more, or purchasing any other graces for us than those for which he has already paid the price of his blood.

5. Nevertheless for the daily *application* of

this one eternal redemption to our souls, and that the mercy, grace, and salvation which he has purchased for us may be actually communicated to us, he not only continually appears in our behalf in the sanctuary of heaven, there representing and offering to his Father his death and Passion for us ; but has also instituted the *Blessed Eucharist,* the night before his Passion, in which he has bequeathed us his body and blood under the sacramental veils, to be not only received by us as a *sacrament,* for the food and nourishment of our souls ; but also to be offered and presented by his ministers to his Father (mystically broken and shed) as a sacrifice : not by way of a new death, but by way of a standing memorial of his death ; a daily celebrating and representing this death to God, and an applying to our souls the fruits of it.

6. This Eucharistic sacrifice of the body and blood of Christ, daily offered under the forms of *bread* and *wine,* in remembrance of his Passion, is what we call the *Mass.* This is the solemn liturgy of the Catholic Church. This is that *pure offering* made to God *in every place* among the Gentiles, according to the prophecy of *Malachi* i. *v.* 10, 11. By this Christ is a priest for ever according to the order of *Melchisedech, Ps.* cix. whose sacrifice was bread and wine, *Gen.* xv.

7. This sacrifice of the Mass is the same in substance with that which Christ offered

for us upon the cross : because both the
victim offered, and the priest, or *principal
offerer*, is the same Jesus Christ. The difference is only in the manner of the offering ;
because upon the cross our Saviour offered
himself in such manner as really to shed his
blood and die for us ; whereas now he does
not really shed his blood or die any more.
And therefore this is called an *unbloody
sacrifice ;* and that of the cross a *bloody
sacrifice.*

8. By reason of this near alliance which this
sacrifice of the Mass has with the sacrifice
of the cross, it completely answers all the
different ends of sacrifice, and that in a
manner infinitely more perfect than any of
the ancient sacrifices. Christ is here both
priest and victim, representing in person
and offering up his death and Passion to his
Father : First, for the *adoration*, praise,
honour and glory of the divine majesty.
Secondly, in *thanksgiving* for all his benefits.
Thirdly, for the obtaining of *pardon* for our
sins. Fourthly, for the obtaining of *grace*
and salvation for us by the merits of that
same death and Passion. And therefore this
sacrifice, in order to all these ends, must be
infinitely beyond all the *holocausts, thank-
offerings, sin-offerings,* and *peace-offerings* of
the ancient law.

9. This sacrifice of the Mass then is offered
up to God in the Catholic Church, *first,* as a
daily *remembrance* of the Passion of Christ :

This do in remembrance of me, St. *Luke* xxii.
Secondly, as a most solemn *worship* of the
divine majesty. *Thirdly*, as a most acceptable
thanksgiving to God, from whence it has the
name of *Eucharist*. *Fourthly*, as a most
powerful means to move God to shew mercy
to us in the *forgiveness of our sins ;* for which
reason we call it *propitiatory :* and *lastly*, as a
most effectual way to *obtain* of God all that
we want, coming to him (as we here do) with
Christ, and through Christ.

10. For these ends both priest and people
ought to offer up the sacrifice of the Mass :
the priest as Christ's minister, and in his
person ; and the people by the hands of the
priest ; and both the one and the other by
the hands of the great high-priest Jesus
Christ. And with this offering of Christ's
both the one and the other ought to make
a total offering of themselves also by his
hands, and in union with him.

11. Hence the best devotion for hearing
Mass is that which has for its object the
Passion of Christ, and which tends to unite
the soul to Christ, and through him to his
Father ; and which most perfectly answers
all the other ends of this sacrifice, *viz.* the
adoration of God, thanksgiving for all his
benefits, the obtaining pardon for all our
sins, and grace in all our necessities.

THE ORDINARY OF THE MASS

The Priest at the foot of the altar says :

IN the Name of the Father, and of the Son, and of the Holy Ghost. *Amen.*

P. I will go unto the altar of God.

R. To God, who giveth joy to my youth.

Psalm 42

P. Judge me, O God, and distinguish my cause from the nation that is not holy, deliver me from the unjust and deceitful man.

R. For Thou, O God, art my strength : why hast thou cast me off ? And why do I go sorrowful, whilst the enemy afflicteth me ?

P. Send forth Thy light and Thy truth : they have conducted me and brought me unto Thy holy mount and into Thy tabernacles.

R. And I will go unto the altar of God : to God who giveth joy to my youth.

P. To Thee, O God, my God, I will give praise upon the harp : why art thou sad, O my soul ? and why dost thou disquiet me ?

R. Hope in God : for I will still give praise to Him ; the salvation of my countenance, and my God.

P. Glory be to the Father, and to the Son, and to the Holy Ghost.

R. As it was in the beginning, is now, and ever shall be, world without end. *Amen.*

P. I will go unto the altar of God.

R. To God, who giveth joy to my youth.

P. Our help is in the Name of the Lord.

R. Who made heaven and earth.

P. I confess to Almighty God, &c.

R. May Almighty God have mercy upon thee, and forgiving thee thy sins, bring thee to life everlasting.

P. Amen.

R. I confess to Almighty God, to blessed Mary ever Virgin, to blessed Michael the Archangel, to blessed John the Baptist, to the holy Apostles Peter and Paul, to all the Saints, and to you, Father, that I have sinned exceedingly, in thought, word, and deed, through my fault, through my fault, through my most grievous fault. Therefore I beseech the blessed Mary ever Virgin, blessed Michael the Archangel, blessed John the Baptist, the holy Apostles Peter and Paul, and all the Saints, and you, Father, to pray to the Lord our God for me.

P. May Almighty God have mercy upon you, and, forgiving you your sins, bring you to life everlasting.

R. Amen.

P. May the almighty and most merciful Lord grant us pardon, absolution, and remission of all our sins.

R. Amen.

P. Turn Thee, O God and quicken us

R. And Thy people shall rejoice in Thee.

P. Show us, O Lord, Thy mercy.

R. And grant us Thy salvation.

P. O Lord, hear my prayer.

R. And let my cry come unto Thee.

P. The Lord be with you.

R. And with thy spirit.

The Priest, going up to the altar, says :

TAKE away from us our iniquities, we beseech Thee, O Lord, that we may be worthy to enter with pure minds into the Holy of Holies. Through Christ our Lord. *Amen.*

WE beseech Thee, O Lord, by the merits of Thy Saints, whose relics are here, and of all the Saints, that Thou wouldst vouchsafe to forgive me all my sins. *Amen.*

In Solemn Mass the altar is here incensed.

The Introit, Collect, Epistle, Gradual, Gospel, Offertory, and Communion Verses, with the Secret and Post-Communion, vary according to the day or feast. The varying portions of Mass here given are taken from the Mass of the Blessed Trinity.

The Introit

BLESSED be the holy Trinity, and the undivided Unity ; we will praise Him, because He hath shown His mercy to us (*Ps.* viii. 2). O Lord, our God, how won-

derful is Thy Name over the whole earth !
Glory be to the Father, and to the Son, and
to the Holy Ghost ; as it was in the beginning, is now, and ever shall be, world without
end. *Amen.*

After which is alternately said :

P.   Lord have mercy on us.
R.   Lord have mercy on us.
P.   Lord have mercy on us.
R.   Christ have mercy on us.
P.   Christ have mercy on us.
R.   Christ have mercy on us.
P.   Lord have mercy on us.
R.   Lord have mercy on us.
P.   Lord have mercy on us.

The *Gloria* is omitted whenever the colour
of the vestments used at Mass is either
black or purple.

GLORY be to God on high, and peace on
earth to men of good will ; we praise
Thee ; we bless Thee ; we adore Thee ; we
glorify Thee ; we give Thee thanks for Thy
great glory, O Lord God, heavenly King,
God the Father Almighty. O Lord Jesus
Christ, the only begotten Son : O Lord God,
Lamb of God, Son of the Father, who
takest away the sins of the world, have
mercy on us. Thou who takest away the sins
of the world, receive our prayer. Thou who
sittest at the right hand of the Father, have

mercy on us. For Thou alone art holy : Thou
alone art the Lord : Thou alone, O Jesus
Christ, with the Holy Ghost, art most high
in the Glory of God the Father. *Amen.*

Turning towards the people, the priest says :

P. 	The Lord be with you.
R. 	And with thy spirit.

The Collect

ALMIGHTY everlasting God, who hast
granted unto Thy servants, in the
confession of the true faith, to acknowledge
the glory of the Eternal Trinity, and to
adore the unity in the power of Thy majesty,
we beseech Thee, that by the strength of
this faith, we may be defended from all
adversity. Through Christ our Lord. *Amen.*

The Epistle

O THE depth of the riches of the wisdom
and of the knowledge of God ! How
incomprehensible are His judgments, and
how unsearchable His ways ! For who hath
known the mind of the Lord ? Or who hath
been His counsellor ? Or who hath first given
to Him, and recompense shall be made Him ?
For of Him, and by Him, and in Him, are all
things : to Him be glory for ever. *Amen.*

At the end of the Epistle the clerk answers.
R. 	Thanks be to God.

The Gradual

BLESSED art Thou, O Lord, who beholdest the deep and sittest on the Cherubim.

Blessed art Thou, O Lord, in the firmament of heaven, and praiseworthy for ever.

Alleluia. Alleluia. Blessed art Thou, O Lord, the God of our fathers, and praiseworthy for ever. Alleluia.

Munda cor meum,

the prayer said by the Priest before the Gospel.

CLEANSE my heart and my lips, O Almighty God, who didst cleanse the lips of the prophet Isaiah with a burning coal; and vouchsafe, through Thy gracious mercy, so to purify me, that I may worthily proclaim Thy holy Gospel. Through Christ our Lord. *Amen.*

May the Lord be in my heart, and on my lips, that I may worthily, and in a becoming manner, announce His holy Gospel. *Amen.*

P. The Lord be with you.

R. And with thy spirit.

P. The continuation (*or* beginning) of the holy Gospel according to N.

R. Glory be to Thee, O Lord.

The Gospel

AT that time, Jesus said to His disciples :
All power is given to Me in heaven and
on earth : Going therefore, teach ye all nations : baptizing them in the Name of the
Father, and of the Son, and of the Holy
Ghost ; teaching them to observe all things
whatsoever I have commanded you ; and
behold I am with you all days, even to the
consummation of the world.

R.   Praise be to Thee, O Christ.

The Priest kisses the Gospel, and says :

BY the words of the Gospel may our
sins be blotted out.

The Nicene Creed

I BELIEVE in one God, the Father
Almighty, Maker of heaven and earth,
and of all things, visible and invisible. And
in one Lord Jesus Christ, the only-begotten
Son of God, born of the Father before all
ages ; God of God ; Light of Light ; true
God of true God ; begotten, not made ;
consubstantial with the Father, by whom
all things were made. Who for us men,
and for our salvation, came down from
heaven, and was incarnate by the Holy
Ghost of the Virgin Mary : *and was made
man. He was crucified also for us, suffered
under Pontius Pilate, and was buried. The

* Here all genuflect.

third day He rose again according to the Scriptures : and ascended into heaven, and sitteth at the right hand of the Father : and He shall come again with glory to judge both the living and the dead ; of whose kingdom there shall be no end.

And I believe in the Holy Ghost, the Lord and lifegiver, who proceedeth from the Father and the Son ; who, together with the Father and the Son, is adored and glorified ; who spake by the prophets. And one holy Catholic and Apostolic Church. I confess one Baptism for the remission of sins. And I look for the resurrection of the dead, and the life of the world to come. *Amen.*

P. The Lord be with you.

R. And with thy spirit.

P. Let us pray.

The Offertory

BLESSED be God the Father, and the only-begotten Son of God, and the Holy Spirit ; for He hath dealt with us according to His mercy.

Offering of the Host

ACCEPT, O Holy Father, Almighty, Eternal God, this immaculate Host, which I, Thy unworthy servant, offer unto Thee, my living and true God, for my innumerable sins, offences, and negligences ; and for all here present ; as also for all faithful Christians, both living and dead, that it may be profitable for my own and for their salvation unto life everlasting. *Amen.*

When the Priest pours wine and water into the chalice,

O GOD, ✠ who, **in creating human** nature, didst wonderfully dignify it, and hast still more wonderfully renewed it: grant that, by the mystery of this water and wine, we may be made partakers of His divinity, who vouchsafed to become partaker of our humanity, Jesus Christ Thy Son, our Lord ; who with Thee liveth and reigneth, in the unity of the Holy Ghost, one God, world without end. *Amen.*

Offering of the Chalice

WE offer unto Thee, O Lord, the Chalice of salvation, beseeching Thy clemency, that in the sight of Thy Divine Majesty, it may ascend with the odour of sweetness, for our salvation, and for that of the whole world. *Amen.*

In the spirit of humility, and with a contrite heart, let us be received by Thee, O Lord : and grant that the sacrifice we offer in Thy sight this day, may be pleasing to Thee, O Lord God.

Come, O Sanctifier, Almighty, Eternal God, and bless this ✠ Sacrifice prepared to Thy holy Name.

Here at Solemn Mass the incense is
blessed, and the bread and wine and
the altar are incensed.

MAY the Lord, by the intercession of
blessed Michael the Archangel, standing at the right hand of the altar of incense,
and of all His elect, vouchsafe to bless ✠
this incense, and receive it as an odour of
sweetness. Through Christ, etc. *Amen.*
May this incense which Thou hast blest,
O Lord, ascend to Thee, and may Thy
mercy descend upon us.
Let my prayer, O Lord, ascend like incense
in Thy sight: and the lifting up of my
hands be as an evening sacrifice. Set a watch,
O Lord, before my mouth, and a door round
about my lips, that my heart may not incline
to evil words, to make excuses in sins.
May the Lord enkindle in us the fire of His
love, and the flame of everlasting charity.
Amen.

The Lavabo

I WILL wash my hands among the inno-
cent: and will encompass Thy altar,
O Lord.
That I may hear the voice of praise; and
tell of all Thy marvellous works.
I have loved, O Lord, the beauty of Thy
house, and the place where Thy glory
dwelleth.
Destroy not my soul with the wicked, O
God: nor my life with men of blood.

In whose hands are iniquities : their right hand is filled with gifts.
But I have walked in my innocence : redeem me and have mercy upon me.
My foot hath stood in the right path : in the churches I will bless Thee, O Lord.
Glory be to the Father, &c.

RECEIVE, O holy Trinity, this offering which we make to Thee in memory of the Passion, Resurrection, and Ascension of our Lord Jesus Christ, and in honour of the blessed Mary ever a virgin, of blessed John the Baptist, the holy Apostles Peter and Paul, of these and all the Saints : that it may be available to their honour and our salvation ; and may they vouchsafe to intercede for us in heaven, whose memory we celebrate on earth. Through the same Christ our Lord. *Amen.*

The Orate Fratres

BRETHREN pray that my sacrifice and yours may be acceptable to God the Father Almighty.
R.   May the Lord receive the sacrifice from Thy hands, to the praise and glory of His Name, to our benefit, and to that of all His holy Church. *Amen.*

The Secret

SANCTIFY, we beseech Thee, O Lord our God, by the invocation of Thy holy

Name, the Victim of this oblation ; and by it make us ourselves an eternal offering unto Thee. Through Thy Son Jesus Christ our Lord, who liveth and reigneth with Thee, in the unity of the Holy Spirit, God, for ever and ever.

P. World without end.

R. Amen.

P. The Lord be with you.

R. And with thy spirit.

P. Lift up your hearts.

R. We have lifted them up unto the Lord.

P. Let us give thanks to the Lord our God.

R. It is meet and just.

The Preface

IT is truly meet and just, right and salutary, that we should at all times and in all places give thanks to thee, O holy Lord, Father Almighty, Everlasting God : who together with Thine only-begotten Son and the Holy Ghost art one God and one Lord ; not in the singleness of one Person, but in the Trinity of one substance. For that which, by Thy revelation, we believe of Thy glory, the same also do we hold as to Thy Son, the same as to the Holy Ghost, without difference or distinction. That in the confession of the true and everlasting Godhead, distinction in Person, unity in Essence, and equality in Majesty may be adored : which the Angels and Archangels, the Cherubim also and Seraphim praise ; who cease not daily to cry out with one voice : saying,

Sanctus

Holy, Holy, Holy, Lord God of hosts. Full are the heavens and the earth of Thy glory ; Hosanna in the highest. Blessed is He that cometh in the Name of the Lord: Hosanna in the heights.

The Canon of the Mass

WE humbly pray and beseech Thee, therefore, most merciful Father, through Jesus Christ Thy Son our Lord, that Thou wouldst vouchsafe to accept and bless these gifts, these presents, these holy, unspotted sacrifices, which in the first place we offer Thee for Thy holy Catholic Church, to which vouchsafe to grant peace ; as also to preserve, unite, and govern it throughout the world, together with Thy servant our Pope, *N.*, and our Bishop, *N.*, as also all orthodox believers and professors of the Catholic and Apostolic Faith.

Commemoration of the Living

BE mindful, O Lord, of Thy servants, men and women, *N.* and *N.*

The Priest joins his hands, and prays silently for those he intends to pray for.

AND of all here present, whose faith and devotion are known unto Thee; for whom we offer, or who offer up to Thee this sacrifice of praise for themselves, their families, and friends, for the hope of their safety and salvation, and who pay their vows to Thee, the eternal, living, and true God.

COMMUNICATING with, and honouring in the first place the memory of the glorious and ever Virgin Mary, Mother of our Lord and God Jesus Christ ; as also of the blessed Apostles and Martyrs, Peter and Paul, Andrew, James, John, Thomas, James, Philip, Bartholomew, Matthew, Simon and Thaddeus, Linus, Cletus, Clement, Xystus, Cornelius, Cyprian, Lawrence, Chrysogonus, John and Paul, Cosmas and Damian, and of all Thy Saints ; by whose merits and prayers grant that we may be always defended by the help of Thy protection. Through the same Christ our Lord. *Amen.*

At the Consecration

WE, therefore, beseech Thee, O Lord, graciously to accept this oblation of our service, as also of Thy whole family ; dispose our days in Thy peace, command us to be delivered from eternal damnation, and to be numbered in the flock of Thy elect. Through Christ our Lord. *Amen.*

WHICH oblation do Thou, O God, vouchsafe in all things to make blessed, approved, ratified, reasonable, and acceptable, that it may become to us the Body and Blood of Thy most beloved Son, Jesus Christ our Lord.

WHO the day before He suffered, took bread (*he takes the Host*) into His holy and venerable hands (*he raises his eyes to heaven*), and with His eyes lifted up towards heaven, to God, His Almighty Father, giving thanks to Thee, did bless, break, and give to His disciples, saying : " Take, and eat ye all of This ; *for this is my body.*"

The bell is rung. The priest, kneeling, adores, and then elevates the sacred Host.

IN like manner, after He had supped, taking also this excellent Chalice into His holy and venerable hands, and giving Thee thanks, He blessed, and gave to His disciples, saying : Take and drink ye all of This : *for this is the Chalice of My Blood of the new and eternal testament ; the Mystery of faith ; which shall be shed for you, and for many, to the remission of sins.* As often as ye do these things, ye shall do them in remembrance of Me.

The bell is rung. The Priest, kneeling, adores, and then elevates the Chalice.

WHEREFORE, O Lord, we Thy servants, as also Thy holy people, calling to mind the blessed Passion of the same Christ Thy Son our Lord, His Resurrection from the dead, and glorious Ascension into heaven, offer unto Thy most excellent Majesty, of Thy gifts and grants, a pure Host, a holy Host, an immaculate Host, the holy Bread of eternal life, and the Chalice of everlasting salvation.

UPON which vouchsafe to look with a propitious and serene countenance, and to accept them, as Thou wast graciously pleased to accept the gifts of Thy just servant Abel, and the sacrifice of our Patriarch Abraham, and that which Thy high Priest Melchisedech offered to Thee, a Holy Sacrifice, an Immaculate Host.

WE most humbly beseech Thee, Almighty God, let these Offerings be carried by the hands of Thy holy Angel to Thy Altar on high, in the sight of Thy Divine Majesty, that as many of us *(he kisses the altar)* as by participation at this altar, shall receive the most sacred Body and Blood of Thy Son, may be filled with all heavenly benediction and grace. Through the same Christ our Lord. *Amen.*

The Commemoration of the Dead

BE mindful, O Lord, of Thy servants, men and women, *N.* and *N.*, who are gone before us with the sign of faith, and sleep in the sleep of peace.

Here the dead for whom it is intended specially to pray are named.

TO these, O Lord, and to all that rest in Christ, grant, we beseech Thee, a place of refreshment, light, and peace. Through the same Christ our Lord. *Amen.*

The Priest, striking his breast, says :

AND to us sinners, Thy servants, hoping in the multitude of Thy mercies, vouchsafe to grant some part and fellowship with Thy holy Apostles and Martyrs : with John, Stephen, Mathias, Barnabas, Ignatius, Alexander, Marcellinus, Peter, Felicity, Perpetua, Agatha, Lucy, Agnes, Cecily, Anastasia, and with all Thy Saints : into whose company we beseech Thee to admit us, not considering our merits, but freely pardoning our offences. Through Christ our Lord.

By whom, O Lord, Thou dost always create, sanctify, quicken, bless, and give us all these good things.

Through Him, and with Him, and in Him, is to Thee, God the Father Almighty, in the unity of the Holy Ghost, all honour and glory.

P.   For ever and ever.

R.   Amen.

Let us pray.

INSTRUCTED by Thy saving precepts, and following Thy Divine institution, we presume to say :

Our Father, who art in heaven, hallowed be Thy Name : Thy kingdom come ; Thy will be done on earth as it is in heaven. Give us this day our daily bread : and forgive us our trespasses, as we forgive them that trespass against us. And lead us not into temptation.

R. But deliver us from evil.

P. Amen.

DELIVER us, we beseech Thee, O Lord, from all evils, past, present, and to come : and by the intercession of the blessed and glorious Mary ever Virgin, Mother of God, together with Thy blessed Apostles Peter and Paul, and Andrew and all the Saints, mercifully grant peace in our days : that by the assistance of Thy mercy we may be always free from sin, and secure from all disturbance. Through the same Jesus Christ, Thy Son, our Lord. Who with Thee in the unity of the Holy Ghost liveth and reigneth God.

P. World without end.

R. Amen.

P. May the peace of the Lord be always with you.

R. And with thy spirit.

MAY this mingling and consecration of the Body and Blood of our Lord Jesus

3

Christ be to us that receive it effectual to eternal life. *Amen.*

The Agnus Dei

LAMB of God, who takest away the sins of the world, have mercy upon us.
Lamb of God, who takest away the sins of the world, have mercy upon us.
Lamb of God, who takest away the sins of the world, grant us peace.

LORD Jesus Christ, who saidst to Thy Apostles, peace I leave with you, My peace I give unto you; regard not my sins, but the faith of Thy Church; and vouchsafe to it that peace and unity which is agreeable to Thy will: who livest and reignest God for ever and ever. *Amen.*

LORD Jesus Christ, Son of the living God, who, according to the will of the Father, through the co-operation of the Holy Ghost, hast by Thy death given life to the world; deliver me by this Thy most sacred Body and Blood from all mine iniquities and from all evils, and make me always adhere to Thy commandments, and never suffer me to be separated from Thee; who with the same God the Father and Holy Ghost livest and reignest God for ever and ever. Amen.

LET not the participation of Thy Body, O Lord Jesus Christ, which I, unworthy, presume to receive, turn to my judgment and condemnation; but through Thy goodness, may it be to me a safeguard and remedy, both of soul and body. Who with God the Father, in the unity of the Holy Ghost, livest and reignest God for ever and ever. *Amen.*

I WILL take the Bread of heaven, and call upon the Name of the Lord.

At the Communion

LORD, I am not worthy that Thou shouldst enter under my roof ; say but the word, and my soul shall be healed. (Thrice.)

MAY the Body of our Lord Jesus Christ preserve my soul to life everlasting. *Amen.*

Taking the Chalice, the Priest says :

WHAT shall I render to the Lord for all He hath rendered unto me ? I will take the Chalice of salvation, and call upon the Name of the Lord. I will call upon the Lord and praise Him, and I shall be saved from mine enemies.

THE Blood of our Lord Jesus Christ preserve my soul to everlasting life. *Amen.*

GRANT, O Lord, that what we have taken with our mouth, we may receive with a pure mind ; and of a temporal gift may it become to us an eternal remedy.

MAY Thy Body, O Lord, which I have received, and Thy Blood which I have drunk, cleave to my heart, and grant that no stain of sin may remain in me, who have been refreshed with pure and holy Sacraments. Who livest, &c. *Amen.*

The Communion

WE bless the God of heaven, and shall praise Him before all things living; because He hath dealt with us according to His mercy.

P.   The Lord be with you.
R: And with thy spirit.

The Post-Communion

MAY the reception of this Sacrament, O Lord our God, as also the confession of the holy and everlasting Trinity, and of its undivided Unity, profit us unto the health of body and soul.
Through, etc.

P.   The Lord be with you.
R.   And with thy spirit.
P.   Go, the Mass is ended; *or,* Let us bless the Lord.
R.   Thanks be to God.

In Masses for the Dead:

P.   May they rest in peace.
R.   Amen.

O HOLY Trinity, let the performance of my homage be pleasing to Thee; and grant that the sacrifice which I, unworthy, have offered up in the sight of Thy Majesty, may be acceptable to Thee, and through Thy mercy be a propitiation for me, and all those for whom I have offered it. Through Christ our Lord. *Amen.*

At the Blessing

MAY Almighty God, the Father, Son, and Holy Ghost, bless you.

℟. Amen.

The blessing is omitted in Masses for the Dead.

℣. The Lord be with you.

℟. And with thy spirit.

℣. The beginning of the holy Gospel according to Saint John.

℟. Glory be to Thee, O Lord.

IN the beginning was the Word, and the Word was with God, and the Word was God : the same was in the beginning with God. All things were made by Him, and without Him was made nothing that was made : in Him was life, and the Life was the light of men : and the Light shineth in darkness, and the darkness did not comprehend it. There was a man sent from God, whose name was John. This man came for a witness, to give testimony of the Light, that all men might believe through Him. He was not the Light, but came to give testimony of the Light. He was the true Light which enlighteneth every man that cometh into this world. He was in the world, and the world was made by Him, and the world knew Him not. He came unto His own and His own received Him not. But as many as received Him, to them gave He power to become the sons of God : to those that believe in His Name, who are born not of blood, nor of the will of the flesh, nor of the will of man, but of God. *And the Word was made flesh, and dwelt among us ; and we saw His glory, the glory as it were of the only-begotten of the Father, full of grace and truth.

R. Thanks be to God.

*Here all genuflect.

DEVOTIONS
FOR HOLY COMMUNION

Before Communion

O LORD Jesus Christ, King of everlasting glory, behold I desire to come to Thee this day, and to receive Thy Body and Blood in this heavenly Sacrament, for Thy honour and glory, and the good of my soul. I desire to receive Thee, because it is Thy desire, and Thou hast so ordained : blessed be Thy Name for ever. I desire to come to Thee like Magdalen, that I may be delivered from all my evils, and embrace Thee, my only good. I desire to come to Thee, that I may be happily united to Thee, that I may henceforth abide in Thee, and Thou in me ; and that nothing in life or death may ever separate me from Thee.

Commemorate the Passion of Christ

I DESIRE, in these holy mysteries, to commemorate, as Thou hast commanded, all Thy sufferings : Thy agony and bloody sweat ; Thy being betrayed and apprehended ; all the reproaches and calumnies, all the scoffs and affronts, all the blows and buffets, Thou hast endured for me ; Thy being scourged, crowned with thorns, and loaded with a heavy cross for my sins, and for those of the whole world ; Thy Cruci-

fixion and Death, together with Thy glorious
Resurrection and triumphant Ascension. I
adore Thee, and give Thee thanks for all
that Thou hast done and suffered for us ;
and for giving us, in the most blessed Sacrament, this pledge of our redemption, this
victim of our ransom, this Body and Blood
which was offered for us.

Make an Act of Faith

I MOST firmly believe, O Jesus, that in
this holy Sacrament Thou art present
verily and indeed ; that here are Thy Body
and Blood, Thy soul and Thy divinity. I
believe that Thou, my Saviour, true God
and true Man, art really here, with all Thy
treasures ; that here Thou communicatest
Thyself to us, makest us partakers of the
fruit of Thy Passion, and givest us a pledge
of eternal life. I believe there cannot be a
greater happiness than to receive Thee worthily, nor a greater misery than to receive
Thee unworthily. All this I most steadfastly
believe, because it is what Thou hast taught
us by Thy Church.

Make an Act of Contrition

O LORD, I detest, with my whole heart,
all the sins by which I have offended
Thy Divine Majesty, from the first moment
that I was capable of sinning to this very
hour ; I desire to lay them all at Thy feet,

to be cancelled by Thy precious Blood. Hear me, O Lord, by that infinite love by which Thou hast shed Thy Blood for me. O let not that Blood be shed in vain ! I detest my sins, because they have offended Thy infinite goodness. By Thy grace I will never commit them any more. I am sorry for them, and will be sorry for them as long as I live, and, according to the best of my power, will do penance for them. Forgive me, dear Lord, for Thy mercy's sake ; pardon me all that is past ; and be Thou my keeper for the time to come, that I may never more offend Thee.

When the time comes to receive Holy Communion, join with the clerk in saying the Confiteor, *and with the Priest when he says the* Domine, non sum dignus. *Approach the altar rails quietly and devoutly. At the moment you receive say :*

May the Body of our Lord Jesus Christ preserve my soul to life everlasting. Amen.

AFTER COMMUNION

After Communion, always spend at least a quarter of an hour in thanksgiving.

Acts of Devotion, Praise, and Thanksgiving

O LORD Jesus Christ, my Creator and my Redeemer, my God and my All, whence is this to me, that my Lord, and so great a Lord, whom heaven and earth cannot contain, should come into this poor dwelling, this house of clay of my earthly habitation. Bow down thyself, with all thy powers, O my soul, to adore the Sovereign Majesty which hath vouchsafed to come to visit thee ; pay Him the best homage thou art able, as to thy first beginning and thy last end ; pour thyself forth in His presence in praises and thanksgiving, and invite all heaven and earth to join with thee in magnifying their Lord and thine for His mercy and bounty to thee.

What return shall I make to Thee, O Lord, for all Thou hast done for me ? Behold, when I had no being at all, Thou didst create me ; and when I was gone astray, and lost in my sins, Thou didst redeem me by dying for me. All that I have, all that I am, is Thy gift ; and now, after all Thy other favours, Thou hast given me Thyself. Blessed be Thy name for ever. Thou art great, O Lord, and exceedingly to be praised : great are Thy works, and of Thy wisdom there is no end ; but Thy tender mercies, Thy bounty and goodness to me, are above all Thy works. These I desire to confess and extol for ever.

Bless then, thy Lord, O my soul, and let all that is within thee praise and magnify His Name. Bless thy Lord, O my soul, and see thou never forget all that He hath done

for thee. O all ye works of the Lord, bless
the Lord, praise and glorify Him for ever.
O all ye angels of the Lord, bless the Lord,
praise and glorify His holy Name. Bless
the Lord, all ye Saints, and let the whole
Church of heaven and earth join in praising
and giving Him thanks for all His mercies
and graces to me, and so, in some measure,
supply what is due from me. But as all this
still falls short of what I owe Thee for Thy
infinite love, I offer to Thee, O Eternal
Father, the same Son of Thine whom Thou
hast given me, and His Thanksgiving, which
is infinite in value. Look not, then, upon my
insensibility and ingratitude, but upon the
face of Thy Christ, and with Him, and
through Him, receive this offering of my
poor self, which I desire to make to Thee.

Petitions after Communion

O MOST merciful Saviour, behold I have
presumed to receive Thee this day into
my house, relying on Thy infinite goodness
and mercy, and hoping, like Zaccheus, to
obtain Thy benediction. But, alas ! with how
little preparation, with how little devotion!
From my heart I beg pardon for my great
unworthiness, and for my innumerable sins,
which I detest for the love of Thee. Thou
seest, O Searcher of hearts, all my maladies,
and all the wounds of my soul. Thou knowest
how prone I am to evil, and how backward

and sluggish to good. Who can heal all these
my evils but Thou, the true Physician of my
soul, who givest me Thy Body and Blood in
this blessed Sacrament, as a sovereign medi-
cine for all my infirmities? Dispel the darkness of ignorance from my understanding by
Thy heavenly light; drive away the corruption and malice of my will by the fire of
Divine love and charity; strengthen my
weakness with heavenly fortitude; subdue in
me all evil passions, particularly that which
is most deeply rooted in me; stand by me
henceforward in all my temptations, that I
may never more be overcome; and grant me
that I may rather die a thousand deaths
than live to offend Thee mortally.

O my Jesus, Thou art infinitely rich, and
all the treasures of Divine grace are locked
up in Thee! These treasures Thou bringest
with Thee when Thou dost visit us in this
blessed Sacrament, and Thou takest an
infinite pleasure in opening them to us to
enrich our poverty. This it is that gives
me confidence to present Thee now with
my petitions, and to beg of Thee those
graces and virtues which I stand so much in
need of. Oh, increase and strengthen my
belief of Thy heavenly truths, and grant
that henceforward I may ever live by faith,
and be guided by the maxims of Thy Gospel.
Teach me to be poor in spirit, and take off
my heart from the love of these transitory
things, and fix it upon eternity: teach me,

by Thy Divine example, and by Thy most
efficacious grace, to be meek and humble of
heart, and in my patience to possess my
soul. Grant that I may ever keep my body
and soul chaste and pure ; that I may ever
bewail my past sins, and by a daily mortification, restrain all irregular inclinations
and passions for the future. Teach me to love
Thee, to be ever recollected in Thee, and to
walk always in Thy presence ; teach me to
love my friends in Thee, and my enemies for
Thee ; grant me grace to persevere to the
end in this love, and so to come one day to
that blessed place where I may love and
enjoy Thee for ever.

Have mercy also on my parents, friends,
and benefactors, and on all those for whom
I am bound to pray, that we may all love
Thee and faithfully serve Thee. Have
mercy on Thy whole Church, especially on
the clergy and religious men and women,
that all may live up to their callings and
sanctify Thy Name. Give Thy grace and
blessing to all princes and magistrates, and
to all Christian people ; convert all un-
believers and sinners, and bring all strayed
sheep back to Thy fold ; particularly have
mercy on N. and N., etc.

O Blessed Virgin, Mother of my God and
Saviour, recommend all these my petitions
to your Son. O all ye Angels and Saints,
citizens of heaven, unite your prayers with
mine ; you ever stand before the throne,

and see Him face to face whom I here receive hidden under the sacramental veil; be ever mindful of me, and obtain from Him, and through Him, that with you I may bless Him and love Him for ever. *Amen.*

PRAYER BEFORE A CRUCIFIX

To which Pope Pius IX has annexed a plenary Indulgence, applicable to the souls in purgatory, which all the faithful may obtain, who, after having confessed their sins with contrition, and received the Holy Communion, and prayed for the intentions of the Sovereign Pontiff, shall devoutly recite it before an image or representation of Christ crucified.

BEHOLD, O kind and most sweet Jesus, I cast myself upon my knees in Thy sight, and with the most fervent desire of my soul I pray and beseech Thee that Thou wouldst impress upon my heart lively sentiments of faith, hope, and charity, with true repentance for my sins, and a firm desire of amendment, whilst with deep affection and grief of soul I ponder within myself, and mentally contemplate Thy five most precious wounds; having before my eyes that which David spake in prophecy: "They pierced My hands and My feet; they have numbered all My bones."

INVOCATIONS TO BE SAID
AFTER HOLY COMMUNION

*(300 days ; plenary each month if said every
day.)*

SOUL of Christ, be my sanctification ;
'Body of Christ, be my salvation ;
Blood of Christ, fill all my veins ;
Water of Christ's side, wash out my stains ;
Passion of Christ, my comfort be ;
O good Jesu, listen to me ;
In Thy wounds I fain would hide,
Ne'er to be parted from Thy side ;
Guard me, should the foe assail me ;
Call me when my life shall fail me ;
Bid me come to Thee above,
With Thy Saints to sing Thy love
World without end.   *Amen.*

MANNER OF SERVING AT MASS

The Clerk or Server, kneeling at the left hand of the Priest, answers him as follows :

Priest. Introíbo ad altáre Dei.

Server. Ad Deum, qui laetíficat juventútem meam.

(In Masses for the Dead the following Psalm is omitted):

Psalm xlii.

Pr. Júdica me, Deus, et discérne causam meam de gente non sancta : ab hómine iníquo et dolóso érue me.

Ser. Quia tu es, Deus, fortitúdo mea : quare me repulísti ? et quare tristis incédo, dum afflígit me inimícus ?

Pr. Emítte lucem tuam et veritátem tuam : ipsa me deduxérunt, et adduxérunt in montem sanctum tuum, et in tabernácula tua.

Ser. Et introíbo ad altáre Dei : ad Deum, qui laetíficat juventútem meam.

Pr. Confitébor tibi in cíthara, Deus, Deus meus : quare tristis es ánima mea ? et quare contúrbas me ?

Ser. Spera in Deo quóniam adhuc confitébor illi : salutáre vultus mei, et Deus meus.

Pr. Glória Patri, et Filio, et Spirítui Sancto.

Ser. Sicut erat in princípio, et nunc et semper, et in sǽcula sæculórum. Amen.

Pr. Introíbo ad altáre Dei.

Ser. Ad Deum, qui lætíficat juventútem meam.

Pr. Adjutórium ✠ nostrum in nómine Dómini.

Ser. Qui fecit cœlum et terram.

Then the Priest says :

Confíteor, etc. . . . oráre pro me ad Dóminum Deum nostrum.

Ser. Misereátur tui omnípotens Deus, et dimíssis peccátis tuis, perdúcat te ad vitam ætérnam.

Pr. Amen.

Ser. Confíteor Deo omnipoténti, beátæ Maríæ semper Vírgini, beáto Micháeli Archángelo, beáto Joánni Baptístæ, sanctis Apóstolis Petro et Paulo, ómnibus Sanctis, et tibi, pater, quia peccávi nimis, cogitatióne, verbo et ópere, mea culpa, mea culpa, mea máxima culpa. Ideo precor beátam Maríam semper Vírginem, beátum Micháelem Archángelum, beátum Joánnem Baptístam, sanctos Apóstolos Petrum et Paulum, ómnes Sanctos, et te, pater, oráre pro me ad Dóminum Deum nostrum.

Pr. Misereátur vestri omnípotens Deus, et dimíssis peccátis vestris, perdúcat vos ad vitam ætérnam.

Ser. Amen.

Pr. Indulgéntiam ✠ absolutiónem et remissiónem peccatórum nostrórum, tríbuat nobis omnípotens et miséricors Dóminus.

(When a Bishop says Mass the Server here gives him the Maniple.)

Ser.   Amen.

Pr.   Deus, tu convérsus vivificábis nos.

Ser.   Et plebs tua lætábitur in te.

Pr.   Osténde nobis, Dómine, misericórdiam tuam.

Ser.   Et salutáre tuum da nobis.

Pr.   Dómine, exáudi oratiónem meam.

Ser.   Et clamor meus ad te véniat.

Pr.   Dóminus vobíscum.

Ser.   Et cum spíritu tuo.

After the Introit :

Pr.   Kyrie eléison.

Ser.   Kyrie eléison.

Pr.   Kyrie eléison.

Ser.   Christe eléison.

Pr.   Christe eléison.

Ser.   Christe eléison.

Pr.   Kyrie eléison.

Ser.   Kyrie eléison.

Pr.   Kyrie eléison.

After the Gloria :

Pr.   Dóminus vobíscum.

(*A Bishop says :*   Pax vobis.)

Ser.   Et cum spíritu tuo.

At the end of the Epistle the Server answers :
Deo grátias.

The Epistle, Gradual, Alleluia, or Tract being read, the Server takes the missal to the Gospel side. of the Altar.

Pr. Dóminus vobíscum.
Ser. Et cum spíritu tuo.
Pr. Sequéntia (Inítium) sancti Evangélii secúndum (*N*).
Ser. Glória tibi, Dómine.

At the end of the Gospel the Server answers :
Ser. Laus tibi, Chríste.

Before the Offertory :

Pr. Dóminus vobíscum.
Ser. Et cum spíritu tuo.

Here give the wine and water, and afterwards prepare the basin, water and lavabo cloth for the Priest. When the Priest has washed his fingers, kneel in your former place and answer :

Pr. Oráte fratres, etc.
Ser. Suscípiat Dóminus sacrifícium de mánibus tuis ad laudem et glóriam nóminis sui, ad utilitátem quoque nostram, totiúsque ecclésiæ suæ sanctæ.

At the Preface :

Pr. Per ómnia sǽcula sæculórum.
Ser. Amen.
Pr. Dóminus vobíscum.
Ser. Et cum spíritu tuo.
Pr. Sursum corda.

Ser. Habémus ad Dóminum.
Pr. Grátias agámus Dómino Deo nostro.
Ser. Dignum et justum est.

At the Sanctus ring the bell three times. When the Priest spreads his hands over the chalice ring the bell once. Then holding up the Vestment with your left hand and having the bell in the right ring three times during the elevation of the ·Host, and three times during the elevation of the chalice.

At the Pater Noster :

Pr. Per ómnia sǽcula sæculórum.
Ser. Amen.
Pr. Præcéptis salutáribus, etc. Et ne nos indúcas in tentatiónem.
Ser. Sed líbera nos a malo.

A little later on the Priest says :
Pr. Per ómnia sǽcula sæculórum.
Ser. Amen.
Pr. Pax Dómino sit semper vobíscum.
Ser. Et cum spíritu tuo.

Ring the bell once each time the Priest says Dómine non sum dignus. *If there be communicants, give them the communion paten, and say the* Confiteor. *Afterwards serve first the wine and then the wine and water to the Priest. Remove the missal to the Epistle side of the altar.*

(A Bishop must here be served with water to wash his hands as at the offertory.)

Pr. Dóminus vobíscum.
Ser. Et cum spíritu tuo.

*At the end of the Post-Communion the Server
answers* Amen.

*If after the Post-Communion the Priest,
returning to the middle of the altar, leaves the
missal open, the Server takes it to the Gospel
side.*

Pr. Dóminus vobíscum.
Ser. Et cum spíritu tuo.
Pr. Ite, missa est (*or* Benedicámus Dómino).
Ser. Deo grátias.

(*In Masses for the Dead*):
Pr. Requiescant in pace.
Ser. Amen.

(*At a Bishop's Mass*) :
Bishop. Sit nomen Dómini benedíctum.
Ser. Ex hoc nunc et usque in sǽculum.
Bishop. Adjutórium nostrum in nómine
Dómini.
Ser. Qui fecit cœlum et terram.

*Then the Priest gives the Blessing, except in
Masses for the Dead :*
Pr. Benedícat vos omnípotens Deus, Pater,
et Fílius, et Spíritus Sanctus.
Ser. Amen.

At the last Gospel :
Pr. Dóminus vobíscum.
Ser. Et cum spíritu tuo.

Pr.   Inítium (Sequéntia) sancti Evangélii secúndum (*N.*).

Ser.   Glória tibi, Dómine.

At the end of the last Gospel the Server says
Deo grátias.

BAPTISM

BAPTISM is necessary for salvation, for Christ has said : Unless a man be born again of water and *The Holy Ghost* he cannot enter into the kingdom of God (*John* iii. 5).

In Case of Necessity

When an infant is in danger of death, and a priest is not at hand, any lay person may baptise it. *The water must be poured on the head of the child while the words are being said.* The words are : " I baptise thee in the Name of the Father and of the Son and of the Holy Ghost."

The ritual of Baptism begins at the entrance to the church, as a symbol that the child is not yet admitted into the Church, though by the desire of its sponsors it has been brought into the " outer courts " of God's House.

Priest. N., What dost thou ask of the Church of God ?
Godfather. Faith.
Priest. What doth faith offer thee ?
Godfather. Life everlasting.
Priest. If then thou wilt enter into life, keep the commandments. Thou shalt love the Lord thy God with thy whole heart, with thy whole soul, and with thy whole mind, and thy neighbour as thyself.

Then the Priest breathes gently thrice upon the face of the child, and says once :

Go out of him, thou unclean spirit, and give room to the Holy Spirit, the Paraclete.

Then the Priest makes the sign of the Cross with his thumb on the forehead and breast of the child, saying :

Receive the sign of the Cross both upon thy forehead ✠ and also upon thy heart ✠; take unto thee the faith of heavenly doctrine, and in thy manners be such, that thou mayest now be the temple of God.

Then the Priest says the following prayers, during the second of which he lays his hand on the head of the child.

Let us pray.

WE beseech Thee, O Lord, mercifully hear our prayers; and guard by Thine unceasing power this Thy chosen child, N., signed with the sign of the Lord's Cross; that possessing now the first beginnings of Thy great glory, he may, by the keeping of Thy commandments, be brought to attain unto the glory of New Birth. Through Christ our Lord.
R. Amen.

Let us pray.

ALMIGHTY, everlasting God, Father of our Lord Jesus Christ, deign to look down upon this Thy servant N., whom Thou hast been pleased to call to the first beginnings of the faith ; drive out from him all blindness of heart ; break all the bonds of Satan, wherewith he was bound ; open unto him, O Lord, the gate of Thy mercy, that, being safely signed with the sign of Thy wisdom, he may be free from the reek of all wicked lusts ; and, following the sweet fragrance of Thy precepts, may joyfully serve Thee in Thy Church, and go forward from day to day. Through the same Christ our Lord.

R. Amen.

Then the Priest puts a small quantity of blessed salt into the mouth of the child, saying :

N., Receive the salt of wisdom ; let it be for thee as an appeal for mercy, unto ever-lasting life.

R. Amen.

V. Peace be with thee.

R. And with thy spirit.

Let us pray.

O GOD of our fathers, O God the author of all truth, we humbly beseech Thee, graciously deign to look down upon this Thy servant N., and, now that he tastes this first savour of salt, suffer him no longer to hunger for want of being filled with heavenly food, so that he may be always fervent in spirit, rejoicing in hope, ever serving Thy

Name. Bring him, O Lord, we beseech Thee, to the bath of New Birth, that, with Thy faithful, he may be made to attain to the everlasting rewards of Thy promises. Through Christ our Lord.

R. Amen.

I exorcize thee, unclean spirit, in the name of the Father ✠, and of the Son ✠, and of the Holy ✠ Ghost, that thou go out and withdraw from this servant of God, N. For it is He commands thee, accursed damned spirit, who walked on foot upon the sea, and stretched out His right hand to Peter in his sinking.

Therefore, accursed devil, acknowledge thy sentence, and give honour to the living and true God; give honour to Jesus Christ, His Son, and to the Holy Ghost; and withdraw from this servant of God N., because God, even our Lord Jesus Christ, hath vouchsafed to call him to His holy grace and benediction, and to the font of baptism.

Here, with his thumb, he signs the child on the forehead.

And this sign of the holy Cross ✠ which we put upon his forehead, do thou, accursed devil, never dare to violate. Through the same Christ our Lord.

R. Amen.

With his hand on the head of the child he continues :

Let us pray.

I BESEECH Thy eternal and most just goodness, O holy Lord, Father Almighty, eternal God, author of light and truth, in behalf of this Thy servant N. that Thou wouldst vouchsafe to enlighten him with the light of Thy wisdom : cleanse him and sanctify him : give unto him true knowledge, that, being made worthy of the grace of Thy Baptism, he may hold firm hope, right counsel, holy doctrine. Through Christ our Lord.

R. Amen.

The Priest puts the end of his stole on the child, leading him into the church, saying :

N., Enter into the temple of God, that thou mayest have part with Christ unto life everlasting.

R. Amen.

When they have entered the church, the Priest says along with the godparents aloud the Apostles' Creed and the Our Father.

I BELIEVE in God, the Father Almighty, Creator of heaven and earth ;—and in Jesus Christ, His only Son, our Lord ;— who was conceived by the Holy Ghost, born of the Virgin Mary ;—suffered under Pontius Pilate, was crucified, dead, and buried ;— He descended into hell ; the third day He rose again from the dead ;—He ascended into heaven; sitteth at the right hand of God the Father Almighty;—from thence He shall come to judge the living and the dead.—I believe in the Holy Ghost;— the Holy Catholic Church; the Communion of Saints;—the forgiveness of sins;—the resurrection of the body; and life everlasting. *Amen.*

OUR Father, who art in heaven, hallowed be thy name, thy kingdom come; thy will be done on earth as it is in heaven. Give us this day our daily bread; and forgive us our trespasses, as we forgive them that trespass against us. And lead us not into temptation. But deliver us from evil. *Amen.*

Before entering the Baptistery the Priest shall say :

I exorcise thee, every unclean spirit, in the name of God the Father ✠ Almighty, and in the name of Jesus Christ His Son, our Lord and Judge ✠, and in the power of the Holy Ghost ✠, that thou depart from this creature of God N., whom Our Lord hath vouchsafed to call unto His holy temple, that he may be made the temple of the living God, and that the Holy Ghost may dwell in him. By the same Christ our Lord, who shall come to judge the living and the dead, and the world by fire.

R. Amen.

Then the Priest, moistening his thumb on his lips, shall touch therewith, in the form of a cross, the ears and nostrils of the child.

Touching the right and the left ear, he shall say :

Ephpheta, that is to say, Be opened.

Then he touches the nostrils, saying :

For a fragrant sweetness.
But thou, devil, begone ; for the judgment of God draws near.

The Priest then questions the person to be baptised, by name, saying :

N., dost thou renounce Satan ?
R. I do renounce him.
Priest. And all his works ?
R. I do renounce them.
Priest. And all his pomps ?
R. I do renounce them.

Then the Priest dips his thumb in the oil of Catechumens and anoints the child on the breast, and between the shoulders, in the form of a cross, saying :

I anoint thee ✠ with the oil of salvation, in Christ Jesus our Lord, that thou mayest have life everlasting.
R. Amen.
N., dost thou believe in God the Father Almighty, Creator of heaven and earth ?
R. I do believe.

Priest. Dost thou believe in Jesus Christ, His only Son, our Lord, who was born and suffered ?

R. I do believe.

Priest. Dost thou believe also in the Holy Ghost, the Holy Catholic Church, the communion of saints, the forgiveness of sins, the resurrection of the body, and life everlasting ?

R. I do believe.

Then, pronouncing the name of the person to be baptized, the Priest says :

N., wilt thou be baptized ?

The godfather answers :

R. I will.

Then while the godfather or the godmother holds the child, the Priest takes baptismal water in a small vessel, and thereof thrice pours on the head of the child in the form of a cross, and at the same time pronouncing the words, he says once only, distinctly and attentively :

N., I baptize thee in the name of the Father ✠ (*he pours the first time*) and of the Son ✠ (*he pours the second time*), and of the Holy ✠ Ghost (*he pours the third time*).

This done, he dips his thumb in the holy chrism, and anoints the child on the top of the head in the form of a cross, saying :

Almighty God, the Father of Our Lord Jesus Christ, who has regenerated thee by water and the Holy Ghost, and who has given unto thee remission of all thy sins (*here he anoints*), may He anoint thee with the chrism of salvation ✠ in the same Christ Jesus our Lord, unto life everlasting.

R.   Amen.

Priest.   Peace be to thee.

R.   And with thy spirit.

Then he puts on the head of the child a white linen cloth, and says :

Receive this white garment, and see thou carry it without stain before the judgment-seat of our Lord Jesus Christ, that thou mayest have eternal life.

R.   Amen.

Then the Priest places a lighted candle in the hand of the person baptized, or of the godfather.

Receive this burning light, and keep thy baptism without blame : observe the commandments of God, that when the Lord shall come to the nuptials thou mayest be able to meet Him together with all the Saints in the heavenly court, and live for ever and ever.

R.   Amen.

Finally he says :

N., go in peace, and the Lord be with thee.

R.   Amen.

PENANCE

WE must try to avoid the danger of allowing our confession to become a matter of mere routine, entered into lightly without due thought and consideration.

Remember that three things are required on the part of the penitent: *Contrition, Confession, Satisfaction.*

Contrition.—Our sorrow should arise less from fear of hell, and more from the love of God; we must also have a firm purpose of amendment.

Confession.—We are bound to confess all mortal sins committed since our last confession.

Satisfaction.—Is to do the penance given us by the priest.

How to go to Confession

1. Pray for grace to make a good confession.
2. Examination of conscience.

Prayer before Examination of Conscience

O MOST Merciful God, I most humbly thank Thee for all Thy mercies unto me, and particularly at this time, for Thy forbearance and long suffering with me, in spite of my many and grievous sins. It is of Thy great mercy that I have not fallen into greater and more grievous sins than those which I have committed, and that I

have not been cut off and been cast into
hell. O my God, although I have been so
ungrateful to Thee in times past, yet I now
beseech Thee to accept me, returning to
Thee with an earnest desire to repent and
devote myself to Thee, my Lord and my
God, and to praise Thy holy Name for ever.
Receive my confession, and spare me, O
most gracious Lord Jesus Christ, whom I,
an unworthy sinner, am not worthy to
name, because I have so often offended
Thee. Rebuke me not in Thine anger, and
cast me not away from Thy face, O good
Jesus, who has said that Thou willest not
the death of a sinner, but rather that he
should be converted and live.

Receive me, I beseech Thee, returning to
Thee with a penitent and contrite heart.
Spare me, O most kind Jesus, who didst die
upon the cross that Thou might save
sinners. To whom shall I flee but unto
Thee, my only hope and salvation ? Have
mercy on me, O most gracious Lord, and
despise not the humble and contrite heart
of Thy servant. I know Thy mercies are
above all Thy works, and I most confidently
hope that as in Thy mercy Thou hast
spared me so long, and hast now given me
this desire of returning to Thee, so Thou wilt
finish the work Thou hast begun, and bring
me to perfect reconciliation with Thee.

I beg of you, most gracious Virgin Mary,
beloved Mother of Jesus Christ my Re-

deemer, intercede for me with Him. Obtain
for me the full knowledge of all my sins, with
the grace of a sincere sorrow, and a firm
determination to amend my life, to the
salvation of my soul and the glory of His
Name.

I implore the same grace through thee, O
my Angel Guardian ; through you, my holy
patrons N.N. ; through you, O holy St. Peter
and holy Magdalen, and through all the holy
saints of God.

Intercede for me, a sinner, repenting of my
sins, and resolving to confess and amend
them.

Examination of Conscience

1. Have you been guilty of :
    Negligence in the worship of God.
    Heresy, disbelief, or doubt of any
        article of faith.
    Exposing yourself to the danger of
        losing your faith by reading bad
        books, etc.
    Despair or Presumption.
2. Taken God's Name in vain, by swearing,
    blaspheming, or rash oaths.
3. Neglected to hear Mass on Sunday or
    Holyday of Obligation, or performed un-
    necessary servile works ?
    Kept the days of fasting and abstinence ?
    Made your Easter duties ? .... received
    any Sacrament unworthily ?

4. Children, have you neglected your duty towards your parents ?
Parents, have you neglected to provide for the Spiritual and Temporal needs of your children ?
Do you bring up your children in the knowledge and practice of their religion ?

5. Have you been guilty of violence towards your neighbour, scandal or bad example ?

6. Have you been guilty of impurity of thought, word or action ?

7. Have you been guilty of stealing, cheating, or keeping that which does not belong to you ? have you paid your debts ?
If you have wronged your neighbour, either in his person or in his goods, you are bound to make restitution.

8. Have you been guilty of telling lies, calumny or detraction ?

9. Have you been guilty of unchaste thoughts or desires, pride, gluttony, or avarice ?

10. Have you been envious of your neighbour's goods ?

Having examined your conscience make a good act of contrition.

ACT OF CONTRITION

O MY GOD, because Thou art so good, I am very sorry that I have sinned against Thee and I will not sin again.

METHOD OF CONFESSION

Kneeling down, make the sign of the cross, saying :

IN the Name of the ✠ Father, and of the Son, and of the Holy Ghost. *Amen.*

Then ask a blessing in these words :

Pray, Father, give me your blessing, for I have sinned.

The Priest's blessing :

May the Lord be in your heart, and on your lips, that you may, with truth and with humility, confess all your sins, in the Name of the Father, and of the Son, and of the Holy Ghost. *Amen.*

Then say the first part of the Confiteor, *as follows :*

I CONFESS to Almighty God, to Blessed Mary, ever Virgin, to blessed Michael the Archangel, to blessed John Baptist, to the holy Apostles Peter and Paul, to all the Saints, and to you, Father, that I have sinned exceedingly in thought, word, and deed, through my fault, through my fault, through my most grievous fault.

Then say :

Since my last confession, which was (*mention how long since*), I accuse myself, etc.

After this accuse yourself of your sins, either according to the order of God's commandments, or such other order as you find most helpful to

*your memory, adding after each sin the number
of times that you have been guilty of it, and
such circumstances as may very considerably
aggravate the guilt, but carefully abstaining
from such as are irrelevant or unnecessary, and
from excuses and long narrations.*

*After you have confessed all that you can
remember, conclude with this or the like form :*

For these and all other my sins, which I
cannot at present call to my remembrance,
I am heartily sorry, purpose amendment for
the future, and most humbly ask pardon of
God, and penance and absolution of you, my
ghostly Father.

Therefore I beseech thee blessed Mary,
ever Virgin, blessed Michael the Archangel,
blessed John Baptist, the holy Apostles
Peter and Paul, and all the Saints, and you,
Father, to pray to the Lord our God for me.

*Then give attentive ear to the instructions and
advice of your Confessor, and humbly accept
of the penance enjoined by him.*

*Whilst the Priest gives you absolution, bow
down your head, with great humility call upon
God for mercy, and repeat once again the Act
of Contrition.*

THANKSGIVING AND
SATISFACTION

*Having received from God the great blessing of
the pardon of your sins, be careful at once to
thank Him for His goodness.*

A Prayer after Confession

WHAT thanks are not due to Thee, O my Jesus, for Thy great goodness to me? When I was faithless to Thy goodness and loving-kindness Thou hast had patience with me; and even when I offended Thee Thy grace waited for me. It is to Thy infinite grace and goodness that I am indebted for this sacrament, in which Thou hast reconciled me to Thyself. To Thee, and to Thy precious Blood, I desire to offer all the love of my heart, just cleansed from sin. Humbled before Thee, I cried out like David, Have mercy on me, O God, according to Thy great mercy; and Thou hast heard my prayer, O my God, Thou hast forgiven me my sins, Thou hast restored unto me the joy of Thy salvation. Join with me, O my dear Mother Mary, and you, my Angel Guardian and holy Patron, in thanking our dear Jesus for His goodness and mercy to me.

I desire once again, O my Jesus, to express the grief and contrition of my heart for having offended Thee. Whilst thanking Thee for having released me from my sins, I renew the hatred and detestation of them, with which Thou hast inspired me. Reject not, I beseech Thee, the sacrifice of a contrite and humble heart. It is to Thee that I have returned, sinful and sorrowing; it is through Thy mercy that I have received the pardon of my sins. Blessed and praised for evermore be Thy infinite goodness and mercy. *Amen.*

A Prayer for Perseverance

AS Thou hast given me, O my God, the grace once again to return to Thee, I am resolved from henceforth to live wholly for Thee. I belong to Thee, O my God ; keep me as the pupil of Thine eye, protect me under the shadow of Thy wing. I will fly from sin, I will avoid the occasions, and abstain even from the appearances of sin. From henceforth my whole life shall be devoted to Thee ; I will seek in all things to do Thy most holy will. Assist me, O my God, to keep these holy resolutions ; guide my feet in the way of Thy commandments ; permit not that iniquity should have any dominion over me. Let me not receive Thy grace in vain, but do Thou, O my God, complete the work Thou hast wrought in me, and bestow on me that sorrow which leads to true repentance. Grant me the grace of perseverance, that I may faithfully serve Thee all the days of my life. *Amen.*

Satisfaction is an integral part of the Sacrament of Penance ; we must therefore be most careful to perform the penance given us by our confessor. It is best to do so before leaving the church.

MATRIMONY

IT is the wish of the Church that, whenever possible, Catholics should marry Catholics. Mixed marriages, while permitted in certain circumstances, are discouraged by the Church. Such marriages often bring difficulties and troubles to the Catholic party; especially where the children are concerned.

What to do when you wish to be married :

Visit your Parish Priest, taking with you your Baptismal certificate, and arrange for your banns to be called.

Where both parties are Catholic they should try to have a Nuptial Mass if this can be suitably arranged.

In the case of mixed marriages the non-Catholic will be required to sign the following promises before a dispensation will be granted :—

1. Not to interfere with the religious beliefs of the Catholic.

2. That the marriage shall not be preceded nor followed by any other religious ceremony.

3. That all children of both sexes shall be brought up in the knowledge and practice of the Catholic religion.

93

THE MARRIAGE SERVICE

The priest questions the man and woman concerning their consent to marry. The Priest first asks the bridegroom, who stands at the right hand of the bride :

N— WILT thou take N., here present, for thy lawful wife, according to the rite of our holy mother the Church ?
R.   I will.

Then the Priest asks the bride :
N., wilt thou take N., here present, for thy lawful husband, according to the rite of our holy mother the Church ?
R.   I will.

The woman is now given away by her father or her friends. The man holds her right hand in his own right hand, and, taught by the Priest, plights her his troth in these words :

I, N., take thee, N., to my wedded wife, to have and to hold, from this day forward, for better, for worse, for richer, for poorer, in sickness and in health, till death do us part; and thereto I plight thee my troth.

Now loosing their hands and joining them again, the woman, taught by the Priest, says :

I., N., take thee, N., to my wedded husband, to have and to hold, from this day forward, for better, for worse, for richer, for poorer, in sickness and in health, till death do us part; and thereto I plight thee my troth.

Their troth thus plighted, and their hands being joined, the Priest says :

I join you together in marriage, in the Name of the Father ✠ and of the Son, and of the Holy Ghost. *Amen.*

He sprinkles them with holy water. Now the bridegroom puts upon a salver, gold and silver, and also a ring, which the Priest blesses in these words :

V. Our help is in the name of the Lord :
R. Who made heaven and earth.
V. O Lord, hear my prayer :
R. And let my cry come unto Thee.
V. The Lord be with you :
R. And with thy spirit.

Let us pray.

BLESS ✠ O Lord, this ring, which we bless ✠ in Thy name, that she who shall wear it, keeping true faith unto her husband, may abide in Thy peace and according to Thy will, and may ever live with him in mutual love. Through Christ our Lord.
R. Amen.

The Priest now sprinkles the ring with holy water in the form of a cross. The bridegroom receives the ring from the hand of the Priest

*and gives the gold and silver to the bride,
saying :*

With this ring I thee wed ; this gold and
silver I thee give ; with my body I thee
worship ; and with all my worldly goods I
thee endow.

*Now the bridegroom places the ring on the
thumb of the left hand of the bride, saying :*
In the name of the Father ; *then on the
second finger, saying :* and of the Son ; *then
on the third finger, saying :* and of the Holy
Ghost ; *lastly, on the fourth finger, saying :*
Amen.

Which being finished, the Priest says :
V. Confirm that, O God, which Thou hast
wrought in us :
R. From thy holy temple, which is in
Jerusalem.
Lord, have mercy.
Christ, have mercy.
Lord, have mercy.
Our Father, *etc., secretly.*
V. And lead us not into temptation :
R. But deliver us from evil.
V. Save Thy servants :
R. Who hope in Thee, O my God.
V. Send them help, O Lord, from the
Sanctuary :
R. And defend them out of Sion.
V. Be unto them, O Lord, a tower of
strength :

R. From the face of the enemy.
V. O Lord, hear my prayer :
R. And let my cry come unto Thee.
V. The Lord be with you :
R. And with thy spirit.

Let us pray.

LOOK down, we pray Thee, Lord, upon these Thy servants, and lovingly be present at this Thine institution, which Thou hast ordained for the furtherance of mankind ; so that they who by Thine authority are united, may by Thine assistance be preserved, through Christ our Lord. *Amen.*

EXTREME UNCTION

THIS Sacrament is administered when a person is in danger of death by sickness Do not wait until the person is actually at the point of death before you send for the Priest; remember that one of the effects f this Sacrament is to restore health, if God sees it to be expedient.

Prepare for the coming of the priest by placing in the sickroom a table with a clean white cloth, two wax candles, and a crucifix.

A Prayer proper to be Daily Repeated in Time of Sickness

LORD Jesus Christ, behold I receive this sickness, with which Thou art pleased to visit me, as coming from Thy Fatherly hand. It is Thy will it should be thus with me, and therefore I submit : Thy will be done on earth, as it is in heaven. May this sickness be to the honour of Thy Holy Name, and for the good of my soul. For this end I here offer myself with an entire submission to all Thy appointments; to suffer whatever Thou pleasest, as long as Thou pleasest, and in what manner Thou pleasest. For I am Thy creature, O Lord, who have most ungratefully offended Thee ; and since my sins have a long time cried aloud to heaven for justice, why shall I now complain if I feel Thy hand upon me ? No, my God, Thou art just in all Thy ways ; I have truly deserved Thy punishments, and therefore I have no reason to complain of Thee, but only of my own wickedness.

But rebuke me not, O Lord, in Thy fury, nor chastise me in Thy wrath ; but have regard to my weakness. Thou knowest how frail I am ; that I am nothing but dust and ashes : deal not with me therefore according to my sins, neither punish me according to my iniquities ; but according to the multitude of Thy most tender mercies, have compassion on me. O let Thy justice be tempered with mercy ; and let Thy heavenly grace come in to my assistance, to support me under this my illness. Confirm my soul with strength from above, that I may bear with a true Christian patience all the uneasiness, pains, disquiets and difficulties of my sickness ; and that I may cheerfully accept them as the just punishment of my offences : preserve me from all temptations, and be Thou my defence against all the assaults of the enemy, that in this illness I may no way offend Thee. And if this is to be my last, I beg of Thee so to direct me by Thy grace, that I may no ways neglect, or be deprived of those helps, which Thou hast, in Thy mercy, ordained for the good of my soul, to prepare it for its passage into eternity ; that being perfectly cleansed from all my sins, I may believe in Thee, put my whole trust in Thee, love Thee above all things, and, through the merits of Thy death and Passion, be admitted into the company of the blessed, where I may praise Thee for ever. *Amen.*

Short Acts of the Most Necessary Virtues, proper to be inculcated in the Time of Sickness

LORD, I accept this sickness from Thy hands, and entirely resign myself to Thy blessed will, whether it be for life or death : not my will, but Thine be done : Thy will be done on earth as it is in heaven. Lord, I submit to all the pains and uneasinesses of this my illness : my sins have deserved infinitely more. Thou art just, O Lord, and Thy judgment is right.

Lord, I offer up to Thee all that I now suffer, or may have yet to suffer, to be united to the sufferings of my Redeemer, and sanctified by his Passion.

I adore Thee, O my God and my All, as my first beginning and last end : and I desire to pay Thee the best homage I am able, and to bow down all the powers of my soul to Thee.

Lord, I desire to praise Thee for ever, in sickness as well as in health : I desire to join my heart and voice with the whole

and take full possession of my whole soul, and teach me to love Thee for ever.

I desire to be dissolved, and to be with Christ. Oh ! when will Thy kingdom come ? O Lord, when wilt Thou perfectly reign in all hearts ? When shall sin be no more ?

I desire to embrace every neighbour with perfect charity for the love of Thee. I forgive from my heart all that have any ways offended or injured me, and ask pardon of all whom I have any ways offended.

Have mercy on me, O God, according to Thy great mercy; and according to the multitude of Thy tender mercies, blot out all my iniquities.

O ! who will give water to my head and fountains of tears to my eyes, that night and day I may bewail all my sins !

O ! that I had never offended so good a God ! O that I had never sinned ! Happy those souls that have always preserved their baptismal innocence.

Lord, be merciful to me a sinner; sweet Jesus, Son of the living God, have mercy on me.

I commend my soul to God my Creator, who made me out of nothing ; to Jesus Christ my Saviour, who redeemed me with his precious blood ; to the Holy Ghost, who sanctified me in baptism. Into Thy hands, O Lord, I commend my spirit.

I renounce from this moment, and for all eternity, the devil and all his works : and I abhor all his suggestions and temptations. O suffer not this mortal enemy, O Lord, of my soul to have any power over me, either now, or at my last hour. O let Thy holy angels defend me from all the powers of darkness.

O holy Mary, Mother of God, pray for us sinners now and at the hour of our death. O all you blessed angels and saints of God, pray for me a poor sinner.

It may be proper also in time of sickness to read to the sick person leisurely, and as he is able to bear it, the Passion of Christ, or some meditations on His Passion; as also the paraphrase on the Lord's Prayer, the Miserere, and the other penitential psalms; devout acts of contrition, etc. But not too much at once; for that might fatigue him, and do him harm.

A Short Exercise in Preparation for Death, which may be used every day

1. MY heart is ready, O God, my heart is ready; not my will, but Thine be done. O my Lord, I resign myself entirely to Thee, to receive death at the time, and in the manner, it shall please Thee to send it.

2. I most humbly ask pardon for all my sins committed against Thy sovereign goodness, and repent me of them all from the bottom of my heart.

3. I firmly believe whatsoever the holy Catholic Church believes and teaches; and by Thy grace I will die in this belief.

4. I hope to possess eternal life by Thy infinite mercy, and by the merits of my Saviour Jesus Christ.

5. O my God, I desire to love Thee as my sovereign good above all things, and to despise this miserable world : I desire to love my neighbour as myself for the love of Thee; and to forgive all injuries from my heart.

6. O my divine Jesus, how great is my desire to receive Thy sacred body ! O come now into my soul, at least by a spiritual communion ! O grant that I may worthily receive Thee before my death ! I desire to unite myself to all the worthy communions which shall be made in Thy holy church even to the end of the world.

7. Grant me the grace, O my divine Saviour, perfectly to efface all the sins I have committed by any of my senses, by applying daily to my soul Thy blessed merits, the holy unction of Thy precious blood.

8. Holy Virgin, Mother of my God, defend me from my enemies in my last hour, and present me to thy divine Son. Glorious St. Michael, prince of the heavenly host, and thou my angel guardian, and you my blessed patrons, intercede for me and assist me in this last and dreadful passage.

9. O my God, I renounce all temptations of

the enemy, and in general whatsoever may displease Thee. I adore and accept Thy divine judgments with regard to my soul, and entirely abandon myself to them as most just and equitable.

THE BURIAL SERVICE

The priest, in the house of the deceased, or, at least, meeting the remains at the churchyard gate, sprinkles them with holy water, and begins the Antiphon.

If thou, O Lord, shalt observe iniquities.

De Profundis

Psalm 129

OUT of the depths have I cried to thee, O Lord, Lord, hear my voice.

Let thine ears be attentive to the voice of my supplication.

If thou, O Lord, shalt observe iniquities, Lord, who shall abide it ?

For with thee there is merciful forgiveness, and by reason of thy law have I waited for thee, O Lord.

My soul hath relied on his word, my soul hath hoped in the Lord.

From the morning watch even until night let Israel hope in the Lord.

For with the Lord there is mercy, and with him plentiful redemption.

And he shall redeem Israel from all his iniquities.

Eternal rest give unto him (her), O Lord.

And let perpetual light shine upon him (her).

If thou, O Lord, shalt observe iniquities, Lord, who shall abide it ?

Then, while the remains are being carried to the church, the priest thus continues :

The bones that have been humbled shall rejoice.

Miserere

Psalm 50

HAVE mercy upon me, O Lord, according to thy great mercy.

And according to the multitude of thy tender mercies blot out my iniquity.

Wash me yet more from my iniquity, and cleanse me from my sin.

For I acknowledge my iniquity, and my sin is always before me.

Against thee only have I sinned, and done evil in thy sight ; that thou mayest be justified in thy words and overcome when thou art judged.

For behold, I was conceived in iniquities ; and in sins did my mother conceive me.

For behold, thou hast loved truth : the uncertain and hidden things of thy wisdom thou hast made manifest unto me.

Thou shalt sprinkle me with hyssop, and I shall be cleansed : thou shalt wash me, and I shall be made whiter than snow.

To my hearing thou shalt give joy and gladness ; and the bones that were humbled shall rejoice.

Turn away thy face from my sins, and blot out all my iniquities.

Create in me a clean heart, O God; and renew a right spirit within my bowels.

Cast me not away from thy face; and take not thy holy spirit from me.

Restore unto me the joy of thy salvation; and strengthen me with a perfect spirit.

I will teach the unjust thy ways; and the wicked shall be converted unto thee.

Deliver me from blood, O God, thou God of my salvation; and my tongue shall extol thy justice.

O Lord, thou wilt open my lips; and my mouth shall declare thy praise.

For if thou hadst desired sacrifice, I would indeed have given it; with burnt offerings thou wilt not be delighted.

The sacrifice of God is an afflicted spirit : a contrite and humble heart, O God, thou wilt not despise.

Deal favourably, O Lord, in thy good will with Sion, that the walls of Jerusalem may be built up.

Then shalt thou accept the sacrifice of justice, oblations and whole burnt-offerings; then shalt thou lay calves upon thine altars.

Eternal rest give unto him (her), O Lord.

And let perpetual light shine upon him (her).

The bones that have been humbled shall rejoice in the Lord.

After entering the Church, the following Responsory is said :

COME to his (her) assistance, all ye saints of God ; meet him (her) all ye angels of the Lord, receiving his (her) soul, offering it in the sight of the Most High.

May Christ receive thee, who hath called thee, and may the angels conduct thee to Abraham's bosom. Receiving his (her) soul, offering it in the sight of the Most High.

Eternal rest give to him (her), O Lord.

And let perpetual light shine upon him (her).

Offering it in the sight of the Most High.

If the Office of the Dead is to be said, it follows here.

After the Antiphon the officiating priest intones :

Our Father, *silently.*

V.   And lead us not into temptation.

R.   But deliver us from evil.

V.   From the gate of hell.

R.   Deliver his (her) soul, O Lord.

V.   May he (she) rest in peace.   Amen.

V.   O Lord, hear my prayer.

R.   And let my cry come to thee.

V.   The Lord be with you.

R.   And with thy spirit.

Let us pray.

ABSOLVE, we beseech thee, O Lord, the soul of thy servant *N*, from every chain of sin ; that he (she) may be raised up in the glory of the resurrection and live anew amid thy saints and elect. Through Jesus Christ, thy Son, our Lord, who liveth and reigneth with thee in the unity of the Holy Ghost, world without end. *Amen.*

THE MASS FOR THE DEAD

The Mass follows the ordinary form (see p 36) but with the following special parts.

Introit

ETERNAL rest give to them, O Lord; and let perpetual light shine upon them. A hymn, O God, becometh thee in Sion; and a vow shall be paid to thee in Jerusalem : O Lord, hear my prayer ; all flesh shall come to thee. Eternal rest, &c.

Prayer for Bishops or Priests

O GOD, who didst raise thy servants to the dignity of bishops or priests in the apostolic priesthood ; grant, we beseech Thee, that they may be joined in fellowship with thine apostles for evermore.

For Deceased Brethren, Kinsfolk and Benefactors

O GOD, who grantest forgiveness and desirest the salvation of mankind, we beseech thee in thy mercy to grant that the brethren of our congregation with their kinsfolk and benefactors who have passed out of this life, by the intercession of blessed Mary ever Virgin and of all thy saints, may partake of everlasting bliss.

For all the Faithful Departed

O GOD, the creator and redeemer of all the faithful; grant to the souls of thy servants departed the remission of all their sins, that through pious supplications they may obtain the pardon which they have always desired : who livest.

Lesson : Apoc. 14

IN those days : I heard a voice from heaven, saying to me, Write, Blessed are the dead, who die in the Lord. From henceforth now, saith the Spirit, that they may rest from their labours, for their works follow them.

Gradual

ETERNAL rest give to them, O Lord : and let perpetual light shine upon them. The just shall be in everlasting remembrance ; he shall not fear the evil hearing.

Tract

ABSOLVE, O Lord, the souls of all the faithful departed from every bond of sins. And by the help of thy grace may they be enabled to escape the judgment of punishment, and enjoy the happiness of light eternal.

Sequence

DAY of wrath and doom impending,
  David's word with Sibyl's blending !
Heaven and earth in ashes ending !
Oh, what fear man's bosom rendeth,
When from heaven the Judge descendeth,
On whose sentence all dependeth !
Wondrous sound the trumpet flingeth,
Through earth's sepulchres it ringeth,
All before the throne it bringeth.
Death is struck and nature quaking,
All creation is awaking,
To its Judge an answer making.
Lo ! the book exactly worded,
Wherein all hath been recorded ;
Thence shall judgment be awarded.
When the Judge His seat attaineth,
And each hidden deed arraigneth.
Nothing unavenged remaineth.
What shall I, frail man, be pleading ?
Who for me be interceding,
When the just are mercy needing ?
King of majesty tremendous,
Who dost free salvation send us,
Fount of pity, then befriend us.
Think, kind Jesu, my salvation
Caused Thy wondrous Incarnation ;
Leave me not to reprobation.
Faint and weary Thou hast sought me,
On the Cross of suffering bought me ;
Shall such grace be vainly brought me ?
Righteous Judge, for sin's pollution

Grant Thy gift of absolution,
Ere that day of retribution.
Guilty now I pour my moaning,
All my shame with anguish owning;
Spare, O God, Thy suppliant groaning.
Through the sinful woman shriven,
Through the dying thief forgiven,
Thou to me a hope hast given.
Worthless are my prayers and sighing,
Yet, good Lord, in grace complying,
Rescue me from fires undying.
With Thy sheep a place provide me,
From the goats afar divide me,
To Thy right hand do Thou guide me.
When the wicked are confounded,
Doomed to flames of woe unbounded,
Call me, with Thy Saints surrounded.
Low I kneel, with heart submission;
See, like ashes my contrition!
Help me in my last condition!
Ah! that day of tears and mourning!
From the dust of earth returning,
Man for judgment must prepare him;
Spare, O God, in mercy spare him!
Lord, all pitying, Jesu blest,
Grant them Thine eternal rest. *Amen.*

Gospel. John v. 25-29

AT that time, Jesus said to the multitudes of the Jews, Amen, Amen, I say unto you, that the hour cometh, and now is, when the dead shall hear the voice of the Son of God; and they that hear shall live.

For as the Father hath life in himself, so
He hath given to the Son also to have life
in himself : and he hath given him power
to do judgment, because he is the Son of
Man. Wonder not at this, for the hour
cometh wherein all that are in the graves
shall hear the voice of the Son of God ; and
they that have done good things shall come
forth unto the resurrection of life, but they
that have done evil, unto the resurrection
of judgment.

Offertory

O LORD Jesus Christ, King of Glory,
deliver the souls of all the faithful
departed from the pains of hell and from
the deep pit : deliver them from the mouth
of the lion, that hell may not swallow them
up, and they may not fall into darkness, but
may the holy standard-bearer Michael intro-
duce them to the holy light; which thou
didst promise of old to Abraham and to his
seed. We offer thee, O Lord, sacrifices and
prayers; do thou receive them in behalf of
those souls whom we commemorate this day.
Grant them, O Lord, to pass from death to
that life which thou didst promise of old to
Abraham and to his seed.

Secret

For Bishops and Priests

RECEIVE, O Lord, we beseech thee, the
sacrifice which we offer up on behalf

of the souls of thy servants who are bishops
or priests ; so that those whom in this world
thou didst raise to episcopal or priestly rank
may, by thy command, be gathered to thy
saints in the kingdom of heaven. Through
Our Lord.

For Brethren, Kinsfolk and Benefactors

O GOD, whose mercy is boundless,
favourably receive our humble prayers
and by means of these sacraments of our
salvation, grant to the souls of our brethren,
kinsfolk and benefactors, who by thy grace
did confess thy name, the remission of all
their sins.

For All the Faithful Departed

LOOK down in thy mercy, we beseech
thee, O Lord, upon this sacrifice, which
we offer up to thee for the souls of thy
servants ; that to those to whom thou
didst grant the merit of Christian faith, thou
mayest also grant its reward.

Communion

MAY light eternal shine upon them, O
Lord. With thy saints for ever, because
thou art merciful. Eternal rest give to them,
O Lord; and let perpetual light shine upon
them.

Post Communion

For Bishops and Priests

WE beseech thee, O Lord, that thy
clemency which we implore, may

church of heaven and earth in blessing Thee for ever.

I give Thee thanks from the bottom of my heart for all Thy mercies and blessings, bestowed upon me, and Thy whole church, through Jesus Christ Thy Son ; and above all, for Thy having loved me from all eternity, and redeemed me with His precious blood : O, let not that blood be shed for me in vain !

Lord, I believe all those heavenly truths which Thou hast revealed, and which Thy holy Catholic Church believes and teaches : Thou art the sovereign truth, who neither canst deceive, nor be deceived : and Thou hast promised the spirit of truth to guide Thy church into all truth. *I believe in God the Father Almighty, etc.* In this faith I resolve, through Thy grace, both to live and die : O Lord, strengthen and increase this my faith.

O my God, all my hopes are in Thee : and through Jesus Christ my Redeemer, and through his Passion and death, I hope for mercy, grace and salvation from Thee. In Thee, O Lord, have I put my trust ; O, let me never be confounded !

O sweet Jesus, receive me into Thy arms in this day of my distress ; hide me in Thy wounds, bathe my soul in Thy precious blood. I love Thee, O my God, with my whole heart and soul above all things : at least I desire so to love Thee. O come now,

benefit the souls of thy servants who are bishops or priests ; that by thy mercy they may partake of all that in which they hoped and believed.

For Brethren, Kinsfolk and Benefactors

GRANT, we beseech thee, Almighty and merciful God, that the souls of our brethren, kinsfolk and benefactors, for whom we offer up to thy majesty this sacrifice of praise, may by virtue of this sacrament be cleansed from all sin and by thy mercy receive the happiness of eternal light.

For All the Faithful Departed

LET the prayer of those who humbly pray to thee avail for the souls of thy servants and handmaids, O Lord, we beseech thee, so that thou mayst loose them from all sin, and let them share in thy redemption.

After the Mass for the Dead, the following prayer is recited :

ENTER not into judgment with thy servant, O Lord, for in thy sight shall no man be justified, unless thou grant him remission of all his sins. Therefore we beseech thee, let not the sentence of thy judgment fall heavy upon him, whom the true and humble prayer of Christian faith recommends unto thee, but by the help of thy grace let him be found worthy to escape the judgment of condemnation, who in life was signed with the sign of the blessed Trinity. Who livest and reignest world without end: Amen.

The Responsory

DELIVER me, O Lord, from everlasting death in that dread day, when heaven and earth shall quake; when thou shalt come to judge the world by fire.

I tremble, and am sore afraid for the judgment and wrath to come. When heaven and earth shall quake.

O that day! that day of wrath, of woe and of tribulation! a great day and exceeding bitter. When thou shalt come to judge the world by fire. Eternal rest give unto him (her), O Lord, and let perpetual light shine upon him (her). Deliver me, O Lord, from everlasting death in that dread day. When heaven and earth shall quake. When thou shalt come to judge the world by fire.

Lord, have mercy.

Christ, have mercy.

Lord, have mercy.

Our Father, etc., *silently.*

Meanwhile the priest goes round the bier and sprinkles the remains with holy water thrice on each side. He then incenses them in the same way.

V.   And lead us not into temptation.

R.   But deliver us from evil.

V.   From the gate of hell.

5

R.   Deliver his (her) soul, O Lord.
V.   May he (she) rest in peace.   *R.*   Amen.
V.   O Lord, hear my prayer.
R.   And let my cry come unto thee.
V.   The Lord be with you.
R.   And with thy spirit.

Let us pray.

O GOD, whose property it is always to have mercy and to spare, we humbly beseech thee for the soul of thy servant *N*, which to-day thou hast taken out of this world, that thou deliver it not into the hands of the enemy, nor forget it for ever ; but command the holy angels to receive it, and lead it home to heaven ; so that, inasmuch as it hath believed and hoped in thee, it may not suffer the pains of hell, but may have everlasting joys. Through Christ our Lord. *Amen.*

Here the remains are carried to the grave, and in the meantime is said or sung the following :

MAY the angels lead thee into paradise: may the martyrs receive thee at thy coming, and lead thee into the holy city of Jerusalem. May the choir of angels receive thee, and mayest thou, like the poor man Lazarus of old, have everlasting rest.

When the grave is reached, it is blessed with the following prayer, which is omitted if the cemetery be already blessed :

Let us pray.

O GOD, by whose mercy the souls of the
faithful find rest, vouchsafe to bless this
grave, and appoint thy holy angel to keep
it ; and release the souls of all those whose
bodies are buried here from every bond of
sin, that they may always rejoice in thee
with thy saints for ever. Through Christ our
Lord. *Amen.*

*Here the remains and grave are sprinkled with
holy water, and incensed ; and when the
remains are laid in the grave, the following is
said :*

I am the Resurrection.

The Canticle of Zachary.   Luke i.

BLESSED be the Lord God of Israel ;
because he hath visited and wrought
the redemption of his people.
And he hath raised up the horn of salvation
to us, in the house of David his servant.
As he spoke by the mouth of his holy prophets, who are from the beginning.
Salvation from our enemies, and from the
hand of all that hate us.
To work mercy with our fathers ; and remember his holy testament.
The oath which he swore to Abraham our
father, that he would grant us.
That being delivered from the hand of our
enemies, we may serve him without fear.

In holiness and justice before him, all our days.

And thou, child, shalt be called the prophet of the highest; for thou shalt go before the face of the Lord to prepare his ways.

To give the knowledge of salvation to his people, unto the remission of their sins.

Through the bowels of the mercy of our God, in which the orient from on high hath visited us.

To enlighten them that sit in darkness and in the shadow of death : to direct our feet in the way of peace.

Eternal rest grant to him (her), O Lord.

And let perpetual light shine on him (her).

I am the resurrection and life; he that believeth in me, though he be dead, shall live; and every one that liveth and believeth in me shall not die for ever.

Lord, have mercy.

Christ, have mercy.

Lord, have mercy.

Our Father. etc.

In the meantime the remains are sprinkled with holy water.

V.   And lead us not into temptation.

R.   But deliver us from evil.

V.   From the gate of hell.

R.   Deliver his (her) soul, O Lord.

V.   May he (she) rest in peace.   *R.*   Amen.

V.   O Lord, hear my prayer.

R.   And let my cry come to thee.

V. The Lord be with you.

R. And with thy spirit.

Let us pray.

GRANT to thy servant (handmaid) departed, O Lord, we beseech thee, this favour, that he (she) who prayed that thy will might be done may not receive punishment for his (her) deeds ; and that even as here on earth the true faith joined him (her) to the ranks of the faithful, so in heaven by thy mercy he (she) may have fellowship with the choirs of angels. Through Christ our Lord. *Amen.*

V. Eternal rest give to him (her), O Lord.

R. And let perpetual light shine upon him (her)

V. May he (she) rest in peace. *R* Amen. May his (her) soul, and the souls of all the faithful departed, through the mercy of God, rest in peace. *Amen.*

Then is said :

COME to his assistance, all ye saints of God ; meet him all ye angels of God : receiving his soul, offering it in the sight of the Most High. May Christ receive thee, who hath called thee, and may the angels conduct thee to Abraham's bosom. Receiving his soul and offering it in the sight of the Most High.

V. Eternal rest give to him, O Lord : and let perpetual light shine upon him.

R. Offering it in the sight of the Most High.

V. Lord, have mercy on him.

R. Christ, have mercy on him.

V. Lord, have mercy on him.

Our Father, etc.

V. And lead us not into temptation.

R. But deliver us from evil.

V. Eternal rest give to him, O Lord.

R. And let perpetual light shine upon him.

V. From the gates of hell.

R. Deliver his soul, O Lord.

V. May he rest in peace.

R. Amen.

V. O Lord, hear my prayer.

R. And let my cry come unto thee.

Let us pray.

TO thee, O Lord, we commend the soul of thy servant *N.*, that being dead to this world he may live to thee ; and whatever sin he has committed in this life through human frailty, do thou in thy most merciful goodness forgive. Through Christ our Lord. *Amen.*

Then, for a conclusion, may be added the following prayer for those who are present :

GRANT, O God, that while we lament the departure of this thy servant, we may always remember that we are most certainly to follow him. And give us grace to prepare for that last hour by a good life, that we may not be surprised by a sudden and unprovided death, but be ever watching, that, when thou shalt call, we may, with the bridegroom, enter into eternal glory : through Christ our Lord. *Amen.*

THE BURIAL OF INFANTS

The priest, meeting the remains at the church-yard gates (if he cannot do so sooner), sprinkles them with holy water, saying :

Blessed be the name of the Lord.

Psalm 112.

PRAISE the Lord, ye children : praise ye the name of the Lord.
Blessed be the name of the Lord, from henceforth now and for ever.
From the rising of the sun to the going down of the same, the name of the Lord is worthy of praise.
The Lord is high above all nations : and his glory above the heavens.
Who is like to the Lord our God, who dwelleth on high, and looketh down on the low things in heaven and in earth ?
Raising up the needy from the earth, and lifting up the poor out of the dung-hill.
That he may place him with princes, with the princes of his people.
Who maketh a barren woman to dwell in a house, the joyful mother of children.

Glory be to the Father, and to the Son, and to the Holy Ghost.

As it was in the beginning, is now, and ever shall be, world without end. *Amen.*

Blessed be the name of the Lord from henceforth now and for ever.

PRAYERS FOR THE DEAD

A Prayer upon the Day of a Person's Decease, or Burial

O GOD, whose property is always to have mercy and to spare, we humbly beseech thee for the soul of thy servant *N.* which thou hast this day called out of the world, that thou wouldst not deliver it up into the hands of the enemy, nor forget it unto the end : but command it to be received by thy holy angels, and to be carried to paradise, its true country ; that as in thee it had faith and hope, it may not suffer the pains of hell, but may take possession of everlasting joys : through our Lord Jesus Christ. *Amen.*

Another

WE beseech thee, O Lord, admit the soul of thy servant, *N.* which this day has departed out of this world, into the fellowship of the saints, and pour forth upon it the dew of thy eternal mercy ; through our Lord Jesus Christ, &c.

On the Anniversary Day

O LORD, the God of mercy and pardon, grant to the soul of thy servant *N.* whose anniversary we commemorate, the seat of refreshment, the happiness of rest, and the brightness of light : through our Lord Jesus Christ, &c.

A Prayer for One Lately Deceased

ABSOLVE, we beseech thee, O Lord, the soul of thy servant *N.*, that being dead to the world, he may live to thee : and whatever he has committed in this life through human frailty, do thou of thy most merciful goodness forgive : through our Lord Jesus Christ, &c.

For Father and Mother

O GOD, who hast commanded us to honour our father and mother, have mercy on the souls of my father and mother : and grant that I may see them in the glory of eternity : through our Lord Jesus Christ, &c.

For Brethren, Relations and Benefactors

O GOD, the giver of pardon, and lover of the salvation of men, we beseech thy clemency in behalf of our brethren, kinsfolk, and benefactors, who are departed this life, that by the intercession of the Blessed Virgin *Mary*, and of all thy saints, thou wouldst receive them into the joys of thy eternal kingdom : through our Lord Jesus Christ, &c.

For All that lie in the Church or Churchyard

O GOD, by whose mercy the souls of the faithful find rest, grant to all thy servants here or elsewhere, that have slept in Christ, the full pardon of their sins ; that being discharged from all guilt, they may rejoice with thee for all eternity : through our Lord Jesus Christ, &c.

For a Man Deceased

HEAR, we beseech thee, O Lord, our prayers, which we humbly address to thy mercy, that the soul of thy servant which thou hast called out of this world, may be received into the region of light and peace, and be numbered amongst the blessed : through our Lord Jesus Christ, &c.

For a Woman Deceased

WE beseech thee, O Lord, according to thy great goodness, to shew mercy to the soul of thy servant, that being now delivered from the corruptions of this mortal life, she may be received into the inheritance of eternal bliss : through our Lord Jesus Christ, &c.

For Many Deceased

O GOD, whose property is always to have mercy and to spare, be favourably propitious to the souls of thy servants ; and grant them the remission of all their sins, that being delivered from the bonds of this mortal life, they may be admitted to life everlasting. Through our Lord Jesus Christ thy Son, &c.

DEVOTIONS
TO THE SACRED HEART

THERE are some who think that this is a new devotion; this is not the case, as there is ample evidence to show that it was practised by St. Gertrude (1302) and before her time.

It was St. Margaret Mary who was chosen by God to make this devotion public and spread it through the world.

Our Divine Lord appeared to her on several occasions urging her to propagate the devotion to His Sacred Heart. The most famous of these visions took place during the octave of Corpus Christi in the year 1675, when Christ appeared with His Heart aflame, saying :

" Behold the Heart that has so loved men that It has spared nothing, even to exhausting and spending Itself utterly, in order to testify to them Its love ; while in return I receive for the most part nothing but the ingratitude, contempt, irreverence, sacrileges and coldness which they show Me in this Sacrament of Love . . . Therefore I ask of thee, that the first Friday after the Octave of the Blessed Sacrament be kept as a particular feast in honour of My Heart, by communicating on that day, and making an act of reparation to It, in order to atone for the indignities which It has received while It is exposed upon the altars."

Since the death of St. Margaret Mary the devotion to The Sacred Heart has spread throughout the whole church. The Friday after the Octave of Corpus Christi has become the Feast of The Sacred Heart, and in June 1899 Pope Leo XIII ordered the whole of mankind to be consecrated solemnly to The Sacred Heart.

Promises given to St. Margaret Mary by Our Lord in favour of persons devoted to the Sacred Heart :

1. I will give them all the graces necessary to their state.
2. I will give peace to their families.
3. I will comfort them in all their trials.
4. I will be their sure refuge during life, and especially at the hour of death.
5. I will shed abundant blessings upon all their undertakings.
6. Sinners shall find in My Heart the source and ocean of infinite mercy.
7. Tepid souls shall become fervent.
8. Fervent souls shall rise rapidly to a high degree of perfection.
9. I will bless the houses wherein the image of My Sacred Heart shall be exposed and honoured.
10. I will give to Priests the power to touch the hardest hearts.

11. Those who propagate this Devotion shall have their names written in My Heart, whence they shall never be effaced.

12. I promise them in the abundance of My Heart's Mercy that It's all-powerful love shall secure for all those who communicate on the first Fridays of nine consecutive months the grace of final perseverance so that they shall not die in my displeasure, or without receiving the last Sacraments: and that My Heart shall be to them a sure refuge in that last hour.

PRAYER OF ST. MARGARET MARY

ETERNAL Father, suffer me to offer Thee the Heart of Jesus Christ, Thy beloved Son, as He himself offered it in sacrifice to Thee. Receive this offering for me, as well as all the desires, sentiments, affections, movements and acts of this Sacred Heart. They are all mine, since He offered Himself for me, and henceforth I wish to have no other desires but His. Receive them in satisfaction for my sins, and in thanksgiving for all Thy benefits. Grant me through His merits all the graces necessary for my salvation, especially that of final perseverance. Receive them as so many acts of love, adoration, and praise, which I offer to Thy divine Majesty, since it is through the Heart of Jesus, that Thou art worthily honoured and glorified. *Amen.*

LITANY OF THE SACRED HEART

LORD, have mercy on us.
Christ, have mercy on us.
Lord, have mercy on us.
Christ, have mercy on us.
Christ, hear us.
Christ, graciously hear us.
God, the Father of heaven, *have mercy on us.*
God the Son, Redeemer of the world, *
God the Holy Ghost,
Holy Trinity, one God,
Heart of Jesus, Son of the Eternal Father,
Heart of Jesus, formed by the Holy Ghost, in the womb of the Virgin Mother,
Heart of Jesus, substantially united to the Word of God,
Heart of Jesus, of infinite majesty,
Heart of Jesus, Sacred Temple of God,
Heart of Jesus, tabernacle of the Most High,
Heart of Jesus, House of God and Gate of heaven,
Heart of Jesus, burning furnace of charity,
Heart of Jesus, abode of justice and love,
Heart of Jesus, full of goodness and love,
Heart of Jesus, abyss of all virtues,
Heart of Jesus, most worthy of all praise,
Heart of Jesus, king and centre of all hearts,
Heart of Jesus, in Whom are all the treasures of wisdom and knowledge,
     * *have mercy on us.*

Heart of Jesus, in Whom dwells the fulness
of divinity,*

Heart of Jesus, in Whom the Father was
well pleased,

Heart of Jesus, of Whose fulness we have all
received,

Heart of Jesus, desire of the everlasting
hills,

Heart of Jesus, patient and most merciful,

Heart of Jesus, enriching all who invoke
Thee,

Heart of Jesus, fountain of life and holiness,

Heart of Jesus, propitiation for our sins,

Heart of Jesus, loaded down with oppro-
brium,

Heart of Jesus, bruised for our offences,

Heart of Jesus, obedient unto death,

Heart of Jesus, pierced with a lance,

Heart of Jesus, source of all consolation,

Heart of Jesus, our life and resurrection,

Heart of Jesus, our peace and reconciliation,

Heart of Jesus, victim for sin,

Heart of Jesus, salvation of those who trust
on Thee,

Heart of Jesus, hope of those who die in
Thee,

Heart of Jesus, delight of all the Saints,
have mercy on us.

Lamb of God, Who takest away the sins of
the world, *spare us, O Lord.*

Lamb of God, Who takest away the sins of
the world, *graciously hear us, O Lord.*

* *have mercy on us.*

Lamb of God, Who takest away the sins of the world, *have mercy on us.*

V.   Jesus meek and humble of heart,

R.   Make our hearts like unto Thine.

Let us pray.

O ALMIGHTY and eternal God, look upon the Heart of Thy dearly beloved Son, and upon the praise and satisfaction He offers Thee in the name of sinners and for those who seek Thy mercy ; be Thou appeased, and grant us pardon in the Name of the same Jesus Christ, Thy Son, Who liveth and reigneth with Thee, in the unity of the Holy Ghost, world without end. *Amen.*

FORM OF
CONSECRATION TO THE SACRED HEART OF JESUS

O SWEETEST Jesus, Redeemer of the human race, look down upon us, humbly prostrated before Thine altar. We are Thine, and Thine we would ever be : and in order that we may live more closely united to Thee, behold here to-day every one of us consecrates himself to Thy Sacred Heart. Many, alas ! have never known Thee ; many, despising Thy commandments, have rejected Thee. Have mercy on them all, O most loving Jesus, and draw them to Thy Sacred Heart. O Lord, be Thou King, not only of the faithful who have never forsaken Thee, but also of the prodigal children, who have abandoned Thee ; grant that they may quickly return to their Father's house, lest they die of misery and hunger. Be Thou King of those who live in the delusion of error, or who are separated from Thee by schism, call them back to the haven of truth and to the unity of faith, so that soon there may be but one fold and one Shepherd. And, lastly, be Thou King of all those who sit in the ancient superstition of paganism ; and refuse not to deliver them out of darkness into light and to the Kingdom of God. Grant, O Lord, safety and liberty to Thy Church ; give peace and order to all nations ; make the earth resound from pole to pole with one cry : Praise to the divine Heart whence comes our salvation, to It be glory and prayer for ever. *Amen.*

PRAYER OF
ST. ALPHONSUS LIGUORI TO
THE SACRED HEART

O ADORABLE Heart of my Jesus, Heart created expressly for the love of men ! Until now I have shown towards Thee only ingratitude. Pardon me, O my Jesus. Heart of my Jesus, abyss of love and of mercy, how is it possible that I do not die of sorrow when I reflect on Thy goodness to me and my ingratitude to Thee ? Thou, my Creator,

after having created me, hast given Thy
Blood and Thy life for me ; and not content
with this, Thou hast invented a means of
offering Thyself up every day for me in the
holy Eucharist, exposing Thyself to a thousand insults and outrages. Ah, Jesus, do
Thou wound my heart with a great contrition for my sins, and a lively love for Thee ;
through Thy tears and Thy Blood give me
the grace of perseverance in Thy fervent love
until I breathe my last sigh. *Amen.*

LITANY OF THE MOST HOLY NAME OF JESUS

(300 *days' indulgence*)

LORD, have mercy on us.
Christ, have mercy on us.
Lord, have mercy on us.
Jesus, hear us.
Jesus, graciously hear us.
God the Father of Heaven,*
God the Son, Redeemer of the world,
God the Holy Ghost,
Holy Trinity, one God,
Jesus, Son of the living God,
Jesus, splendour of the Father,
Jesus, brightness of eternal light,
Jesus, King of glory,
Jesus, sun of justice,
Jesus, Son of the Virgin Mary,
Jesus, most amiable,
Jesus, most admirable,
Jesus, mighty God,
Jesus, Father of the world to come,
Jesus, Angel of great counsel,
Jesus, most powerful,
Jesus, most patient,
Jesus, most obedient,
Jesus, meek and humble of heart,

* *have mercy on us.*

136

Jesus, lover of chastity,*
Jesus, lover of us,
Jesus, God of peace,
Jesus, Author of life,
Jesus, example of virtues,
Jesus, zealous lover of souls,
Jesus, our God,
Jesus, our refuge,
Jesus, Father of the poor,
Jesus, treasure of the faithful,
Jesus, Good Shepherd,
Jesus, true light,
Jesus, eternal wisdom,
Jesus, infinite goodness,
Jesus, our way and our life,
Jesus, joy of Angels,
Jesus, King of Patriarchs,
Jesus, Master of Apostles,
Jesus, Teacher of Evangelists,
Jesus, strength of Martyrs,
Jesus, light of Confessors,
Jesus, purity of Virgins,
Jesus, crown of all Saints,

Have mercy on us.

Be merciful unto us ;
Spare us, O Jesus.
Be merciful unto us ;
Graciously hear us, O Jesus
From all evil,*
From all sin,

* *Jesus, deliver us.*

From Thy wrath,*
From the snares of the devil,
From the spirit of uncleanness,
From everlasting death,
From the neglect of Thy inspirations,
Through the mystery of Thy holy
   incarnation,
Through Thy nativity,
Through Thine infancy,
Through Thy most Divine life,
Through Thy labours,
Through Thine agony and passion,
Through Thy cross and dereliction,
Through Thy faintness and weariness,
Through Thy death and burial,
Through Thy resurrection,
Through Thine ascension,
Through Thy institution of the most
  Holy Eucharist,
Through Thy joys,
Through Thy glory,
       *Jesus, deliver us.
Lamb of God, who takest away the sins of
the world,
Spare us, O Lord Jesus.
Lamb of God, who takest away the sins of
the world,
Graciously hear us, O Lord Jesus.
Lamb of God, who takest away the sins of
the world,
Have mercy on us, O Lord Jesus.
Jesus, hear us.
Jesus, graciously hear us.

Let us pray.

O LORD Jesus Christ, who hast said : Ask, and ye shall receive ; seek, and ye shall find ; knock, and it shall be opened unto you ; grant, we beseech Thee, to us who ask, the grace of Thy most Divine love, that with all our heart, words, and works, we may love Thee, and never cease to praise Thee.

Make us, O Lord, to have a perpetual fear and love of Thy holy Name ; for Thou never failest to govern those whom Thou dost solidly establish in Thy love. Through Jesus Christ our Lord. *Amen.*

THE WAY OF THE CROSS

(A plenary indulgence may be gained at each recitation.)

The Priests and Acolytes, kneeling before the altar, say as follows :

O JESUS, our adorable Saviour, behold us prostrate at Thy feet, imploring Thy mercy for ourselves, and for the souls of all the faithful departed. Vouchsafe to apply to us the infinite merits of Thy Passion, on which we are now about to meditate. Grant that while we trace this path of sighs and tears, our hearts may be so touched with contrition and repentance, that we may be ready to embrace with joy all the crosses, sufferings, and humiliations of this our life and pilgrimage.

V. Thou shalt open my lips, O Lord.
R. And my mouth shall show forth Thy praise.
V. O God, come to my assistance.
R. O Lord, make haste to help me.
V. Glory be, etc.
R. As it was, etc.

Then the Priest and people move in procession to the First Station.

FIRST STATION

Jesus Christ is Condemned to Death.

V. We adore Thee, O Christ, and we bless Thee.

R. Because by Thy holy Cross Thou hast redeemed the world.

Priest :

LEAVING the house of Caiphas, where He had been blasphemed, and the house of Herod, where He had been mocked, Jesus is dragged before Pilate, His back torn with scourges, His head crowned with thorns ; and He, who on the last day will judge the living and the dead, is Himself condemned to a disgraceful death.

Prayer

IT was for us that Thou didst suffer, O blessed Jesus ; it was for our sins Thou wast condemned to die. Oh, grant that we may detest them from the bottom of our hearts, and by this repentance obtain Thy mercy and pardon.

An Act of Contrition

O GOD, we love Thee with our whole hearts and above all things, and are heartily sorry that we have offended Thee. May we never offend Thee any more. Oh, may we love Thee without ceasing, and make it our delight to do in all things Thy most holy will.

Our Father. Hail Mary. Glory be to the Father.

Have mercy on us, O Lord; have mercy on us.

V.   May the souls of the faithful departed, through the mercy of God, rest in peace.

R.   Amen.

This Act of Contrition is to be repeated after each Station.

While passing from one Station to another, a verse of the Stabat Mater *is sung or said.*

> *V.*   Stabat Mater dolorosa
> Juxta crucem lacrymosa
> Dum pendebat Filius.
>
> *R.*   Sancta Mater, istud agas,
> Crucifixi fige plagas
> Cordi meo valide.

SECOND STATION
Jesus Receives the Cross.

V.   We adore Thee, O Christ, and we bless Thee.

R.   Because by Thy holy Cross Thou hast redeemed the world.

Priest :

A HEAVY cross is laid upon the bruised shoulders of Jesus. He receives it with meekness, nay, with a secret joy, for it is the instrument with which He is to redeem the world.

Prayer

O JESUS ! grant us, by virtue of Thy Cross, to embrace with meekness and cheerful submission the difficulties of our state, and to be ever ready to take up our cross and follow Thee.

Act of Contrition, etc., as before.

V. Cujus animam gementem,
Contristatam, et dolentem,
Pertransivit gladius.

R. Sancta Mater, etc.

THIRD STATION
Jesus Falls the First Time under the Weight of the Cross.

V. We adore Thee, O Christ, and we bless Thee.
R. Because by Thy holy Cross Thou hast redeemed the world.

Priest :

BOWED down under the weight of the cross, Jesus slowly sets forth on the way to Calvary, amidst the mockeries and insults of the crowd. His agony in the garden has exhausted His body ; He is sore with blows and wounds ; His strength fails Him ; He falls to the ground under the cross.

Prayer

O JESUS ! who for our sins didst bear the heavy burden of the Cross, and fell under its weight, may the thoughts of Thy sufferings make us watchful over ourselves, and save us from any grievous fall into sin.

Act of Contrition, etc., as before.

V. O quam tristis et afflicta
Fuit illa benedicta
Mater Unigeniti !
R. Sancta Mater, etc.

FOURTH STATION
Jesus is met by his Blessed Mother.

V. We adore Thee, O Christ, and we bless Thee.
R. Because by Thy holy Cross Thou hast redeemed the world.

Priest :

STILL burdened with His cross, and wounded yet more by His fall, Jesus proceeds on His way. He is met by His Mother. What a meeting must that have been ! What a sword of anguish must have pierced that Mother's bosom ! What must have been the compassion of that Son for His holy Mother !

Prayer

O JESUS ! by the compassion which Thou didst feel for Thy Mother, have compassion on us, and give us a share in her intercession. O Mary, most afflicted Mother ! intercede for us that, through the sufferings of thy Son, we may be delivered from the wrath to come.

Act of Contrition, etc., as before.

V   Quæ mœrebat et dolebat,
     Pia Mater, dum videbat
     Nati pœnas inclyti.
R.   Sancta Mater, etc.

FIFTH STATION
The Cross is laid upon Simon of Cyrene.

V.   We adore Thee, O Christ, and we bless Thee.
R.   Because by Thy holy Cross Thou hast redeemed the world.

Priest :

AS the strength of Jesus fails, and He is unable to proceed, the executioners seize and compel Simon of Cyrene to carry His cross. The virtue of that cross changed his heart, and from a compulsory task it became a privilege and a joy.

Prayer

O LORD Jesus ! may it be our privilege also to bear Thy cross ; may we glory in nothing else ; by it may the world be crucified unto us, and we unto the world ;

may we never shrink from sufferings, but rather rejoice if we may be counted worthy to suffer for Thy Name's sake.

Act of Contrition, etc., as before.

V.   Quis est homo qui non fleret,
  Matrem Christi si videret
  In tanto supplicio ?

R.   Sancta Mater, etc.

SIXTH STATION
The Face of Jesus is Wiped by Veronica.

V. We adore Thee, O Christ, and we bless Thee.

R. Because by Thy holy Cross Thou hast redeemed the world.

Priest :

AS Jesus proceeds on the way, covered with the sweat of death, a woman, moved with compassion, makes her way through the crowd, and wipes His face with a handkerchief. As a reward of her piety, the impression of His sacred countenance is miraculously imprinted upon the handkerchief.

Prayer

O JESUS ! may the contemplation of Thy sufferings move us with the deepest compassion, make us to hate our sins, and kindle in our hearts more fervent love to Thee. May Thy image be graven on our minds, until we are transformed into Thy likeness.

Act of Contrition, etc., as before.

V. Quis non posset contristari,
Christi Matrem contemplari
Dolentem cum Filio ?

R. Sancta Mater, etc.

SEVENTH STATION
Jesus Falls a Second Time.

V. We adore Thee, O Christ, and we bless Thee.
R. Because by Thy holy Cross Thou hast redeemed the world.

Priest :

THE pain of His wounds and the loss of blood increasing at every step of His way, again His strength fails Him, and Jesus falls to the ground a second time.

Prayer

O JESUS ! falling again under the burden of our sins, and of Thy sufferings for our sins, how often have we grieved Thee by our repeated falls into sin ! Oh, may we rather die than ever offend Thee again !

Act of Contrition, etc., as before.

V. Pro peccatis suae gentis
   Vidit Jesum in tormentis,
   Et flagellis subditum.
R. Sancta Mater, etc.

EIGHTH STATION
The Women of Jerusalem Mourn for Our Lord.

V. We adore Thee, O Christ, and we bless Thee.
R. Because by Thy holy Cross Thou hast redeemed the world.

Priest :

AT the sight of the sufferings of Jesus some holy women in the crowd were so touched with sympathy that they openly bewailed and lamented Him. Jesus knowing the things that were to come to pass upon Jerusalem because of their rejection of Him, turned to them and said, "Daughters of Jerusalem, weep not for Me, but weep for yourselves and for your children."

Prayer

O LORD Jesus, we mourn, and will mourn, both for Thee and for ourselves; for Thy sufferings and for our sins which caused them. Oh, teach us so to mourn, that we may be comforted, and escape those dreadful judgments prepared for all who reject or neglect Thee in this life.

Act of Contrition, etc., as before.

V. Vidit suum dulcem Natum
Moriendo desolatum,
Dum emisit spiritum.
R. Sancta Mater, etc.

NINTH STATION

Jesus Falls the Third Time under the Cross.

V. We adore Thee, O Christ, and we bless Thee.
R. Because by Thy holy Cross Thou hast redeemed the world.

Priest :

JESUS had now arrived almost at the summit of Calvary; but before He reached the spot where He was to be crucified, His strength again fails Him, and He falls the third time, to be again dragged up and goaded onward by the brutal soldiers.

Prayer

O LORD Jesus ! we entreat Thee, by the merits of this Thy third most painful fall, to pardon our frequent relapses and our long continuance in sin; and may the thought of these Thy sufferings make us to hate our sins more and more.

Act of Contrition, etc., as before.

6

V.   Eia Mater, fons amoris,
        Me sentire vim doloris
        Fac, ut tecum lugeam.
R.   Sancta Mater, etc.

TENTH STATION
Jesus is stripped of his Garments.

V. We adore Thee, O Christ, and we
bless Thee.
R. Because by Thy holy Cross Thou hast
redeemed the world.

Priest :

ARRIVED at last at the place of sacrifice,
they prepare to crucify Him. His garments are torn from His bleeding body, and
He, the Holy of Holies, stands exposed to the
vulgar gaze of the rude and scoffing multitude.

Prayer

O LORD Jesus, Thou didst endure this
shame for our most shameful deeds.
Strip us, we beseech Thee, of all false
shame, conceit, and pride, and make us so
to humble ourselves voluntarily in this
life, that we may escape everlasting ignominy in the world to come.

Act of Contrition, etc., as before.

V.   Fac ut ardeat cor meum
        In amando Christum Deum
        Ut sibi complaceam.
R.   Sancta Mater, etc.

ELEVENTH STATION
Jesus is Nailed to the Cross.

V. We adore Thee, O Christ, and we bless Thee.
R. Because by Thy holy Cross Thou hast redeemed the world.

Priest :

THE cross is laid upon the ground, and Jesus is stretched upon His bed of death. At one and the same time He offers His bruised limbs to His Heavenly Father on behalf of sinful man, and to His fierce executioners to be nailed by them to the disgraceful wood. The blows are struck! The blood gushes forth!

Prayer

O JESUS, nailed to the cross, fasten our hearts there also, that they may be united to Thee until death shall strike us with its fatal blow, and with our last breath we shall have yielded up our souls to Thee.

Act of Contrition, etc., as before.

V. Sancta Mater, istud agas ;
Crucifixi fige plagas
Cordi meo valide.

R. Sancta Mater, etc.

TWELFTH STATION
Jesus Dies upon the Cross.

V. We adore Thee, O Christ, and we bless Thee.

R. Because by Thy holy Cross Thou hast redeemed the world.

Priest :

FOR three hours has Jesus hung upon His transfixed hands ; His blood has run in streams down His body, and bedewed the ground ; and, in the midst of excruciating sufferings, He has pardoned His murderers, promised the bliss of paradise to the good thief, and committed His blessed Mother and beloved disciple to each other's care. All is now consummated ; and meekly bowing down His head, he gives up the ghost.

Prayer

O JESUS ! we devoutly embrace that honoured cross where Thou didst love us even unto death. In that death we place all our confidence. Henceforth let us live only for Thee ; and in dying for Thee, let us die loving Thee, and in Thy sacred arms.

Act of Contrition, etc., as before.

V.   Tui Nati vulnerati,
       Tam dignati pro me pati,
       Pœnas mecum divide.

R.   Sancta Mater, etc.

THIRTEENTH STATION
Jesus is laid in the Arms of his Sacred Mother.

V. We adore Thee, O Christ, and we bless Thee.

R. Because by Thy holy Cross Thou hast redeemed the world.

Priest :

THE multitude have left the heights of Calvary, and none remain save the beloved disciple and the holy women, who, at the foot of the cross, are striving to stem the grief of Christ's inconsolable Mother. Joseph of Arimathea and Nicodemus take down the body of her Divine Son from the cross and deposit it in her arms.

Prayer

O THOU, whose grief was boundless as an ocean that hath no limits, Mary, Mother of God, give us a share in thy most holy sorrow in the sufferings of thy Son, and have compassion on our infirmities. Accept us as thy children with the beloved disciple. Show thyself a mother unto us ; and may He, through thee, receive our prayer, who for us vouchsafed to be thy Son.

Act of Contrition, etc., as before.

V. Fac me tecum pie flere,
Crucifixo condolere,
Donec ego vixero.

R. Sancta Mater, etc.

Fourteenth Station
Jesus is laid in the Sepulchre.

V. We adore Thee, O Christ, and we bless Thee.

R. Because by Thy holy Cross Thou hast redeemed the world.

Priest :

THE body of her dearly beloved Son is taken from His Mother, and laid by the disciples in the tomb. The tomb is closed, and there the lifeless body remains until the hour of its glorious resurrection.

Prayer

WE, too, O God, will descend into the grave whenever it shall please Thee, as it shall please Thee, and wheresoever it shall please Thee. Let Thy just decrees be fulfilled; let our sinful bodies return to their parent dust, but do Thou, in Thy great mercy, receive our immortal souls, and when our bodies have risen again, place them likewise in Thy kingdom that we may love and bless Thee for ever and ever. *Amen.*

Act of Contrition, etc., as before.

V. Juxta crucem tecum stare,
Et me tibi sociare
In planctu desidero.

R. Sancta Mater, etc.

THE PSALTER OF JESUS

" There is no other name under heaven given to men whereby we must be saved."—Acts iv. 12.

This Psalter is divided into three parts ; each part consisting of five Petitions, and each Petition prefaced by tenfold repetition of the sacred name of Jesus. As it is not to be run over in a hasty manner, but performed with the utmost reverence and recollection, the whole may be said without interruption ; or, each part, at three distinct periods of time, according to the leisure which persons may find, after discharging the indispensable duties of their several states and conditions of life.

FIRST PART

" At the name of Jesus let every knee bow, both in heaven, on earth, and under the earth ; and let every tongue acknowledge that the Lord Jesus Christ is in the glory of God the Father."—Phil. ii.

The First Petition

JESUS ! (*repeated ten times*) thou God of compassion, have mercy on me, and forgive the many and great offences I have committed in Thy sight. Many have been the follies of my life, and great are the miseries I have deserved for my ingratitude. Have mercy on me, dear Jesus, for I am weak; heal me, O Lord, for I am unable to help myself. Deliver me from an inordinate affection for any of Thy creatures, which may divert my eyes from incessantly looking up to Thee. For the love of Thee, grant me henceforth the grace to hate sin, and, out of a just esteem of Thee, to despise all worldly vanities.

Have mercy on all sinners, I beseech Thee, dear Jesus: turn their vices into virtues; and making them sincere lovers of Thee, and observers of Thy law, conduct them to bliss in everlasting glory. For the sake of Thy glorious name, Jesus, and through the merits of thy bitter passion, have mercy also on the souls in purgatory. O Blessed Trinity, one eternal God, have mercy on me. Our Father. Hail Mary.

The Second Petition

JESUS! (*repeated ten times*) help me to overcome all temptations to sin, and the malice of my ghostly enemy. Help me to spend my time in virtuous actions, and in such labours as are acceptable to Thee. Enable me to resist and repel every inordinate emotion of sloth, gluttony, and carnality. Render my heart enamoured of virtue, and inflamed with desires of Thy glorious presence. Help me to merit and preserve a good name by a peaceable and pious life, to Thy honour, O Jesus ! to my own comfort, and the edification of others. Have mercy on all sinners, etc., *as in the first petition.* Our Father. Hail Mary.

The Third Petition

JESUS ! (*repeated ten times*) grant me effectual strength of soul and body, to please Thee in the performance of such virtuous actions as may bring me to Thy everlasting joy and felicity. Grant me, O merciful Saviour, a firm purpose to amend my life, and to make atonement for the years past; those years, which I have lavished, to Thy displeasure, in vain or wicked thoughts, evil words, deeds, and habits. Make my heart obedient to Thy will, and ready, for Thy love, to perform all the works of mercy. Grant me the gifts of the Holy Ghost, which, through a virtuous life, and devout frequenting of Thy most holy sacraments, may at length conduct me to Thy heavenly kingdom. Have mercy, etc. Our Father. Hail Mary.

The Fourth Petition

JESUS ! (*repeated ten times*) comfort me, and grant me grace to fix in Thee my chief joy and only felicity ; inspire me with heavenly meditations, spiritual sweetness, and fervent desires of Thy glory; ravish my soul with the contemplation of heaven, where I hope to dwell everlastingly with Thee. Bring Thy unspeakable goodness to my frequent recollection, and let me always, with gratitude, remember Thy gifts; but when Thou bringest the multitude of the sins whereby I have so ungratefully offended Thee to sad remembrance, comfort me with the assurance of pardon; and by the spirit of true penance, purging away my guilt, prepare me for the possession of Thy heavenly kingdom.

Have mercy, etc.   Our Father.   Hail Mary.

The Fifth Petition

JESUS! (*repeated ten times*) make me constant in faith, hope, and charity. Grant me perseverance in virtue, and a resolution never to offend Thee. May the memory of Thy passion, and of those bitter pains Thou didst suffer for my sake, fortify my patience, and refresh my soul under every tribulation and adversity. Render me a strenuous professor of the Catholic faith, and a diligent frequenter of my religious duties. Let me not be blinded by the delights of a deceitful world, nor my fortitude shaken by internal frauds or carnal temptations. My heart has for ever fixed its repose in Thee, and resolved to contemn all things for Thine eternal reward.

Have mercy, etc. Our Father. Hail Mary.
"The Lord Jesus Christ, for our sakes,
became obedient unto death, even the death
of the cross."—*Phil.* ii.
Hear these petitions, O most merciful
Saviour, and grant me the grace frequently
to repeat and consider them, that they may
serve as so many easy steps, whereby my
soul may ascend to Thy knowledge and love,
and to a diligent performance of my duty
to Thee and my neighbour, through the
whole course of my life. *Amen.*
Our Father. Hail Mary. I believe in God.

SECOND PART

*Begin as before, saying, "At the name of
Jesus let every knee bow, both in heaven, on
earth, and under the earth," etc., as in part
the first, page* 155.

The Sixth Petition

JESUS ! (*repeated ten times*) enlighten me
with spiritual wisdom, whereby I may
arrive at a knowledge of Thy goodness, and
of everything which is most acceptable to
Thee. Grant me a perfect apprehension of
my only good, and a discretion to regulate
my life accordingly. Grant me wisely to
proceed from virtue to virtue, till at length
I enjoy a clear sight of Thy glory. Forbid,

dear Lord, that I return to the sins of which
I accused myself at the tribunal of confession. Let others be edified by my pious
example, and my enemies mollified by my
good counsel.
Have mercy upon all sinners, etc.,
page 156. Our Father. Hail Mary.

The Seventh Petition

JESUS ! (*repeated ten times*) grant me
grace inwardly to fear Thee, and avoid
every occasion whatsoever of offending
Thee. Let the threats of the torments
prepared for sinners, the dread of the loss of
Thy love, and of Thy heavenly inheritance,
always keep me in awe. Suffer me not to
slumber in sin, but rather rouse me to
repentance, lest through Thine anger I may
be overtaken by the sentence of eternal
wrath and endless damnation. Let the
powerful intercession of Thy blessed Mother
and all Thy saints, but above all Thine own
merits and mercy, serve as a rampart
between my poor soul and Thine avenging
justice. Enable me, O my God ! to work out
my salvation with fear and trembling, and
the apprehension of Thy sacred judgments.
Make me a more humble and diligent suitor
to the throne of Thy mercy.
Have mercy, etc. Our Father. Hail Mary.

The Eighth Petition

JESUS ! (*repeated ten times*) grant me the grace truly to love Thee, for Thine infinite goodness and those excessive bounties I have received, or shall ever hope to receive from Thee. Let the recollection of Thy benignity and patience conquer the malice and wretched propensity of my perverse nature. May the consideration of the many deliverances, frequent calls, and continual helps I have received from Thee during the course of my life, make me blush at my ingratitude. Ah, what return dost Thou require of me for all Thy mercies, but that I love Thee ! And why dost Thou require it ? Because Thou art my only good !—Thou art my dear Lord ! the sole object of my life ; and I will diligently keep Thy commandments, because I truly love Thee.

Have mercy, etc.   Our Father.   Hail Mary.

The Ninth Petition

JESUS ! (*repeated ten times*) grant me the grace always to remember my latter end, and the account I am to give after death ; that my soul may be always well disposed, and ready to depart out of this life in Thy grace and favour. At that hour, by the powerful intercession of Thy blessed Mother, the glorious assistance of St. Michael, and my good angel, rescue my poor soul, O Lord, from the snares of the enemy of my salvation. Remember, then, Thy mercy, O dear Jesus ! and hide not Thy face from me on account of my offences. Secure me against the terrors of that awful period, by causing me now to die daily to all earthly things, and to have my conversation continually in heaven. Let the remembrance of Thy death teach me to set a just value on life, and the memory of Thy resurrection encourage me to descend cheerfully to the grave.

Have mercy, etc. Our Father. Hail Mary.

The Tenth Petition

JESUS ! (*repeated ten times*) send me my purgatory in this life, and thus prevent me from being tormented in the cleansing fire, which awaits those souls who have not been sufficiently purified in this world. Vouchsafe to grant me those merciful crosses and afflictions which Thou seest necessary for weaning my affections from things here below. Suffer not my heart to find any repose but in sighing after Thee, since no one can see Thee who loves anything which is not for Thy sake. Too bitter, alas ! will be the anguish of the soul that desires to be united to Thee, and whose separation is retarded by the heavy chains of sin. Keep me, then, O my Saviour, continually mortified in this world, that being purified thoroughly with the fire of Thy love, I may pass from hence to the immediate possession of Thee in everlasting glory.

Have mercy on all sinners, etc., *as at the conclusion of the First Petition*, p. 156.

Third Part

Begin as before, saying : At the name of Jesus let every knee bow, etc., p. 155.

The Eleventh Petition

JESUS ! (*repeated ten times*) grant me grace to avoid bad company ; or, if I should chance to come in the midst of such, preserve me from being infected with the least temptation to mortal sin, through the merits of Thine uncorrupt conversation among sinners. Art Thou not always present, O Lord ? And wilt Thou not take an exact account of all our words and actions, and judge us accordingly ? How then dare I converse with liars, slanderers, drunkards, or blasphemers ; or with those whose discourse is either vain, quarrelsome, or dissolute. Repress in me, dear Jesus, every inordinate affection to carnal pleasures and to delights of taste ; and strengthen me by Thy grace to avoid such company as would enkindle the flames of those unruly appetites. May Thy power, Thy wisdom, and Thy fatherly compassion defend, direct and chastise me ; and cause me to lead such a life that I may be fit hereafter for the conversation of angels.

Have mercy, etc.   Our Father.   Hail Mary.

The Twelfth Petition

JESUS ! (*repeated ten times*) grant me the grace to call on Thee for help in all my necessities, and frequently to remember Thy death and resurrection. Wilt Thou be deaf to my cries, Who hast laid down Thy life for my ransom ? Or canst Thou not save me who took it up again for my crown ? *Call on me in the day of trouble, and I will deliver thee.* Whom have I in heaven but Thee, O my Jesus ! from whose blessed mouth issued such sweet words ? Thou art my sure rock of defence against all my enemies, and my gracious assistant in every good work. I will then invoke Thee with confidence in all trials and afflictions, and when Thou hearest me, O Jesus ! Thou wilt have mercy on me.

Have mercy, etc.   Our Father.   Hail Mary.

The Thirteenth Petition

JESUS ! (*repeated ten times*) enable me to persevere in a virtuous life, and never to grow weary in Thy service till Thou rewardest me in Thy kingdom. In pious customs, holy duties, and in all honest and necessary employments, continue, O Lord, to strengthen me both in soul and body. My life is nothing on earth but a pilgrimage towards the heavenly Jerusalem, to which he that sits down or turns out of the way can never arrive. May I always, O Jesus! follow Thy blessed example. With how much pain and how little pleasure didst Thou press on to a bitter death—the assured way to a glorious resurrection. Let me frequently meditate on those severe words of Thine: *He only that perseveres to the end shall be saved.*

Have mercy, etc. Our Father. Hail Mary.

The Fourteenth Petition

JESUS! (*repeated ten times*) grant me grace to fix my mind on Thee, especially while I converse with Thee in time of prayer. Check the wanderings of my fanciful brain, put a stop to the desires of my fickle heart, and suppress the power of my spiritual enemies, who at that time endeavour to withdraw my mind from heavenly thoughts to vain imaginations. Thus shall I joyfully look on Thee as my deliverer from all evil, and thank Thee as my benefactor, for all the good I have received, or hope to obtain. I shall be convinced that Thou art my chief good, and that all other things were ordained by Thee only as the means of engaging me to fix my affections on Thee alone : that by persevering till death in Thy love and service, I might be eternally happy. Let all my thoughts, O beloved of my soul ! be absorbed in Thee, that my eyes being shut to all vain and sinful objects may become worthy to behold Thee, face to face, in Thy everlasting glory.

Have mercy, etc.   Our Father.   Hail Mary.

The Fifteenth Petition

JESUS ! (*repeated ten times*) grant me the grace to order my life with reference to my eternal welfare, sincerely intending, and wisely referring all the operations of my soul and body towards obtaining the reward of Thy infinite bliss and eternal felicity. For what use is this world, but a school for the tutoring of souls, created for eternal happiness in the next ? And how are they educated but by an anxious desire of enjoying God, their only end ?   Break my froward spirit, Jesus! by the reins of humility and obedience. Grant me grace to depart hence with the most sovereign contempt for this world, and with a heart overflowing with joy at the thought of going to Thee. Let the memory of Thy passion make me cheerfully undergo every temptation or suffering in this state of probation, for love of Thee;

whilst my soul, in the meantime, languishes after that life of consummate bliss and immortal glory, which Thou hast prepared for Thy servants in heaven. O Jesus, let me frequently and attentively consider, that whatsoever I may gain, if I lose Thee, all is lost; and that whatever I may lose, if I obtain Thee, all is gained.

Have mercy on all sinners, etc., *as at the conclusion of the First Petition.*

DEVOTIONS

TO OUR BLESSED LADY

THE ROSARY

THIS is one of the most popular forms of devotion practised by the faithful throughout the world. The name of St. Dominic will always be associated with the Rosary on account of the revelations he received from Our Blessed Lady concerning it. The Rosary as we know it to-day is divided into fifteen mysteries, or meditations, called the Joyful, Sorrowful, and Glorious Mysteries. During the contemplation of each event presented in each Mystery we should recite one *Our Father*, ten *Hail Marys*, and one *Glory be to the Father*. St. Dominic found this a simple yet effective way of instructing the faithful in the life of Christ. For our part we should try to say some part of the Rosary every day, both for the sake of the meditation and for the sake of the indulgences to be gained.

The Joyful Mysteries
The Annunciation
The Visitation
The Nativity
The Presentation of the Child Jesus in the Temple
The Finding of the Child Jesus in the Temple

The Sorrowful Mysteries

The Agony in the Garden
The Scourging at the Pillar
The Crowning with Thorns
Jesus Carries His Cross
The Crucifixion

The Glorious Mysteries

The Resurrection
The Ascension
The Descent of the Holy Ghost on the Apostles
The Assumption of Our Blessed Lady into
Heaven
The Coronation of Our Blessed Lady

LITANY
OF THE BLESSED VIRGIN
(Indulgence of 300 days, each time)

Kyrie eleison.	Lord have mercy.
Kyrie eleison.	Lord have mercy.
Christe eleison.	Christ have mercy.
Christe eleison.	Christ have mercy.
Kyrie eleison.	Lord have mercy.
Kyrie eleison.	Lord have mercy.
Christe audi nos.	Christ hear us.
Christe exaudi nos.	Christ graciously hear us.

Pater de cœlis Deus,

God the Father of heaven,

Fili, Redemptor mundi Deus,

God the Son, Redeemer of the world,

Spiritus Sancte Deus,

God the Holy Ghost,

Sancta Trinitas, unus Deus,

Holy Trinity, one God,

Miserere nobis.

Have mercy on us.

Sancta Maria,

Holy Mary,

Ora pro nobis.

Pray for us.

Sancta Dei Genitrix,*

Holy Mother of God, *

Sancta Virgo virginum,

Holy Virgin of virgins,

Mater Christi,

Mother of Christ,

Mater divinæ gratiæ,

Mother of Divine grace,

Mater purissima,

Mother most pure,

Mater castissima,

Mother most chaste

Mater inviolata,

Mother inviolate,

Mater intemerata,

Mother undefiled,

Mater amabilis,

Mother most lovable,

Mater admirabilis,

Mother most admirable,

Mater Boni Consilii,

Mother of Good Counsel,

Mater Creatoris,

Mother of our Creator,

* *Ora pro nobis.*

* *Pray for us.*

Mater Salvatoris,*	Mother of our Saviour,*
Virgo prudentissima,	Virgin most prudent,
Virgo veneranda,	Virgin most venerable,
Virgo prædicanda,	Virgin most renowned,
Virgo potens,	Virgin most powerful,
Virgo clemens,	Virgin most merciful,
Virgo fidelis,	Virgin most faithful,
Speculum justitiæ,	Mirror of justice,
Sedes sapientiæ,	Seat of wisdom,
Causa nostræ lætitiæ,	Cause of our joy,
Vas spirituale,	Spiritual Vessel,
Vas honorabile,	Vessel of honour,
Vas insigne Devotionis,	Singular vessel of devotion,
Rosa mystica,	Mystical Rose,
Turris Davidica,	Tower of David,
Turris eburnea,	Tower of ivory,
Domus aurea,	House of gold,
Fœderis arca,	Ark of the covenant,
Janua cœli	Gate of heaven,
Stella matutina,	Morning star,
Salus infirmorum,	Health of the sick,
* *Ora pro nobis.*	* *Pray for us.*

Refugium peccatorum,*

Refuge of sinners,*

Consolatrix afflictorum,

Comfort of the afflicted,

Auxilium Christianorum,

Help of Christians,

Regina Angelorum,

Queen of Angels,

Regina Patriarcharum,

Queen of Patriarchs,

Regina Prophetarum,

Queen of Prophets,

Regina Apostolorum,

Queen of Apostles,

Regina Martyrum,

Queen of Martyrs,

Regina Confessorum,

Queen of Confessors,

Regina Virginum,

Queen of Virgins,

Regina Sanctorum omnium,

Queen of all Saints,

Regina sine labe originali concepta,

Queen conceived without original sin,

Regina sacratissimi Rosarii,

Queen of the most holy Rosary,

Regina Pacis,

Queen of Peace,

*Ora pro nobis.

*Pray for us.

Agnus Dei, qui tollis peccata mundi,

Lamb of God, who takest away the sins of the world,

Parce nobis, Domine.

Spare us, O Lord.

Agnus Dei, qui tollis peccata mundi,

Exaudi nos, Domine.

Agnus Dei, qui tollis peccata mundi,

Miserere nobis.

V. Ora pro nobis, sancta Dei Genitrix.

R. Ut digni efficiamur promissionibus Christi.

Oremus.

GRATIAM tuam quæsumus, Domine, mentibus nostris infunde ; ut qui angelo nuntiante, Christi Filii tui Incarnationem cognovimus, per Passionem ejus et Crucem ad Resurrectionis gloriam perducamur. Per eumdem Christum Dominum nostrum. Amen.

Lamb of God, who takest away the sins of the world,

Graciously hear us, O Lord.

Lamb of God, who takest away the sins of the world,

Have mercy on us.

V. Pray for us, O holy Mother of God

R. That we may be made worthy of the promises of Christ.

Let us pray.

POUR forth, we beseech Thee, O Lord, Thy grace into our hearts ; that we, to whom the Incarnation of Christ Thy Son was made known by the message of an Angel, may by His Passion and Cross be brought to the glory of His Resurrection. Through the same Christ our Lord. Amen.

V. Divinum aux-
ilium maneat sem-
per nobiscum.

R. Amen.

V. May the Di-
vine assistance re-
main always with
us.

R. Amen.

AVE REGINA

*From Compline on the Feast of the Purifica-
tion to Maundy Thursday, exclusively.*

HAIL, O Queen of Heaven enthroned !
Hail, by Angels mistress owned !
Root of Jesse, gate of morn,
Whence the world's true light was born.
Glorious Virgin, joy to thee !
Loveliest whom in heaven they see,
Fairest thou, where all are fair,
Plead with Christ our sins to spare.
V. Vouchsafe that I may praise thee, O
sacred Virgin.
R. Give me strength against thine enemies.

Let us pray.

GRANT, O merciful God, support to our
frailty ; that we who celebrate the
memory of the holy Mother of God may, by
the help of her intercession, arise from our
iniquities. Through the same Christ, our
Lord. *R*. Amen.

REGINA COELI

From Compline on Holy Saturday till Trinity Sunday.

JOY to thee, O Queen of Heaven ! alleluia.
He whom thou wast meet to bear ;
alleluia.
As He promised, hath arisen ; alleluia.
Pour for us to Him thy prayer ; alleluia.
V. Rejoice and be glad, O Virgin Mary ;
alleluia.
R. For the Lord hath risen indeed ; alleluia.

Let us pray.

O GOD, who didst vouchsafe to give joy
to the world through the Resurrection
of Thy Son our Lord Jesus Christ ; grant,
we beseech Thee, that through His Mother,
the Virgin Mary, we may obtain the joys of
everlasting life. Through the same Christ,
our Lord. *R.* Amen.

SALVE REGINA

From first Vespers of Trinity Sunday till Advent.

HAIL, holy Queen, Mother of mercy ;
Hail, our life, our sweetness, and our
hope !
To thee do we cry, poor banished children
of Eve ;

To thee do we send up our sighs, mourning
  and weeping in this vale of tears.
Turn then, most gracious Advocate,
Thy merciful eyes towards us,
And after this our exile, show unto us
The blessed fruit of thy womb, Jesus.
O clement, O loving, O sweet Virgin Mary.

V.   Pray for us, O holy Mother of God.
R.   That we may be made worthy of the
promises of Christ.

Let us pray.

A LMIGHTY, everlasting God, who by
the co-operation of the Holy Ghost,
didst prepare the body and soul of Mary,
glorious Virgin and Mother, to become the
worthy habitation of Thy Son ; grant that
we may be delivered from instant evils and
from everlasting death by her gracious
intercession, in whose commemoration we
rejoice. Through the same Christ our Lord.
R.   Amen.

PRAYER FOR ENGLAND

*Prayer to the Blessed Virgin for the
Conversion of England*

O BLESSED VIRGIN MARY, Mother
of God, and our most gentle Queen and
Mother, look down in mercy upon England,
thy Dowry, and upon us all who greatly
hope and trust in thee.

By thee it was that Jesus, our Saviour and our hope, was given unto the world ; and He has given thee to us that we might hope still more. Plead for us, thy children, whom thou didst receive and accept at the foot of the Cross, O sorrowful Mother.

Intercede for our separated brethren, that with us in the one true fold they may be united to the Chief Shepherd, the Vicar of thy Son. Pray for us all, dear Mother, that by faith, fruitful in good works, we may all deserve to see and praise God, together with thee, in our heavenly home.   Amen.

PRAYER TO OUR LADY

St. Aloysius' Prayer to the Blessed Virgin

TO thee, O holy Mary, my sovereign Mistress, to thy blessed trust and special charge, and to the bosom of thy mercy, this day and every day, and at the hour of my death, do I commit myself, my soul and my body ; to thee I commit all my hope and all my consolation, my distresses and my miseries, my life and the end thereof : that through thy intercession, and through thy merits, all my works may be directed and disposed, according to thy will and the will of thy Son. *Amen.*

PRAYER OF CONSECRATION TO THE IMMACULATE HEART OF MARY

By His Holiness Pope Pius XII

QUEEN of the Most Holy Rosary, Help of Christians, Refuge of the human race, Conqueror in all God's battles, we humbly prostrate ourselves before thy throne. We are confident of obtaining mercy, grace, and help in the present calamities, not for our own merits, to which we make no claim, but only because of the great goodness of thy Maternal Heart.

In this tragic hour of human history we confide, entrust, and consecrate to thy Immaculate Heart the Holy Church, Mystical Body of thy Son, Jesus, which bleeds now from so many wounds and is so sorely tried. We consecrate likewise to thy Immaculate Heart the whole world torn as it is by deadly strife, afire with hatred and paying the penalty of its own wickedness.

Be moved to pity by the sight of so much destruction and ruin of souls, by the grief and agony of fathers and mothers, husbands and wives, brothers, sisters, and innocent children. Look with compassion on the lives cut off in the flower of youth, on the bodies mangled in horrible slaughter, on the many souls torn with anguish, and on all those in danger of being lost forever.

Mother of Mercy, obtain for us peace from God and the grace that is able in an instant to change the heart of man, the grace that brings and fosters peace, and makes it lasting. Queen of Peace, pray for us and give to the warring world that peace for which the nations long, a peace in the truth, in the righteousness, and in the love of Jesus Christ.

Turn their weapons aside and let peace possess their souls so that God's kingdom may be set up in quiet order.

Stretch out a helping hand to the unbeliever and to all who live in the shadow of death. Give them peace and grant that enlightened by the truth they may repeat with us before the one Saviour of the world " Glory to God in the highest and on earth peace to men of good will."

Give peace also to the peoples separated from us by error or strife and in particular to those who have professed a special devotion to thee and in whose homes thine ikon was always an object of veneration. It is hidden away now maybe to await the dawn of better days. Bring them back to the one fold of Christ under the one true shepherd. Grant perfect peace and freedom to the holy Church of God. Stem the flood of modern paganism. Let the love of purity increase among the children of God. Make

us live as true followers of Christ, as zealous
apostles, so that God's servants may grow in
merit and increase in number. And as the
whole human race was consecrated to the
heart of thy Jesus that through hope in
Him He might become for all the sign and
pledge of victory and salvation, so we in
like manner consecrate ourselves forever to
thee and to thy Immaculate Heart, O
Mother and Queen of the world. This we
do so that thy love and protection may
hasten the triumph of God's kingdom.
Thus may all nations at peace with one
another and with God proclaim thee blessed,
and sing with thee from pole to pole the
unending Magnificat of glory, love, and
thanksgiving to the Heart of Jesus in which
alone they can find truth, life, and peace.
Amen.

THE THIRTY DAYS'
PRAYER TO THE B. V. MARY

In Honour of the Sacred Passion of our Lord Jesus Christ

*By the devout recital of this prayer for the
above space of time, we may mercifully hope
to obtain our lawful request. It is particularly recommended as a proper devotion for
every day in Lent, and all Fridays throughout
the year.*

EVER glorious and blessed Mary, Queen
of virgins, Mother of Mercy, hope and
comfort of dejected and desolate souls,
through that sword of sorrow which pierced
thy tender heart, whilst thine only Son,
Christ Jesus our Lord, suffered death and
ignominy on the cross, through that filial
tenderness and pure love He had for thee,
grieving in thy sorrows, whilst from His
cross He recommended thee to the care and
protection of His beloved disciple, St. John ;
take pity, I beseech thee, on my poverty
and necessities ; have compassion on my
anxieties and cares ; assist and comfort me
in all my infirmities and miseries. Thou
art the Mother of Mercies, the sweet consolatrix and refuge of the needy and the
orphan, of the desolate and the afflicted.
Cast, therefore, an eye of pity on a miserable, forlorn child of Eve, and hear my
prayer, for since, in just punishment of my
sins, I may find myself encompassed by a
multitude of evils, and oppressed with much
anguish of spirit, whither can I fly for more
secure shelter, O amiable Mother of my
Lord and Saviour Jesus Christ, than under
the wings of thy maternal protection ?
Attend, therefore, I beseech thee, with an
ear of pity and compassion, to my humble
and earnest request. I ask it through the
bowels of mercy of thy dear Son, through
that love and condescension wherewith He
embraced our nature, when, in compliance
7

with the Divine will, thou gavest thy consent; and whom, after the expiration of nine months, thou didst bring forth from thy chaste womb, to visit this world, and bless it with His presence. I ask it through the anguish of mind wherewith thy beloved Son, our dear Saviour, was overwhelmed on Mount Olivet, when He besought His Eternal Father *to remove from Him, if possible, the bitter chalice* of His future Passion. I ask it through the threefold repetition of His prayer in the garden, from whence afterwards, with dolorous steps and mournful tears, thou didst accompany Him to the doleful theatre of His death and sufferings. I ask it through the welts and sores of His virginal flesh, occasioned by the cords and whips wherewith He was bound and scourged, when stripped of His seamless garment, for which His executioners afterwards cast lots. I ask it through the scoffs and ignominies by which He was insulted, the false accusations and unjust sentence by which He was condemned to death, and which He bore with heavenly patience. I ask it through His bitter tears and bloody sweat, His silence and resignation, His sadness and grief of heart. I ask it through the Blood which trickled from His royal and sacred Head when struck with the sceptre of a reed and pierced with His crown of thorns. I ask it through the excruciating torments He suffered when His hands and feet were fastened with gross nails to the tree of the cross. I ask it through His vehement thirst and bitter potion of vinegar and gall. I ask it through His dereliction on the cross, when He exclaimed, *" My God ! My God ! why hast Thou forsaken me ? "* I ask it through His mercy extended to the repentant thief ; and through His recommending His precious soul and spirit into the hands of His Eternal Father, before He expired, saying *"All is consummated."* I ask it through the Blood mixed with Water, which issued from His sacred Side when pierced with a lance, from whence a flood of grace and mercy has flowed to us. I ask it through His immaculate Life, bitter Passion, and ignominious Death on the cross, at which nature itself was thrown into convulsions by the bursting of rocks, rending of the veil of the Temple, the earthquake, and darkness of the sun and moon. I ask it through His descent into hell, where He comforted the Saints of the Old Law with His presence, and led captivity captive. I ask it through His glorious victory over death, and when He arose again to life on the third day ; and through the joy which His appearance for forty days after gave thee, His blessed Mother, His Apostles, and the rest of His disciples, when, in thine and their presence, He miraculously ascended into heaven. I ask it through the grace of the Holy Ghost, infused into the hearts of

His apostles when He descended upon them in the form of fiery tongues, and by which they were inspired with zeal in the conversion of the world, when they went to preach the Gospel. I ask it through the awful appearance of thy Son at the last dreadful day, when He shall come to judge the living and the dead, and the world by fire. I ask it through the compassion He bore thee in this life, and the ineffable joy thou didst feel at thy assumption into heaven, where thou art eternally absorbed in the sweet contemplation of His Divine perfections. O glorious and ever-blessed Virgin, comfort the heart of thy suppliant, by obtaining for me—

(Here mention or reflect on your lawful request under the reservation of its being agreeable to the will of God, Who sees whether it will contribute towards your spiritual good.)

And as I am persuaded my Divine Saviour doth honour thee as His beloved Mother, to whom He refuses nothing, because you ask nothing contrary to His honour, so let me speedily experience the efficacy of thy powerful intercession, according to the tenderness of thy maternal affection, and His filial, loving heart, who mercifully granteth the requests, and complieth with the desires of those that love and fear Him. Wherefore, O most blessed Virgin, besides the object of my present petition, and whatever else I may stand in need of, obtain for me also of thy dear Son, our Lord and our God, a lively faith, firm hope, perfect charity, true contrition of heart, unfeigned tears of compunction, sincere confession, condign satisfaction, abstinence from sin, love of God and my neighbour, contempt of the world, patience to suffer affronts and ignominies, nay, even, if necessary, an opprobrious death itself, for love of Thy Son, our Saviour Jesus Christ. Obtain likewise for me, O sacred Mother of God, perseverance in good works, performance of good resolutions, mortification of self-will, a pious conversation through life, and at my last moments strong and sincere repentance, accompanied by such a lively and attentive presence of mind, as may enable me to receive the Last Sacraments of the Church worthily, and die in thy friendship and favour. Lastly, obtain, I beseech thee, for the souls of my parents, brethren, relatives and benefactors, both living and dead, life everlasting. *Amen.*

MEMORARE

(300 days' indulgence each time. Plenary once a month, if said each day.)

REMEMBER, O most gracious Virgin Mary, that never was it known that any one who fled to thy protection, implored thy help, and sought thy intercession, was left unaided. Inspired with this confidence, I fly unto Thee, O Virgin of virgins, my Mother : to thee I come. before thee I stand sinful and sorrowful. O Mother of the Word Incarnate, despise not my petitions, but in thy clemency hear and grant them. *Amen.*

MAGNIFICAT

Canticle of B.V.M.

MY soul doth magnify the Lord.
And my spirit hath rejoiced in God my Saviour.
Because He hath regarded the humility of His handmaid : for behold, from henceforth, all generations shall call me blessed.
For He that is mighty hath done great things to me : and holy is His Name.
And His mercy is from generation to generation of them that fear Him.
He hath showed might in His arm : He hath scattered the proud in the conceit of their heart.
He hath put down the mighty from their seat : and hath exalted the humble.
He hath filled the hungry with good things : and the rich He hath sent empty away.
He hath received Israel His servant : being mindful of His mercy.
As He spoke to our fathers : to Abraham. and to his seed for ever.
Glory be to the Father, etc.

LITANY OF ST. JOSEPH

(Approved by Pius X, March 18, 1909)

LORD, have mercy on us.
 Christ, have mercy on us.
Lord, have mercy on us.
Christ, hear us.
Christ, graciously hear us.
God, the Father of heaven,*
God the Son, Redeemer of the world,*
God the Holy Ghost,*
Holy Trinity, one God,*
Holy Mary,†
Saint Joseph,
Illustrious Son of David,
Splendour of Patriarchs,
Spouse of the Mother of God,
Chaste Guardian of the Virgin,
Foster-Father of the Son of God,
Watchful Defender of Christ,
Head of the Holy Family,
Joseph most just,
Joseph most pure,
Joseph most prudent,
Joseph most courageous,
Joseph most obedient,
Joseph most faithful,
Mirror of patience,
Lover of poverty,

Have mercy on us.
†*Pray for us.*

187

Model of all who labour,*
Glory of family life,
Preserver of virgins,
Mainstay of families,
Solace of the afflicted,
Hope of the sick,
Patron of the dying,
Terror of demons,
Protector of Holy Church,
       Pray for us.

Lamb of God, who takest away the sins of the world, *Spare us, O Lord.*

Lamb of God, who takest away the sins of the world, *Graciously hear us, O Lord.*

Lamb of God, who takest away the sins of the world, *Have mercy on us.*

V. He hath made Him master of His House.

R. *And ruler of all His possessions.*

Let us pray.

O GOD, who in Thine ineffable providence didst vouchsafe to choose blessed Joseph to be the spouse of Thy most Holy Mother, grant, we beseech Thee, that we may be worthy to have him for our intercessor in heaven whom on earth we venerate as our protector; who livest and reignest world without end. *Amen.*

PRAYER TO ST. JOSEPH

TO thee, O blessed Joseph, we fly in our tribulation; and after imploring the help of thy most holy spouse, we ask also with confidence for thy intercession. By that tender affection which bound thee to the immaculate Virgin Mother of God, and by the paternal love with which thou didst embrace the child Jesus, we beseech thee to look kindly upon the inheritance which Jesus Christ acquired by His precious blood, and by thy powerful aid to help us in our needs. Protect, O most careful guardian of the Holy Family, the chosen people of Jesus Christ. Keep us, most loving Father, from all pestilence of error and corruption. From thy place in heaven, most powerful protector, be thou mercifully with us, in this warfare with the powers of darkness ; and, as thou didst rescue the child Jesus when in utmost peril of life, so now defend God's holy Church from the snares of the enemy and from all adversity. Guard each of us by thy constant patronage, so that, sustained by thine example and help, we may live in holiness, die a holy death, and obtain everlasting happiness in heaven. *Amen.*

GUILD OF THE
BLESSED SACRAMENT

THE GUILD SERVICE

The Tabernacle

I COME to Thee, my Love,
From ways of grief and pain ;
I come to Thee, my Love,
Who here in light dost reign.
The tempest raves without,
The angry billows roll,
But here Thy peace is mine,
Thou Lover of my soul.

Oh, touch me with Thy hand,
As in the dust I lie ;
Oh, lift me to Thy Heart,
Without Thee I must die.
My soul is faint and dark,
I come to Thee for rest ;
Oh, let me see Thy light
And lie upon Thy Breast.

I long, when far away,
To be with Thee again,
Where treasures of Thy grace
Fall like the silent rain.
O veiled and hidden Love,
O loving, gracious Lord,
From Thee the silver showers
Upon my heart are poured.

The storm of pain and grief
Bends me beneath its power;
I have no help but Thee
In sorrow's darkest hour.
Oh, help me, then, my Love,
For I am dark and lone;
And joy and light are Thine
Upon this Altar Throne.

H. A. Rawes, O.S.C.

Priest.* In the Name . . .

(All stand.)

Priest and People. ✠ In the Name of the Father, and of the Son, and of the Holy Ghost. *Amen.*

Priest. An Act of Faith.

(All kneel.)

Priest. Behold the Lamb of God!

People. Behold Him Who taketh away the sins of the world.

Priest. Acts of Hope and Charity.

Priest and People. O Sacred Banquet! in which Christ is received, the memory of His Passion is renewed, the mind is filled with grace, and the pledge of future glory is given to us.

Priest. Acts of Contrition and Supplication.

Priest and People. Lamb of God, Who takest away the sins of the world, Have mercy on us.

* *The Chaplain of the Guild should conduct the service standing, either in the pulpit or at the altar-rails, facing the people.*

Lamb of God, Who takest away the sins of the world, Have mercy on us.

Lamb of God, Who takest away the sins of the world, Give us peace.

SUMMARY OF THESE ACTS

From the *Adoro Te Devote*

Priest and People :

Increase my faith, fix all my hopes on Thee, And bind my heart to Thine in deathless charity.

> (*Fac me tibi semper magis credere,*
> *In te spem habere, te diligere.*)

The Five Prayers

Priest. In Adoration and in Praise of the Blessed Sacrament ; in Thanksgiving and in Reparation for the Five Sacred Wounds ; and in Commemoration of the Passion perpetually renewed in the adorable Sacrament—let us say five times the following prayers :—

Priest. 1. In Adoration.
Blessed and praised every moment.
People. Be the Most Holy and Divine Sacrament.
Priest and People. Our Father ; Hail Mary ; Glory be to the Father.

Verse

O Sacrament Most Holy, O Sacrament Divine,

All praise and all thanksgiving be every
    moment Thine.

Priest.   2. In Praise,
    Blessed and praised every moment.
People. Be the Most Holy and Divine
Sacrament.
Priest and People. Our Father ; Hail Mary ;
Glory be to the Father.

Verse

O Sacrament Most Holy, O Sacrament
    Divine,
All praise and all thanksgiving be every
    moment Thine.

Priest.   3. In Thanksgiving.
    Blessed and praised every moment.
People. Be the Most Holy and Divine
Sacrament.
Priest and People. Our Father ; Hail Mary ;
Glory be to the Father.

Verse

O Sacrament Most Holy, O Sacrament
    Divine,
All praise and all thanksgiving be every
    moment Thine.

Priest.   4. In Reparation.
    Blessed and praised every moment.
People. Be the Most Holy and Divine
Sacrament.
Priest and People. Our Father ; Hail Mary ;
Glory be to the Father.

Verse

O Sacrament Most Holy, O Sacrament
    Divine,
All praise and all thanksgiving be every
    moment Thine.

Priest. 5. In Commemoration of the Passion.
    Blessed and praised every moment.
People. Be the Most Holy and Divine
Sacrament.
Priest and People. Our Father; Hail Mary;
Glory be to the Father.

Verse

O Sacrament Most Holy, O Sacrament
    Divine,
All praise and all thanksgiving be every
    moment Thine.

Priest. Thou didst give them Bread from
heaven.
People. Containing in itself all sweetness.
Priest. Let us pray.

Priest and People :

O GOD, Who under a wonderful Sacrament, hast left to us a memorial of Thy
Passion, grant us, we beseech Thee, so to
reverence the sacred mysteries of Thy Body
and Blood, that we may ever find in ourselves the Fruit of Thy Redemption, Who
livest and reignest world without end.
Amen.

The Protestation of Faith

Priest.   I believe . . *

(*All stand.*)

Priest and People :

I BELIEVE in God the Father Almighty, Creator of heaven and earth, and in Jesus Christ, His Only Son, Our Lord, Who was conceived by the Holy Ghost, born of the Virgin Mary, suffered under Pontius Pilate, was crucified, dead and buried. He descended into hell, the third day He rose again from the dead ; He ascended into heaven, sitteth at the right hand of God the Father Almighty. From thence He shall come to judge the living and the dead, I believe in the Holy Ghost, the Holy Catholic Church, the Communion of Saints, the forgiveness of sins, the resurrection of the body, and life everlasting. *Amen.*

(*All kneel.*)

For the Sick

Priest.   Let us say a *Hail Mary* for . . .
Members of our Guild, who are sick.

For the Dead

Priest.   Let us say Psalm cxxix., the *De Profundis,* for the repose of the souls of the faithful departed, especially for . . . and for all who have been members of our Guild.

* *As an alternative to the recitation of the* Apostles' Creed *the* Credo *may be sung.*

Priest. Out of the depths have I cried unto Thee, O Lord : Lord, hear my voice.

People. Let Thine ears be attentive to the voice of my supplication.

Priest. If Thou, O Lord, wilt mark iniquities : Lord, who shall endure it ?

People. For with Thee there is merciful forgiveness : and by reason of Thy law I have waited for Thee, O Lord.

Priest. My soul hath relied on His word : my soul hath hoped in the Lord.

People. From the morning watch even until night, let Israel hope in the Lord.

Priest. For with the Lord there is mercy : and with Him plentiful redemption.

People. And He shall redeem Israel from all his iniquities.

Priest. Eternal rest give to them, O Lord.

People. And let perpetual light shine upon them.

Priest. Let us pray.

Priest and People :

O GOD, the Creator and Redeemer of all the faithful, grant to the souls of Thy servants departed the remission of all their sins ; that through pious supplications they may obtain the pardon which they have always desired. Who livest and reignest, world without end. *Amen.*

Priest. May they rest in peace.

People. Amen.

(*All stand.*)

Conclusion

Priest. Let us sing three times the *Glory be to the Father*, in thanksgiving for all the graces received through the adorable Sacrament of the Altar.

Priest and People. *Glory be to the Father.** (Here a short Address is given, followed by Hymn and Benediction).

** The doxology is sung three times—thus, p, f, ff.*

BENEDICTION
OF THE BLESSED SACRAMENT

O Salutaris †   *O Salutaris*

O Salutaris Hostia !

Quæ cœli pandis ostium ;

Bella premunt hostilia,

Da robur, fer auxilium.

Uni trinoque Domino

Sit sempiterna gloria

Qui vitam sine termino

Nobis donet in patria.

Amen.

O saving Victim ! opening wide

The gate of Heaven to man below,

Our foes press on from every side ;

Thine aid supply, Thy strength bestow.

To Thy great **Name** be endless praise,

Immortal Godhead, one in three ;

Oh, grant us endless length of days

In our true native land with Thee.

Amen.

† *When the Guild Service takes place at times of Exposition, such as during the " Holy Hour," the* O Salutaris *is not repeated here.*

ACT OF REPARATION TO JESUS IN THE BLESSED SACRAMENT

Priest and People :

O JESUS, my Lord, Who dwellest night and day in our midst, I am deeply grieved to see Thee so often abandoned by Thy children. Deploring their ingratitude from the bottom of my heart, I desire to make amends by grateful acknowledgment of Thy exceeding love. Behold me, then, humbly prostrate at Thy feet. Adoring Thee profoundly, I have come in reparation, O Jesus, to consecrate myself to Thee once more in the adorable Sacrament. I earnestly purpose, by the help of Thy grace, to do all that I can to atone for sins committed by me and by others against Thee in the Most Holy Sacrament. *Amen.*

Tantum Ergo	*Tantum Ergo*
Tantum ergo Sacramentum	Down in adoration falling,
Veneremur cernui :	Lo ! the sacred Host we hail :
Et antiquum documentum	Lo ! o'er ancient forms departing,
Novo cedat ritui :	Newer rites of grace prevail ;
Præstat fides supplementum	Faith for all defects supplying

Sensuum defectui.

Genitori, Genitoque

Laus et jubilatio :

Salus honor, virtus quoque
Sit et benedictio :

Procedenti ab utro-que
Compar sit laudatio.
            Amen.
V. Panem de cœlo præstitisti eis.
        (Alleluia.)

R. Omne delecta-mentum in se ha-bentem.
        (Alleluia.)

Oremus

DEUS, qui nobis sub Sacramento mirabili passionis tuæ memoriam reliquisti : tribue, quæsumus, ita nos corporis et sanguinis tui sacra mysteria venerari ; ut redemp-

Where the feeble senses fail.

To the everlasting Father,

And the Son Who reigns on high,

With the Holy Ghost proceeding
Forth from each eternally,

Be salvation, honour blessing,
Might, and endless majesty.   *Amen.*
V. Thou didst give them bread from heaven.
        (Alleluia.)

R. Containing in itself all sweetness.
        (Alleluia.)

Let us pray.

O GOD, Who, under a wonderful Sacrament, hast left to us a memorial of Thy Passion, grant us, we beseech Thee, so to reverence the sacred mysteries of Thy Body and Blood,

tionis tuæ fructum in nobis jugiter sentiamus. Qui vivis, etc. *Amen.*

that we may ever find in ourselves the Fruit of Thy Redemption. Who livest, etc. *Amen.*

Divine Praises

Blessed be God.

Blessed be His Holy Name.

Blessed be Jesus Christ, true God and true Man.

Blessed be the Name of Jesus.

Blessed be His Most Sacred Heart.

Blessed be Jesus in the Most Holy Sacrament of the Altar.

Blessed be the great Mother of God, Mary most holy.

Blessed be her holy and Immaculate Conception.

Blessed be the name of Mary, Virgin and Mother.

Blessed be St. Joseph, her chaste spouse.

Blessed be God in His Angels and in His Saints.

Two Minutes' Silence with Our Lord (*during which the Blessed Sacrament is left in exposition on the corporal till the conclusion of the silence*).

In place of the *Adoremus*, the Guild Hymn is sung.

The Blessed Sacrament Guild Hymn

G OD, Creator, Mighty Lord,
    King of Heaven and earth adored,
Thee we praise, we bless Thy Name,
Thee our Sovereign Lord proclaim.

God Incarnate, Mary's Son,
Victor crowned with laurels won,
Source of Life, Eternal King,
Loving homage Thee we bring.

Holy Spirit, Fount of Grace,
Strength and Wisdom to our race,
Sorrows soothe, cold hearts inflame,
" Comforter," Thy thrice blessed Name.

God 'neath sacramental veil,
Angels' Bread for mortals frail,
Come, our souls' most welcome Guest,
Peace in Thee we find, and rest.

Mgr. Grosch.

MEDITATIONS

Instructions for Meditation or Mental Prayer, proper to be made every day in the morning

In the mornings I will meditate upon thee. *Psalm* 62.

The wise man shall give his heart to watch in the morning early to the Lord that made him, and in the sight of the most high shall present his prayer. *Ecclus.* 39.

MEDITATION, consisting of *Considerations* on the great truths of Christianity, pious *Affections* and manifold elevations of the soul to God, and serious *Resolutions* of devoting one's self to him, is allowed to be one of the most important exercises of a Christian life, and such as ought to be performed daily, by as many as would serve God in good earnest. The time most proper for it is in the morning. The most proper place, one's closet, or what other place one can be most recollected in. The chief subjects to be meditated on, especially for beginners, are : the end for which we came into this world; the benefits of God, and the many motives that we have to love and serve him; the vanity of the honours, riches, and pleasures of this life ; and how very suddenly all these things vanish away ;

the enormity of sin, and the multitude of our own sins in particular; the certainty and uncertainty of death ; and the necessity of preparing for it; the account that we must one day give of our whole lives to an all-seeing judge ; the eternal joys of heaven, and the eternal torments of hell : the presence and majesty of God; the life and death of Jesus Christ ; the examples of his saints; the state of our own interior, in order to the knowledge of ourselves ; our passions and vices, &c.

The method of meditation prescribed by that great master in spirituality, St. *Francis de Sales*, in his *Introduction*, part the second, is as follows : first, place yourself in the presence of God, by a lively faith that he sees and beholds you ; and is most intimately present in the very centre of your soul : prostrate yourself in spirit before him, to adore this sovereign Lord, whose majesty fills heaven and earth ; make an offering of your whole being to him ; and humbly beg his pardon for all your past treasons and sins.

Secondly, implore with fervour and humility his light and grace, that you may perform this important exercise as you ought.

Thirdly, consider attentively upon the subject which you have chosen for your meditation (which you ought to have prepared over night) and let the truths of heaven sink deep into your soul. Dwell most upon such points as you find yourself most affected with.

Fourthly, from these considerations draw pious *Affections* of the love of God, of gratitude for his benefits, repentance for your sins, and the like, which are the principal part of mental prayer, and what you ought most to insist upon.

Fifthly, from these affections pass on to good resolutions of a serious amendment of your life, particularly with regard to such failings as you are most subject to : and determine with yourself to begin that very day to put these good purposes in execution on such occasions as shall offer.

Sixthly, conclude by thanksgiving to God for the affections and resolutions he has given you ; offer them to him, and beg his blessing on them.

Seventhly, lay up in your mind such points of your meditation as have touched you most, and oftentimes in the day reflect upon them. Which the saint compares to the gathering, as it were, a nosegay, in this garden of devotion, to smell at all the day.

Eighthly, such as find difficulty in meditation, may help themselves by using some good book, reading leisurely, and pausing upon what they read, and drawing proper affections and resolutions from it.

TEN MEDITATIONS

*Out of the first part of St. Francis de Sales's
Introduction to a Devout Life : which
may serve as examples of this exercise ;
and are very proper to bring a soul to a
resolution of serving God.*

The whole earth is laid waste with desolation, because there is no one that thinks in his heart. *Jeremiah* xii. 11.

THE FIRST MEDITATION

On our Creation

Preparation

1. PLACE yourself in the presence of God. Beseech him to inspire you.

Considerations

1. CONSIDER that so many years ago you were not yet in the world, and that your being was a mere nothing. Where were we, O my soul, at that time ? The world had lasted so many ages, and yet there was no news of us.

2. God has framed you out of this nothing to make you what you are, merely of his own goodness ; having no need at all of you.

3. Consider the being that God has given you ; for it is the highest in this visible

world, capable of eternal life, and of being perfectly united with his divine majesty.

Affections and Resolutions

1. HUMBLE *yourself exceedingly in the presence of God, saying in your heart with the psalmist :* O Lord, I am in thy sight a mere nothing ; and how hadst thou remembrance of me to create me ? Alas, my soul, thou wert ingulfed in that ancient nothing, and hadst yet been there had not God drawn thee thence. And what couldst thou have done remaining there ?

2. *Give thanks to God.* O my great and good creator, how am I obliged to thee, since thou hast vouchsafed to take me out of this nothing, and by thy great mercy to make me what I am ! What can I do to bless thy holy name as I ought, and to render due thanks to thy inestimable goodness ?

3. *Confound yourself.* But, alas ! my creator, instead of uniting myself to thee by love and service, I have been a rebel to thee by my inordinate affections, wandering and straying away from thee, to unite myself to sin ; valuing thy goodness no more than if thou hadst not been my creator.

4. *Prostrate yourself before God.* O my soul, know that the Lord is thy God : It is he that has made thee, and not thou thyself. O God, I am the work of thy hands.

5. I will then no more henceforth take pleasure in myself, since of myself I am nothing. Why dost thou magnify thyself, O dust and ashes ? Yea, rather, O very nothing, why dost thou exalt thyself ? To humble therefore myself, I resolve to do such and such things ; to suffer such and such disgraces : I will change my life, and henceforth follow my creator, and esteem myself honoured with that condition and being which he has given me, employing it entirely in obedience to his will, by such means as shall be taught me, and as I shall learn from my ghostly Father.

Conclusion

1. G*IVE thanks to God.* Bless thy God, O my soul, and let all that is within me praise his holy name ; for his goodness has drawn me, and his mercy has created me out of nothing. 2. *Offer.* O my God, I offer to thee the being which thou hast given me : from my heart I dedicate and consecrate it to thee. 3. *Pray.* O God, strengthen me in these affections and resolutions. O blessed Virgin, recommend them to the mercy of thy Son, with all for whom I ought to pray. *Pater. Ave. Credo.*
After your prayer, out of these considerations which you have made, gather a little nosegay of devotion, to smell to all the rest of the day.

THE SECOND MEDITATION
On the end for which we were Created

Preparation

1. **P**LACE yourself in the presence of God. 2. Beseech him to inspire you.

Considerations

1. **G**OD has not placed you in this world for any need that he has of you, who are altogether unprofitable to him, but only to exercise his goodness in you, by giving you his grace and glory. And to this end he hath enriched you with an understanding to know him ; with a memory to be mindful of him ; with a will to love him ; an imagination to represent to yourself his benefits ; eyes to behold his wondrous works ; a tongue to praise him ; and so of the other faculties.

2. Being created and put into the world for this intent, all actions contrary to it are to be avoided and rejected ; and whatever conduceth not to this end ought to be contemned as vain and superfluous.

3. Consider the wretchedness of worldlings, who never think of this, but live as though they believed themselves created for no other end than to build houses, plant trees, heap up riches, and such like fooleries.

Affections and Resolutions

1. CONFOUND *yourself, reproaching your soul with her misery, which has hitherto been so great, as that she hath seldom or never considered this.* Alas ! shall you say, how did I employ my thoughts, O God, when I placed them not upon thee ? What did I remember when I forgot thee ? What did I love when I loved not thee ? Alas ! I ought to have fed upon truth, and I have glutted myself with vanity ; I have served the world, which was created but to serve me.

2. *Detest your past life.* I renounce you, O vain thoughts and unprofitable fancies : I abjure you, O frivolous and hateful remembrances : O unfaithful and disloyal friendships, lewd and wretched slaveries, ungrateful contentments, and irksome pleasures, I abhor you.

3. *Return to God.* And then, O my God, my Saviour, thou shalt be from henceforth the sole object of my thoughts ; I will no more apply my mind to objects that may be displeasing to thee. My memory shall entertain itself all the days of my life with the greatness of thy clemency so mercifully exercised on me : thou shalt be the delight of my heart, and the sweetness of my affections.

4. Ah ! such and such trash and trifles to which I applied myself, such and such un-

profitable employments, in which I have foolishly squandered away my days, such and such affections which have captivated my heart, shall henceforth be a horror to my thoughts, and to this end I will use such and such good remedies.

Conclusion

1. THANK God *who made you for so excellent an end.* Thou hast created me, O Lord, for thyself, and for the everlasting enjoyment of thy incomprehensible glory : O when shall I be worthy of it ? When shall I praise thee and bless thee as I ought ? 2. *Offer.* I offer to thee, O my dear creator, all these affections and resolutions, with all my heart and soul. 3. *Pray.* I beseech thee, O God, to accept my desires and purposes, and give thy holy benediction to my soul, to the end that it may accomplish them, through the merits of thy blessed Son's blood shed for me upon the cross, &c. *Pater. Ave. Credo.* Make your little nosegay of devotion, as aforesaid.

THE THIRD MEDITATION
On the Benefits of God

Preparation

1. PLACE yourself in the presence of God. 2. Beseech him to inspire you.

Considerations

1. CONSIDER the corporal graces which God has bestowed upon you; what

a body, what conveniences to maintain it,
what health and lawful recreations to entertain it, what friends and assistances ! But
consider all this with respect to many other
persons much more worthy than yourself,
who are destitute of all these blessings ;
some spoiled in their bodies, health and
limbs ; others abandoned to the mercy of
reproaches, contempts, and dishonours ;
others oppressed with poverty ; and God
has not suffered you to become so miserable.
2. Consider the gifts of mind. How many
are in the world stupid, frantic or mad ; and
why are not you of this number ? God has
favoured you. How many are there who have
been brought up rudely and in gross ignorance ? and by God's providence you have
been educated liberally and honourably.

3. Consider the spiritual graces. *O Philothea,* you are a child of the Catholic Church ;
God has taught you to know him even from
your most tender age. How often has he
given you his sacraments ? How many
inspirations, internal illuminations, and
reprehensions for your amendment ? How
frequently has he pardoned you your faults ?
How often has he delivered you from the
occasions of casting yourself away to which
you were exposed ? And were not all these
years past given you as a time and oppor-
tunity to advance the good of your soul ?
Consider in particular how good and gracious
God has always been to you.

Affections and Resolutions

1. ADMIRE *the goodness of God.* O how good is my God towards me ! O how gracious is he ! How rich is thy heart, O Lord, in mercy, and liberal in clemency ! O my soul, let us recount for ever how many favours he has done us.

2. *Be astonished at your ingratitude.* But what am I, O Lord, that thou art so mindful of me ! Ah ! how great is my unworthiness ! Alas, I have even trodden thy blessings under foot. I have dishonoured thy graces, perverting them into abuse and contempt of thy sovereign goodness. I have opposed the depth of my ingratitude to the height of thy grace and favour.

3. *Stir yourself up to acknowledgment.* Well then, my heart, be now no more unfaithful, ungrateful, and disloyal to this great benefactor. And how shall not my soul henceforth be wholly subject to God, who has done so many wonders and favours to me and for me ?

4. Ah ! withdraw then your body, *Philothea*, from such and such sensualities ; and consecrate it to the service of God, who has done so much for it. Apply your soul to know and acknowledge him by such exercises as shall be requisite for that purpose. Employ diligently the means which you have in the church to save your soul, and love Almighty God. Yes, O my God, I will be diligent in

prayer; I will hear thy holy word, and put in practice thy inspirations and counsels.

Conclusion

1. THANK God for the knowledge he hath now given you of your duty, and for the benefits hitherto received. 2. Offer him your heart with all your resolutions. 3. Pray him, that he will strengthen you to practise them faithfully through the merits of his Son's death. Implore the intercession of the Blessed Virgin, and of the saints. *Pater. Ave. Credo.* Make your little spiritual nosegay as before.

THE FOURTH MEDITATION
On Sin

Preparation

1. PLACE yourself in the presence of God. 2. Beseech him to inspire you.

Considerations

1. CALL to mind how long it is since you began to sin, and examine how much since that beginning sins have been multiplied in your heart. How every day you have increased them against God, against yourself, and against your neighbour, by work, by word, or by desire.

2. Consider your evil inclinations, and how far you have followed them : and by these two points you shall find that your sins are

8

greater in number than the hairs of your head, yea than the sands of the sea.

3. Consider in particular the sin of ingratitude against God, which is a general sin, and extends itself over all the rest, making them infinitely more enormous. Consider then how many benefits God has bestowed upon you, and how you have abused them all in prejudice of the giver : and in particular, how many inspirations have you despised ? How many good motions have you made unprofitable ? But above all, how many times have your received the sacraments ? and where are the fruits of it ? What is become of all those precious jewels with which your dear spouse adorned you ? All these have been buried under your iniquities. With what preparation have you received them ? Think on this ingratitude, that God having run so far after you, you have run from him to lose yourself.

Affections and Resolutions.

1. **B**E *confounded at your misery.* O my God ! how dare I appear before thine eyes ? Alas ! I am but the corruption of the world, and a very sink of sin and ingratitude. Is it possible that I have been so disloyal, as not to have left any one of my senses, nor any one of the powers of my soul, which I have not corrupted, violated, and defiled ; and that not so much as one day of my life has passed, in which I have

not brought forth such wicked effects ? Is it thus that I have recompensed the benefits of my creator, and the precious blood of my redeemer ?

2. *Crave pardon*, and cast yourself at the feet of your Lord, like the prodigal child, like a penitent *Magdalene*, or like a woman that has defiled her marriage-bed with all kinds of adultery. Mercy, O Lord, upon this poor sinner ! Alas ! O living fountain of compassion, have pity on this wretch.

3. *Resolve to live better.* No, O Lord, never more, with the help of thy grace, never more will I abandon myself to sin. Alas ! I have loved it too much ; now I detest it, and embrace thee. O Father of Mercy, I will live and die in thee.

4. To expiate my sins past, I will accuse myself of them courageously ; and will not leave one unbanished from my heart.

5. I will use all possible endeavours to extirpate all the roots of sin out of my heart ; and in particular such and such vices, which I am most inclined to.

6. To accomplish this, I will constantly embrace the means which I shall be advised to ; and think I have never done enough to repair so grievous offences.

Conclusion

1. GIVE God thanks for expecting your amendment till this hour ; and bless him that he has given you these affections.

2. Offer him up your heart, that you may put them in execution. 3. Desire him to strengthen you, &c. *Pater. Ave. Credo.* Make your little nosegay of devotion as above.

THE FIFTH MEDITATION
On Death

Preparation

1. PLACE yourself in the presence of God. 2. Beseech him to inspire you with his grace. 3. Imagine yourself to be extremely sick, lying on your bed, and without any hope of recovery.

Considerations

1. CONSIDER the uncertainty of the day of your death. O my soul, thou must one day out of this body ; but when shall that day be ? Shall it be in winter or in summer ? In city or in country ? By day or by night ? Shall it be suddenly, or on notice given thee ? By sickness or by accident ? Shalt thou have leisure to make thy confession ? Shalt thou have the assistance of thy ghostly Father ? Alas ! of all this we know nothing at all : only certain it is, that we shall die, and that always sooner than we imagine.

2. Consider that when the world shall end in regard of you ; for it will last no longer to you, it will turn upside down before your

eyes : for then the pleasures and the vanities, the worldly joys and fond affections of our life will seem to us shadows and airy clouds. Ah wretch ! for what toys and trifles have I offended God ? You shall then see that for a mere nothing you have forsaken him. On the contrary, devotion and good works will then seem to you sweet and delightful. O why did I not follow this lovely and pleasant path ? Then sins which before seemed very little will appear as big as mountains, and your devotion very small.

3. Consider the long and languishing farewells your soul will then give this world : she will then take her leave of riches, vanities, and all idle company ; of pleasures, pastimes, friends and neighbours ; of kindred, children, husband and wife ; in short, of every creature ; and finally of her own body, which she will leave pale, hideous, and loathsome.

4. Consider with what hurrying they will carry away this body, to cover it under the earth : which done, the world will think no more of you, than you have thought on others ; God's peace be with him, they will say, and that's all. O death, how void art thou of regard or pity !

5. Consider how the soul, being departed from the body, takes her way to the right hand, or to the left. Alas ! whither shall yours go ? what way shall it take ? No other than that which it began here in this world.

Affections and Resolutions

1. **P**RAY *to God, and cast yourself into his arms.* Alas! O my Lord, receive me into thy protection at that dreadful day: make that hour happy and favourable to me; and rather let all the other days of my life be sad and sorrowful.

2. *Despise the world.* Since then I know not the hour in which I must leave thee, O wretched world, I will no more set my heart upon thee. O my dear friends and relations, pardon me if I love you no more but with a holy friendship, which may last eternally: for why should I unite myself to you, so as to be forced to break and dissolve that knot?

3. I will then prepare myself against that hour, and take all possible care to end this journey happily. I will secure the state of my conscience to the uttermost of my ability, and take present order for the amendment of such and such defects.

Conclusion

GIVE thanks to God for these resolutions which he has given you. Offer them to his divine majesty. Be instant with him to give you a happy death, by the merits of that of his dearly beloved Son. Implore the assistance of the Blessed Virgin, and of the glorified Saints. *Pater. Ave. Credo.* Make a posy of myrrh.

THE SIXTH MEDITATION
On Judgment

Preparation

1. **P**LACE yourself in the presence of God. Beseech him to inspire you with his grace.

Considerations

1. **A**FTER the time that God hath prescribed for the continuance of the world; after many signs and dreadful presages, which will cause men to pine away through fear and anguish; a fire raging like a torrent shall burn and reduce to ashes every thing that is upon the face of the earth; nothing which we see upon it shall be spared.

2. After these flames and thunderbolts, all men shall arise from their graves (excepting such as are already risen) and at the voice of the angel they shall all appear in the valley of *Josaphat*. But alas! with what difference! for the one sort shall arise in glorified and resplendent bodies; the others in bodies most hideous and horrid.

3. Consider the majesty with which the sovereign judge will appear, environed with all his angels and saints: before him shall be borne his cross, shining much brighter than the sun; an ensign of mercy to the good, and of justice to the wicked.

4. This sovereign judge, by his dreadful command, which shall be suddenly obeyed, will separate the good from the bad, placing the one at his right hand, and the other at his left. O everlasting separation ! after which these two companies shall never meet.

5. This separation being made, and the books of conscience opened, all men shall see clearly the malice of the wicked, and their contempt against God ; and on the other side the penance of the good, and the effects of God's grace which they have received, and nothing shall lie hid. O God, what a confusion will this be to the one, and what a consolation to the other !

6. Consider the last sentence pronounced against the wicked : *Go ye cursed into everlasting fire, prepared for the devil and his angels.* Ponder well those weighty words. *Go,* saith he ; a word of eternal banishment against those miserable wretches, excluding them eternally from his glorious presence. He calls them *cursed :* O my soul, how dreadful a curse ! A general curse, including all manner of *woes ;* an irrevocable curse, comprehending all times and eternity. He adds, *into everlasting fire :* behold, O my heart, this vast eternity : O eternal eternity of pains, how dreadful art thou !

7. Consider the contrary sentence of the good. *Come,* saith the judge ; O sweet word of salvation, by which God draws us to

himself, and receives us into the bosom of his goodness ! *Blessed of my Father ;* O dear blessing, which comprehends all happiness ! *Possess the kingdom which is prepared for you from the beginning of the world :* O good God, what excess of bounty ! For this kingdom shall never have an end.

Affections and Resolutions

1. T*REMBLE, O my soul, at the remembrance of these things.* O my God, who shall secure me in that day when the pillars of heaven shall tremble for fear ?

2. Detest your sins, which only can condemn you in that dreadful day.

3. *Ah! wretched heart of mine, resolve to amend.* O Lord, I will judge myself now, that I may not be judged then. I will examine my conscience, and condemn myself, I will accuse and chastise myself, that the eternal judge may not condemn me in that dreadful day. I will therefore confess my sins, accept of all necessary advice, &c.

Conclusion

T HANK God who has given you means to provide for that day, and time to do penance. Offer him your heart to perform it. Pray him to give you grace duly to accomplish it. *Pater. Ave. Credo, etc.* Make your spiritual nosegay for all the day.

THE SEVENTH MEDITATION
On Hell

Preparation

1. PLACE yourself in the presence of God. 2. Humble yourself and implore his assistance. 3. Represent to yourself a dark city, all burning, all stinking with pitch and brimstone, and full of inhabitants who cannot get out.

Considerations

1. THE damned are in the depth of hell, as within this woeful city, where they suffer unspeakable torments, in all their senses and members ; because as they have employed all their senses and members in sinning, so shall they suffer in them all the punishments due to sin. The eyes for lascivious looks shall be afflicted with the horrid vision of hell and devils. The ears for delighting in vicious discourses shall hear nothing but wailings, lamentations, desperate howlings ; and so of the rest.

2. Besides all these torments there is another greater, which is the loss and privation of God's glory, from the sight of which they are excluded for ever. Now if *Absolom* found it more grievous to him to be denied the seeing the face of his father *David*, than to be banished ; O God, what a grief it will be, to

be for ever excluded from beholding thy most sweet and gracious countenance !

3. Consider above all the eternity of these pains, which above all things makes hell intolerable. Alas ! if a flea in your ear, or if the heat of a little fever make one short night so long and tedious, how terrible will the night of eternity be, accompanied with so many torments ? From this eternity proceeds eternal desperation, infinite rage, and blasphemy, &c.

Affections and Resolutions

1. **T**RRIFY *yourself with the words of the* prophet *Isaiah*. O my soul, art thou able to live for ever in everlasting flames, and amidst this devouring fire ? Wilt thou forfeit the sight of thy God for ever?

2. *Confess that you have deserved hell, yea oftentimes.* From henceforth I will take a new course ; for why should I go down into this bottomless pit ? I will therefore use this or that endeavour to avoid sin, which only can bring me to this eternal death.

Give thanks. Offer. Pray. *Pater. Ave. Credo.*

THE EIGHTH MEDITATION
On Heaven

Preparation

1. **P**LACE yourself in the presence of God. 2. Beseech him to inspire you with his grace.

Considerations

1. CONSIDER a fair and clear night, and think how pleasant it is to behold the sky all spangled with that multitude and variety of stars : join this now with the beauty of as clear a day, so as the brightness of the sun may no ways hinder the lustre of the stars nor moon ; and then say boldly, that all this put together is nothing in comparison with the excellent beauty of the heavenly paradise. Oh ! how this lovely place is to be desired ! Oh ! how precious is this city !

2. Consider the glory, beauty, and multitude of the inhabitants in this blessed country ; those millions of millions of angels, cherubims, and seraphims ! those troops of apostles, prophets, martyrs, confessors, virgins, and holy matrons. The number is innumerable. O how blessed is this company ? The meanest of them is more beautiful to behold than all this world : what a sight then will it be to see them all ? But, O my God, how happy are they ! They sing continually harmonious songs of eternal love ; they always enjoy a constant mirth ; they interchange one with another unspeakable contentments, and live in the comfort of a happy and indissoluble society.

3. In fine, consider how blessed they are to enjoy God, who rewards them for ever with

his lovely aspect, and by the same infuses into their hearts a treasure of delights : how great a happiness it is to be united everlastingly to the sovereign good. They are there like happy birds flying and singing perpetually in the air of his divinity, which encompasses them on all sides with incredible pleasure. There every one does his best, and without envy sings the creator's praise. Blessed be thou for ever, O sweet and sovereign creator and redeemer, who art so bountiful to us, and dost communicate to us so liberally the everlasting treasures of thy glory : blessed be you for ever, says he, my beloved creatures, who have so faithfully served me, and who now shall praise me everlastingly, with so great love and courage.

Affections and Resolutions

1. ADMIRE *and praise this heavenly country.* O how beautiful art thou, my dear *Jerusalem* ! and how happy are thy inhabitants !

2. *Reproach your heart with the little courage it has had hitherto, in wandering so far from the way of this glorious habitation.* O why have I strayed so far from my sovereign good ? Ah ! wretch that I am, for these foolish and trivial pleasures have I a thousand thousand times forsaken eternal and infinite delights ! Was I not mad, to despise

such precious blessings for so vain and con-
temptible affections ?

3. *Aspire now with fervour to this delightful
habitation.* O my gracious God, since it
has pleased thee at length to direct my
wandering steps into the right way, never
hereafter will I turn back. Let us go, my
dear soul, let us go to this eternal repose :
let us walk towards this blessed land that is
promised us : what have we to do in this
Egypt ? I will therefore disburthen myself
of all such things as may divert or retard
me in so happy a journey : I will perform
such and such things as may conduct me
to it.

Give thanks. Offer. Pray. *Pater. Ave.
Credo.*

THE NINTH MEDITATION

By Way of Election and Choice of Heaven

Preparation

1. PLACE yourself in the presence of
God. 2. Humble yourself before his
majesty, and beseech him to inspire you
with his grace. Imagine yourself to be in a
plain field, all alone with your good angel, as
young *Toby* going to *Rages,* and that he
shews you heaven open, with all the
pleasures represented in the former meditation ; then, beneath that, he shews you hell
wide open, with all the torments described
in the meditation of hell : you being thus

piaced in your imagination, and kneeling by your good angel.

Considerations

1. CONSIDER that it is most true, you are between heaven and hell; and that the one and the other is open to receive you, according to the choice you shall make.
2. Consider that the choice which you shall make in this world shall last for all eternity in the other.
3. And though both the one and the other be opened to receive you, according to your choice, yet God, who is ready to give you either the one by his justice, or the other by his mercy, desires notwithstanding with an incomparable desire that you would make choice of heaven; and your good angel also importunes you with all his power, offering you on God's behalf a thousand assistances, and a thousand graces, to help you thither.
4. Consider that Jesus Christ beholds you from above in his clemency, and graciously invites you, saying: Come, my dear soul, to everlasting rest within the arms of my goodness, where I have prepared immortal delights for thee in the abundance of my love. Behold likewise with your inward eyes the Blessed Virgin, who with a motherly love exhorts you, saying : Take courage, my child, despise not the desires of my Son, nor so many sighs which I have cast forth for thee, thirsting with him after thy

eternal salvation. Behold the saints also that exhort you, and millions of blessed souls sweetly inviting you, and wishing nothing more than to see your heart united with theirs in praising and loving God for ever ; assuring you that the way to heaven is not so hard as the world makes it. Be of good courage, dear brother, say they, he that shall diligently consider the way of devotion, by which we ascended hither, shall see that we came to these immortal delights by pleasures incomparably more sweet than those of the world.

Election

1. O HELL, I detest thee now and for evermore : I detest thy torments and pains ; I detest thy miserable and accursed eternity : and above all, I detest those eternal blasphemies and maledictions, which thou vomitest out eternally against my God. And turning my heart and soul to thee, O beautiful paradise, everlasting glory, and endless felicity, I choose my habitation for ever and irrevocably within thy fair and blessed mansions, within thy holy and most lovely tabernacles. I bless thy mercy, O my God, and accept the offer which it pleaseth thee to make me of it. O my sweet Saviour Jesus, I accept thy everlasting love, and the purchase which thou hast made for me of a place in this heavenly Jerusalem, not so much for any other

thing, as to love and bless thee for ever and ever.

2. Accept the favours which the Blessed Virgin and the saints offer you : promise them to advance towards them, and give your hand to your good angel, that he may guide you thither. Encourage your soul to make this choice. *Pater. Ave. Credo.*

THE TENTH MEDITATION

By Way of Election and Choice which the Soul makes of a Devout Life

Preparation

1. PLACE yourself in the presence of God. 2. Prostrate yourself before him, and implore the assistance of his grace.

Considerations

1. IMAGINE yourself again to be in a plain field, all alone with your good angel ; and that you see on your left hand the devil, seated on a great high throne, with many infernal spirits about him, environed with a great troop of worldlings, who all bare-headed acknowledge him for their Lord, and do him homage, some by one sin, and some by another. Observe the countenance of all the wretched courtiers of this abominable king. Behold some of them transported with hatred, envy, and passion ; others killing one another ; others

consumed with cares, pensive and anxious to heap up riches ; others bent upon vanity without any manner of pleasure which is not empty and unprofitable ; others wallowing in the mire, buried and putrified in their brutish affections. Behold how they are all without rest, order, and decency : behold how they despise one another, and love but in show. In a word, you shall see a lamentable commonwealth miserably tyrannized over by this cursed king, which will move you to compassion.

2. On the other side, behold Jesus Christ crucified, who with a cordial love prays for these poor enthralled people, that they may be freed from this tyranny, and calls them to himself. Behold, round about him a troop of devout persons with their angels. Contemplate the beauty of this kingdom of devotion. O what a sight is it to see this troop of virgins, men and women, whiter than the lilies ; that assembly of widows full of holy mortification and humility : see the ranks of divers married people living peaceably together with mutual respect, which cannot be without great charity. Consider how these devout souls join the exterior care of the house with the care of the interior, the love of the husband with that of the celestial bridegroom. Consider them all universally, and you shall see them in a sweet, holy and lovely order, observing our Saviour, whom every one would will-

ingly plant in the midst of his heart. They are full of joy, but that joy is comely, charitable and well ordered ; they love one another, but their love is most pure and holy : such as suffer afflictions amongst this devout company torment not themselves much, nor lose courage. Lastly, behold those eyes of our Saviour, who comforts them, and how they all together aspire to him.

3. You have already shaken off Satan with all his cursed execrable troop, by the good affections and resolutions you have conceived ; but you are not yet arrived at Jesus, nor united with this blessed and holy company of devout people, but have hitherto kept yourself between the one and the other.

4. The Blessed Virgin, with St. *Joseph*, and a hundred thousand others, who are of the squadron of those who have lived in the world, invite and encourage you. And the crucified King himself calls you by your name : Come, my well-beloved, come, that I may crown thee.

Election

O WORLD ! O abominable troop ! No, never more shall you see me under your banner. I have for ever left off your fooleries and vanities. O king of pride, O cursed king, infernal spirit, I renounce thee with all thy vain pomps, I detest thee with all thy works.

2. And turning myself to thee, my dear

Jesus, king of felicity and immortal glory, I embrace thee with all the powers of my soul, I adore thee with all my heart, I choose thee now and ever for my king, and with inviolable fidelity I pay thee irrevocable homage, and submit myself to the obedience of thy holy laws and ordinances.

3. O sacred Virgin, my dear Lady, I choose thee for my guide, I put myself under thy colours, I offer thee a particular respect and special reverence.

4. O my good Angel, present me to this sacred assembly, and forsake me not till I arrive at this blessed company, with whom I say, and will say for ever in testimony of my choice, Live Jesus, Live Jesus. *Pater. Ave. Credo.*

AN UNIVERSAL PRAYER
for all things necessary to salvation

O MY GOD, I *believe* in thee, do thou strengthen my faith. All my *hopes* are in thee, do thou secure them. I *love* thee with my whole heart, teach me to *love* thee daily more and more. I am *sorry* that I have offended thee, do thou increase my *sorrow*. I *adore* thee as my first beginning. I *aspire* after thee as my last end. I give thee *thanks* as my constant benefactor. I *call* upon thee as my sovereign protector.

Vouchsafe, O my God, to conduct me by thy *wisdom*, to restrain me by thy *justice*, to comfort me by thy *mercy*, to defend me by thy *power*.

To thee I desire to consecrate all my thoughts, words, actions, and sufferings; that henceforward I may think of thee, speak of thee, and willingly refer all my actions to thy greater glory; and suffer willingly whatever thou shalt appoint.

Lord, I desire that in all things thy *will* may be done, because it is thy *will*, and in the manner that thou willest.

I beg of thee to enlighten my *understanding*, to enflame my *will*, to purify my *body*, and to sanctify my *soul*.

Give me strength, O my God, to expiate my *offences*, to overcome my *temptations*, to subdue my *passions*, and to acquire the *virtues* proper for my state.

Fill my heart with tender *affection* for thy goodness, a *hatred* for my faults, a *love* for my neighbour, and a *contempt* of the world.

Let me always remember to be submissive to my *superiors*, condescending to my *inferiors*, faithful to my *friends*, and charitable to my *enemies*.

Assist me to overcome sensuality by *mortification*, avarice by *alms-deeds*, anger by *meekness*, and tepidity by *devotion*.

O my God, make me *prudent* in my undertakings, *courageous* in dangers, *patient* in afflictions, and *humble* in prosperity.

Grant, that I may be ever *attentive* at my prayers, *temperate* at my meals, *diligent* in

my employments, and *constant* in my resolutions.

Let my conscience be ever *upright* and *pure*,
my exterior *modest*, my conversation *edify-
ing*, and my comportment *regular*.

Assist me, that I may continually labour to
overcome *nature*, to correspond with thy
grace, to keep thy *commandments*, and to
work out my *salvation*.

Discover to me, O my God, the nothingness
of *this world*, the greatness of *heaven*, the
shortness of *time*, and the length of *eternity*.

Grant that I may prepare for *death*, that I
may fear thy *judgments*, that I may escape
hell, and in the end obtain heaven, through
Jesus Christ. *Amen*.

A PARAPHRASE UPON THE
LORD'S PRAYER

Our Father, who art in heaven

O ALMIGHTY Lord, and maker of
heaven and earth, infinite in majesty,
is it possible that thy love and goodness for
us should be so great as to suffer such poor
worms as we are to call thee *Father* ! O
make us ever dutiful children to such a
parent ! O my soul, ever remember this
dignity to which thou art raised, of being a
child of God ; and see thou never degener-
ate, by making thyself a slave to sin and the
devil. O most holy Father, who dwellest

in heaven, and heavenly souls, raise my heart to thee, and teach me, by thy interior grace, to pray to thee this day with due attention, devotion, humility, and faith.

Hallowed be thy name

THE first thing I beg of thee, O heavenly Father, is the greater honour and glory of thy name. I rejoice with all my soul, that in thyself thou art infinitely happy, and infinitely glorious, and that thou art eternally adored, praised, and glorified, by all thy angels and saints. But alas ! O Lord, how little art thou known in this miserable world, how little art thou loved here, how little art thou served ! How is thy name blasphemed all the day, even by those that call themselves Christians ! How many millions of souls in all parts of the world, though made to thy own image and likeness, and redeemed by the precious blood of thy only Son, live and die in infidelity, error and vice, to the great dishonour of thy holy name ! O when shall so great an evil be remedied ! O that I could do any thing to remedy it ! O that I could worthily promote the honour and glory of thy name ! O that I could make it known to all nations ! O that like the blessed in heaven we were all happily united in praising, blessing, and loving thee ! But this must be the work of thy grace, O Lord : and this grace I beg of thee this day, that so both I and all the world may ever adore, praise, and love thee; and not only in words, but much more in our lives, show forth the glory of thy name.

Thy kingdom come

HEAVEN is the seat of thy eternal kingdom, O Lord; there thou livest and reignest for ever. But whilst we are here in this mortal life, thy *kingdom is within us* as often as thou reignest within our souls by thy grace, and by thy love. I earnestly beg both for myself and for all others a share in thy eternal kingdom, that we may there be witnesses of thy glory, and see, love, praise, and enjoy thee for ever. In the meantime, I beg that the kingdom of thy grace and of thy love may come into our souls; that thou mayst ever reign in us without control, and make us all according to thy own heart, that nothing in us may any more presume to rebel against thee, the true king of hearts; but that we may be ever faithful servants and subjects of thy love.

Thy will be done on earth as it is in heaven

THE blessed in heaven have no other will, O Lord, but thine: this will of thine they ever adore; this they eternally embrace and love; this they readily and cheerfully obey. O that we, poor banished children of *Adam* here upon earth, did in like manner adore, embrace, and love thy

will ! O that we obeyed it in like manner !
Lord, it is my sincere desire, and hearty
prayer, that from henceforward thy holy
will may be done by us all, in all things. O
grant that from this moment thy will may
be the rule of all our actions ; and that in all
our deliberations, like the convert St. *Paul*,
we may ever cry out to thee, *Lord, what
wouldst thou have me to do ?* O grant that in all
our sufferings we may ever have a perfect
conformity to thy holy will.

Give us this day our daily bread

THE bread of our souls, which is to support us during this day of our mortality,
and to feed and nourish us to life everlasting, is no other, O Lord, than thy only
Son, who has said, *I am the living bread that
came down from heaven, he that eateth of this
bread shall live for ever : and the bread that I
will give, is my flesh, for the life of the world.*
This bread of life we earnestly beg of thee :
this we desire often to receive sacramentally;
this we desire daily to receive spiritually, for
the nourishing of our souls with thy heavenly
grace, from this fountain of grace. O come,
dear Jesus, into our poor famished souls,
satisfy our hunger here this day with this
heavenly bread, till we come to the more
happy day of eternity, where all veils being
withdrawn, we shall for ever feed upon thy
divinity. In the meantime, as to the neces-
saries of this life, grant us what in thy wisdom

thou seest best for us, and most conducing to thy honour and our eternal welfare.

And forgive us our trespasses, as we forgive them that trespass against us

OUR sins, O Lord, are innumerable ; the debt that we owe thee is infinite ; and we are poor and miserable, unable of ourselves to discharge the least part of this debt, or to make satisfaction for the least of these sins. But prostrate in spirit before thee we humbly implore thy mercy. We desire to offer thee the sacrifice of a contrite and humble heart. We offer thee the death and Passion of thy only Son, which he hast made over to us for the discharge of our debts. And as he has promised forgiveness to those that forgive, we here from our hearts forgive all that have offended us ; and hope through him to find forgiveness from thee.

Lead us not into temptation

ALAS ! O Lord, man's life upon earth is a continual temptation. We are encompassed on all sides with mortal enemies ; the world, the flesh, and the devil are ever attacking us with united forces. Our only hope in all these dangers and conflicts is in thy strength and protection. O stand thou for us, and we care not who is against us. We believe that thou art faithful, and will not suffer us to be tempted above our strength. O never suffer us to forsake thee ; and we know thou wilt never forsake us. Let not the devil circumvent us by his frauds and deceits ; nor ever glory that he has prevailed over us ; arm us both against the terrors and flatteries of the world, and all the dangers of our passions and concupiscences. And whatever trials thou art pleased to send us, let thy supporting grace ever carry us through them with advantage to our souls : that by thy favour and mercy we may be faithful unto death, and so receive the crown of life.

But deliver us from evil. Amen

O SOVEREIGN good, the fountain of all our good, deliver us from all our evils : from our sins, and the punishments we deserve for them ; from wars, plagues, famines, and such like scourges, which we have too much reason to apprehend hanging over our heads from thy justice, and our impenitence. From heresy and schism, and all that blindness of soul which self-conceit and pride expose us to ; in fine, from a hardened heart, from final impenitence, and everlasting damnation. From all these evils, for thy own goodness sake, O Lord, deliver us, through Jesus Christ thy Son our Lord. *Amen.*

OCCASIONAL PRAYERS

For the Pope

O GOD, the shepherd and ruler of all the faithful, mercifully look upon thy servant N., whom thou hast been pleased to appoint pastor over thy Church. Grant, we beseech thee, that both by word and example, he may edify those over whom he is set, and, together with the flock committed to his care, may attain everlasting life. Through Christ our Lord. *Amen.*

For the King

ALMIGHTY and everliving God, in whose hand are the hearts of kings, we beseech thee to protect and prosper thy servant King George and all the Royal Family. Guide the counsels of his ministers at home and abroad: strengthen with courage and endurance those who fight his battles and all who labour everywhere in the just cause of freedom. Send peace in our days, the reward of victory, and create in us new hearts to deserve these and all thy blessings. Through Jesus Christ our Lord.

For England

O BLESSED Virgin Mary, Mother of God, and our most gentle queen and mother, look down in mercy upon England, thy Dowry, and upon us all who greatly hope and trust in thee. By thee it was that Jesus, our Saviour and our hope, was given unto the world; and He has given thee to us that we may hope still more. Plead for us, thy children, whom thou didst receive and accept at the foot of the Cross, O sorrowful Mother. Intercede for our separated brethren, that with us in the one true fold they may be united to the chief Shepherd, the vicar of thy Son. Pray for us all, dear Mother, that by faith, fruitful in good works, we may be counted worthy to see and praise God, together with thee in our heavenly home. *Amen.*

For any Necessity

O GOD, our refuge and our strength, who art the author of mercy, hearken to the godly prayers of Thy Church and grant that what we ask in faith we may effectually obtain. Through Christ our Lord.

For Peace

O GOD, from whom are holy desires, right counsels and just works, give to thy servants that peace which the world cannot give; that our hearts may be disposed to obey thy commandments, and, the fear of enemies being taken away, our times may by thy protection be tranquil.

In Time of War

O GOD, who bringest wars to nought and shieldest by thy power all who hope in thee, overthrowing all that assail them: help thy servants who implore thy mercy; so that the fierceness of their enemies may be brought low and that we may never cease from praising Thee. Through Christ our Lord.

Prayer on one's Birthday

O GOD, who on this day didst give to me by my parents natural life, and after, by Holy Mother Church in Baptism, supernatural life, grant, I beseech thee, that by perseverance in thy grace I may attain to fulness of life in thy kingdom, through Jesus Christ thy Son, our Lord. *Amen.*

HYMNS
FOR VARIOUS OCCASIONS
PANGE LINGUA

PANGE, lingua, gloriosi
Corporis mysterium,
Sanguinisque pretiosi,
Quem in mundi pretium,
Fructus ventris generosi
Rex effudit gentium.

Nobis datus, nobis natus,
Ex intacta virgine,

Et in mundo conversatus,
Sparso verbi semine,
Sui moras incolatus
Miro clausit ordine.

SING, my tongue, the Saviour's glory,
Of his flesh the mystery sing;
Of the blood all price exceeding,
Shed by our immortal King,
Destined for the world's redemption,
From a noble womb to spring.

Of a pure and spotless virgin,
Born for us on earth below,
He, as man with man conversing,
Stayed, the seeds of truth to sow;
Then he closed in solemn order
Wondrously his life of woe.

In supremæ nocte
   cœnæ,
Recumbens cum fra-
   tribus,
Observata lege plene,
Cibis in legalibus
Cibum turbæ duo-
   denæ,
Se dat suis manibus.

On the night of that
   last supper,
Seated with his chosen
   band,
He the paschal victim
   eating,
First fulfils the law's
   command ;
Then, as food to all
   his brethren,
Gives himself with his
   own hand.

Verbum caro, panem
   verum
Verbo carnem efficit :
Fitque sanguis Christi
   merum,
Et si sensus deficit,
Ad firmandum cor sin-
   cerum
Sola fides sufficit.

Word made flesh, the
   bread of nature
By his word to flesh he
   turns ;
Wine into his blood he
   changes :
What though sense no
   change discerns ?
Only be the heart in
   earnest,
Faith her lesson
   quickly learns.

*(Indulgences : 300 days, once a day, to those
who recite the Pange Lingua, etc., with versicle
and prayer ; 100 days to those who say the
Tantum Ergo, etc., only, with versicle, etc.)*

ADORO TE DEVOTE

ADORO te devote,
latens Deitas,
Quæ sub his figuris
vere latitas ;
Tibi se cor meum to-
tum subjicit,
Quia te contemplans
totum deficit.

O GODHEAD hid,
devoutly I adore
thee,
Who truly art within
the forms before
me ;
To thee my heart I
bow with bended
knee,
As failing quite in
contemplating thee.

Visus, tactus, gustus
in te fallitur,
Sed auditu solo tuto
creditur,
Credo quidquid dixit
Dei Filius ;
Nil hoc verbo veritatis
verius.

Sight, touch, and taste
in thee are each de-
ceived ;
The ear alone most
safely is believed :
I believe all the Son of
God has spoken,
Than truth's own
word there is no
truer token.

In cruce latebat sola
Deitas,
At hic latet simul et
Humanitas,
Ambo tamen credens
atque confitens,
Peto quod petivit la-
tro pœnitens.

God only on the cross
lay hid from view ;
But here lies hid at
once the manhood
too ;
And I, in both pro-
fessing my belief,
Make the same prayer
as the repentant
thief.

9

Plagas, sicut Thomas,
non intueor,
Deum tamen meum te
confiteor.
Fac me tibi semper
magis credere,
In te spem habere, te
diligere.

O memoriale mortis
Domini !
Panis vivus, vitam
præstans homini !
Præsta meæ menti de
te vivere,
Et te illi semper dulce
sapere.

Pie Pelicane, Jesu Do-
mine,
Me immundum mun-
da tuo sanguine :
Cujus una stilla sal-
vum facere
Totum mundum quit
ab omni scelere.

Thy wounds, as
Thomas saw, I do
not see ;
Yet thee confess my
Lord and God to be ;
Make me believe thee
ever more and more ;
In thee my hope, in
thee my love to
store.

O thou memorial of
our Lord's own dy-
ing !
O living bread, to mor-
tals life supplying !
Make thou my soul
henceforth on thee
to live ;
Ever a taste of hea-
venly sweetness
give.

O loving Pelican ! O
Jesu Lord !
Unclean I am, but
cleanse me in thy
blood !
Of which a single
drop, for sinners
spilt,
Can purge the entire
world from all its
guilt.

Jesu, quem velatum nunc aspicio,
Fiat illud, oro, quod tam sitio :
Ut te revelata cernens facie,
Visu sim beatus tuæ gloriæ.

Jesu, whom, for the present, veiled I see,
What I so thirst for, oh ! vouchsafe to me :
That I may see thy countenance unfolding,
And may be blest thy glory in beholding.

TE DEUM

TE Deum laudamus : * te Dominum confitemur.

Te æternum Patrem * omnis terra veneratur.

Tibi omnes angeli, * tibi cœli, et universæ potestates :

Tibi cherubim et seraphim, * incessabili voce proclamant :
Sanctus, sanctus, sanctus, * Dominus Deus Sabaoth :
Pleni sunt cœli et terra, * majestatis gloriæ tuæ.

WE praise thee, O God : we acknowledge thee to be the Lord.

All the earth doth worship thee : the Father everlasting.

To thee all angels cry aloud : the heavens and all the powers therein :

To thee cherubim and seraphim continually do cry :
Holy, holy, holy, Lord God of Sabaoth.

Heaven and earth are full : of the majesty of thy glory.

Te gloriosus * Apostolorum chorus.

The glorious choir of the Apostles : praise thee.

Te Prophetarum * laudabilis numerus.

The admirable company of the Prophets : praise thee.

Te Martyrum candidatus * laudat exercitus.

The white-robed army of Martyrs : praise thee.

Te per orbem terrarum * sancta confitetur Ecclesia.

The Holy Church throughout all the world : doth acknowledge thee.

Patrem * immensæ majestatis.

The Father : of an infinite majesty.

Venerandum tuum verum * et unicum Filium.

Thine adorable, true and only Son.

Sanctum quoque * Paraclitum Spiritum.

Also the Holy Ghost, the Comforter.

Tu Rex gloriæ, * Christe.

Thou art the King of glory : O Christ.

Tu Patris * sempiternus es Filius.

Thou art the everlasting Son : of the Father.

Tu ad liberandum suscepturus hominem, * non horruisti Virginis uterum.

When thou tookest upon thee to deliver man : thou didst not abhor the Virgin's womb.

Tu devicto mortis aculeo, * aperuisti cre-

When thou hast overcome the sting of

dentibus regna cœlorum.

death : thou didst open the kingdom of heaven to all believers.

Tu ad dexteram Dei sedes, * in gloria Patris.

Thou sittest at the right hand of God : in the glory of the Father.

Judex crederis * esse venturus.

We believe that thou shalt come : to be our judge.

† Te ergo quæsumus, tuis famulis subveni, * quos pretioso sanguine redemisti.

We pray thee, therefore, help thy servants : whom thou hast redeemed with thy precious blood.

Æterna fac cum Sanctis, tuis * in gloria numerari.

Make them to be numbered with thy Saints: in glory everlasting.

Salvum fac populum tuum, Domine, * et benedic hæreditati tuæ.

O Lord, save thy people : and bless thine inheritance.

Et rege eos, et extolle illos, * usque in æternum.

Govern them : and lift them up for ever.

Per singulos dies * benedicimus te.

Day by day we magnify thee.

Et laudamus nomen tuum in sæculum, * et in sæculum sæculi.

And we praise thy name for ever : yea, for ever and ever.

Dignare, Domine, die

Vouchsafe, O Lord,

† *Here it is usual to kneel.*

isto, * sine peccato nos custodire.

this day : to keep us without sin.

Miserere nostri, Domine, * miserere nostri.

O Lord, have mercy upon us : have mercy upon us.

Fiat misericordia tua, Domine, super nos : * quemadmodum speravimus in te.

O Lord, let thy mercy be upon us : as we have hoped in thee.

In te Domine, speravi; * non confundar in æternum.

O Lord, in thee have I hoped : let me not be confounded for ever.

AVE VERUM

AVE verum Corpus, natum
Ex Maria virgine,
Vere passum, immolatum
In cruce pro homine.

HAIL to thee ! true Body, sprung
From the Virgin Mary's womb !
The same that on the Cross was hung
And bore for man the bitter doom.

Cujus latus perforatum
Vero fluxit sanguine.
Esto nobis prægustatum
Mortis in examine.

Thou whose side was pierced, and flowed
Both with water and with blood ;
Suffer us to taste of Thee
In our life's last agony.

O clemens, O pie,
O dulcis Jesu, Fili Mariæ.

O kind, O loving one !
O sweet Jesu, Mary's Son !

ADESTE FIDELES

ADESTE fideles,
Læti triumphantes ;
Venite, venite in Bethlehem :
Natum videte,
Regem Angelorum :
Venite adoremus,
Venite adoremus,
Venite adoremus Dominum.

YE faithful, approach ye,
Joyfully triumphing ;
Oh, come ye, oh, come ye, to Bethlehem :
Come and behold him
Born the King of Angels :
Oh, come, let us worship,
Oh, come, let us worship,
Oh, come, let us worship Christ the Lord.

Deum de Deo,
Lumen de lumine,
Gestant puellæ viscera :
Deum verum,
Genitum, non factum,
Venite adoremus, etc.

God of God,
Light of Light,
Lo, He disdains not the Virgin's womb :
Very God,
Begotten, not created:
Oh, come, let us worship, etc.

Cantet nunc Io !
Chorus angelorum ;
Cantet nunc aula cœ-
lestium,
Gloria
In excelsis Deo !
Venite adoremus, etc.

Ergo qui natus
Die hodierna,
Jesu tibi sit gloria ;
Patris æterni
Verbum caro factum !
Venite adoremus, etc.

Sing, choirs angelic,
Io sing exulting ;
Sing, all ye citizens of
heaven above,
Glory to God
In the highest !
Oh, come, let us wor-
ship, etc.

Yea, Lord, we greet
Thee,
Born this happy mor-
ning ;
Jesu, to Thee be glory
given ;
Word of the Father
In our flesh appear-
ing :
Oh, come, let us wor-
ship, etc.

STABAT MATER

STABAT Mater do-
lorosa
Juxta crucem lacry-
mosa,
Dum pendebat Filius.
Cujus animam gemen-
tem,
Contristatam, et do-
lentem,
Pertransivit gladius.

AT the Cross her
station keeping
Stood the mournful
Mother weeping,
Close to Jesus to the
last :
Through her heart, his
sorrow sharing,
All his bitter anguish
bearing,
Now at length the
sword had passed.

O quam tristis et affli-
cta
Fuit illa benedicta
Mater Unigeniti !
Quæ mœrebat, et do-
lebat,
Pia Mater, dum vide-
bat
Nati pœnas inclyti.

Oh, how sad and sore
distressed
Was that Mother high-
ly blest
Of the sole-begotten
One !
Christ above in tor-
ment hangs ;
She beneath beholds
the pangs
Of her dying glorious
Son.

Quis est homo qui non
fleret,
Matrem Christi si vi-
deret
In tanto supplicio ?
Quis non posset con-
tristari,
Christi Matrem con-
templari
Dolentem cum Filio ?

Is there one who
would not weep,
Whelmed in miseries
so deep
Christ's dear Mother
to behold ?
Can the human heart
refrain
From partaking in her
pain,
In that Mother's pain
untold ?

Pro peccatis suæ gen-
tis,
Vidit Jesum in tor-
mentis,
Et flagellis subditum.
Vidit suum dulcem
Natum

Bruised, derided,
cursed, defiled,
She beheld her tender
Child
All with bloody scour-
ges rent,
For the sins of his

Moriendo desolatum,
Dum emisit spiritum.

own nation,
Saw him hang in deso-
lation,
Till his spirit forth he
sent.

Eia Mater, fons
amoris,
Me sentire vim doloris
Fac, ut tecum luge-
am.
Fac ut ardeat cor
meum
In amando Christum
Deum,
Ut sibi complaceam.

O thou Mother ! fount
of love !
Touch my spirit from
above,
Make my heart with
thine accord :
Make me feel as thou
hast felt ;
Make my soul to glow
and melt.
With the love of Christ
my Lord.

Sancta Mater, istud
agas,
Crucifixi fige plagas
Cordi meo valide.
Tui Nati vulnerati,
Tam dignati pro me
pati,
Pœnas mecum divide.

Holy Mother ! pierce
me through ;
In my heart each
wound renew
Of my Saviour cru-
cified :
Let me share with
thee His pain
Who for all my sins
was slain,
Who for me in tor-
ments died.

Fac me tecum pie
  flere,
Crucifixo condolere,
Donec ego vixero.
Juxta Crucem tecum
  stare,
Et me tibi sociare
In planctu desidero.

Let me mingle tears
  with thee,
Mourning him who
  mourned for me,
All the days that I
  may live :
By the Cross with
  thee to stay,
There with thee to
  weep and pray,
Is all I ask of thee to
  give.

Virgo virginum præ-
  clara,
Mihi jam non sis am-
  ara ;
Fac me tecum plan-
  gere.
Fac ut portem Christi
  mortem,
Passionis fac consor-
  tem
Et plagas recolere.

Virgin of all virgins
  best !
Listen to my fond re-
  quest :
Let me share thy
  grief divine,
Let me, to my latest
  breath,
In my body bear the
  death
Of that dying Son of
  thine.

Fac me plagis vulne-
  rari,
Fac me Cruce in-
  ebriari,
Et cruore Filii.
Flammis ne urar suc-
  census,

Wounded with his
  every wound,
Steep my soul till it
  hath swooned
In his very blood
  away :
Be to me, O Virgin,

Per te, Virgo, sim de-
fensus
In die judicii.

nigh,
Lest in flames I burn
and die,
In his awful Judg-
ment Day.

Christe, cum sit hinc
exire
Da per Matrem me ve-
nire
Ad palmam victoriæ.
Quando corpus morie-
tur,
Fac ut animæ donetur
Paradisi gloria.
Amen.

Christ, when thou
shalt call me hence,
Be thy Mother my
defence,
Be thy Cross my vic-
tory;
While my body here
decays,
May my soul thy
goodness praise,
Safe in Paradise with
thee. *Amen.*

VENI CREATOR

VENI, Creator Spi-
ritus,
Mentes tuorum visita,
Imple superna gratia,
Quæ tu creasti pec-
tora.

COME, O Creator
Spirit blest!
And in our souls take
up thy rest;
Come, with thy grace
and heavenly aid,
To fill the hearts
which thou hast
made.

Qui diceris Paraclitus,
Altissimi donum Dei,

Great Paraclete! to
thee we cry,

Fons vivus, ignis, charitas,
Et spiritalis unctio.

O highest gift of God
  most high !
O fount of life ! O fire
  of love !
And solemn Unction
  from above !

Tu septiformis munere,
Digitus paternæ dexteræ,
Tu rite promissum Patris,
Sermone ditans guttura.

Thou in thy sevenfold
  gifts art known ;
The finger of God's
  hand we own ;
The promise of the
  Father thou !
Who dost the tongue
  with power endow.

Accende lumen sensibus,
Infunde amorem cordibus.
Infirma nostri corporis
Virtute firmans perpeti.

Kindle our senses from
  above,
And make our hearts
  o'erflow with love ;
With patience firm,
  and virtue high
The weakness of our
  flesh supply.

Hostem repellas longius,
Pacemque dones protinus ;
Ductore sic te prævio
Vitemus omne noxium.

Far from us drive the
  foe we dread,
And grant us thy true
  peace instead ;
So shall we not, with
  thee for guide,
Turn from the path of
  life aside.

Per te sciamus da
  Patrem,
Noscamus atque Fi-
  lium,
Teque utriusque Spiri-
  tum
Credamus omni tem-
  pore.

Deo Patri sit gloria,
Et Filio, qui a mor-
  tuis
Surrexit, ac Paraclito,
In sæculorum sæcula.
    Amen.

Oh, may thy grace on
  us bestow
The Father and the
  Son to know,
And thee through end-
  less times confessed,
Of both th' eternal
  Spirit blest.

All glory while the
  ages run
Be to the Father, and
  the Son
Who rose from death ;
  the same to Thee,
O Holy Ghost, eter-
  nally.   *Amen.*

LAUDA SION

LAUDA, Sion, Sal-
  vatorem,
Lauda Ducem et Pas-
  torem,
In hymnis et canticis,
Quantum potes, tan-
  tum aude ;
Quia major omni laude
Nec laudare sufficis.

SION, lift thy voice
  and sing,
Praise thy Saviour,
  praise thy King ;
Praise with hymns thy
  Shepherd true :
Strive thy best to
  praise Him well,
Yet doth he all praise
  excel ;
None can ever reach
  his due.

Laudis thema specialis,
Panis vivus et vitalis
Hodie proponitur.
Quem in sacræ mensa
coenæ
Turbæ fratrum duodenæ
Datum non ambigitur.

See to-day before us
laid
Living and life-giving
Bread,
Theme for praise and
joy profound.
Bread which at the
sacred board
Was, by our incarnate
Lord,
Given to his Apostles
round.

Sit laus plena, sit sonora,
Sit jucunda, sit decora
Mentis jubilatio.
Dies enim solemnis
agitur,
In qua mensæ prima
recolitur
Hujus institutio.

Let the praise be loud
and high
Sweet and reverent be
the joy
Felt to-day in every
breast ;
On this festival divine,
Which records the
origin
Of the glorious Eucharist.

In hac mensa novi
Regis,
Novum Pascha novæ
Legis,
Phase vetus terminat.
Vetustatem novitas,
Umbram fugat veritas,

On this table of the
King,
The new Law's paschal Offering
Brings to end the olden Rite.
Here, for empty shadows fled,

Noctem lux eliminat.

Is Reality instead;
Here, instead of dark-
ness, Light.

Quod in cœna Chris-
tus gessit,
Faciendum hoc ex-
pressit
In sui memoriam.
Docti sacris institutis,
Panem, vinum, in sa-
lutis
Consecramus hostiam.

What he did at supper
seated,
Christ ordained to be
repeated,
In his memory divine;
Wherefore we, with
adoration,
Thus the Host of our
salvation
Consecrate from bread
and wine.

Dogma datur Christi-
anis,
Quod in Carnem tran-
sit panis,
Et vinum in Sangui-
nem.
Quod non capis, quod
non vides,
Animosa firmat fides,
Præter rerum ordi-
nem.

Taught by Christ the
Church maintaineth
That the bread its sub-
stance changeth
Into Flesh, the wine
to Blood.
Doth it pass thy com-
prehending?
Faith, the law of sight
transcending,
Leaps to things not
understood.

Sub diversis speciebus,
Signis tantum et non
rebus.
Latent res eximiæ.

Here, beneath these
signs, are hidden
Priceless Things, to
sense forbidden;

Caro cibus, Sanguis
   potus :
Manet tamen Christus
   totus
Sub utraque specie.

A sumente non conci-
   sus,
Non confractus, non
   divisus,
Integer accipitur.
Sumit unus, sumunt
   mille,
Quantum isti, tantum
   ille,
Nec sumptus consu-
   mitur.

Sumunt boni, sumunt
   mali :
Sorte tamen inæquali,
Vitæ vel interitus.
Mors est malis, vita
   bonis,
Vide paris sumptionis
Quam sit dispar exi-
   tus.

Signs, not things, are
   all we see,—
Flesh from bread, and
   Blood from wine,
Yet is Christ in either
   sign,
All entire, confessed
   to be.

They, too, who of him
   partake,
Sever not, nor rend,
   nor break,
But entire, their Lord
   receive,
Whether one, or thou-
   sands eat,
All receive the self-
   same meat,
Nor the less for others
   leave.

Lo, the wicked with
   the good
Eat of this celestial
   food :
Yet with ends how
   opposite !
Life to these, 'tis
   death to those :
See how from like tak-
   ing flows
Difference truly in-
   finite.

Fracto demum Sacramento
Ne vacilles, sed memento
Tantum esse sub fragmento,
Quantum toto tegitur.
Nulla rei fit scissura ;
Signi tantum fit fractura :
Qua nec status, nec statura
Signati minuitur.

Nor do thou doubts entertain
When the Host is broken in twain :
But be sure, each part contains
What was in the whole before ;
'Tis the simple sign alone
Which hath changed in size and form,
Whilst the Signified is one
And the same for evermore.

Ecce Panis Angelorum,
Factus cibus viatorum :
Vere panis filiorum,
Non mittendus canibus.
In figuris præsignatur,
Cum Isaac immolatur :
Agnus Paschæ deputatur :
Datur manna patribus.

Lo, upon the Altar lies,
Hidden deep from human eyes,
Bread of Angels from the skies,
Made the food of mortal man :
Children's meat, to dogs denied ;
In old types foresignified :
In the manna heaven supplied,
Isaac, and the Paschal Lamb.

Bone Pastor, Panis vere,
Jesu, nostri miserere :
Tu nos pasce, nos tuere :
Tu nos bona fac videre
In terra viventium.

Jesu, Shepherd, Bread indeed,
Thou take pity on our need :
Thou thy flock in safety feed,
Thou protect us, thou us lead
To the land of heavenly grace.

Tu, qui cuncta scis et vales,
Qui nos pascis hic mortales :
Tuos ibi commensales,
Cohæredes, et sodales
Fac Sanctorum civium. *Amen.*

Thou, Who feedest us below,
Source of all we have or know,
Grant that, at thy feast of love,
Sitting with the Saints above
We may see thee face to face. *Amen.*

VENI SANCTE SPIRITUS

VENI, Sancte, Spiritus,
Et emitte cœlitus,
Lucis tuæ radium.

COME, O Holy Spirit, come ;
And from thy celestial home
Shed a ray of light divine ;

Veni, Pater pauperum,
Veni, dator munerum,

Come, thou Father of the poor,
Come, thou source of

Veni, lumen cordium.

all our store,
Come, within our bosoms shine.

Consolator optime,
Dulcis hospes animæ,
Dulce refrigerium.

Thou of all consolers best,
Thou the soul's most welcome guest,
Sweet refreshment here below.

In labore requies,
In æstu temperies,
In fletu solatium.

In our labour rest most sweet,
Grateful coolness in the heat,
Solace in the midst of woe.

O Lux beatissima,
Reple cordis intima
Tuorum fidelium.

O most blessed Light Divine,
Shine within these hearts of thine,
And our inmost beings fill.

Sine tuo numine
Nihil est in homine,
Nihil est innoxium.

Where thou art not : man hath naught.
Nothing good in deed or thought,
Nothing free from taint of ill.

Lava quod est sordidum,
Riga quod est aridum,

Heal our wounds ; our strength renew ;
On our dryness pour

Sana quod est sauci-
um.

Flecte quod est rigi-
dum,
Fove quod est frigi-
dum,
Rege quod est devium.

Da tuis fidelibus,
In te confidentibus,
Sacrum septenarium.

Da virtutis meritum,
Da salutis exitum,
Da perenne gaudium.
Amen.

thy dew;
Wash the stains of
guilt away.

Bend the stubborn
heart and will,
Melt the frozen, warm
the chill;
Guide the steps that
go astray.

Thou on those who
evermore
Thee confess and thee
adore,
In thy sevenfold gifts
descend.

Give them virtue's
sure reward,
Give them thy salva-
tion, Lord,
Give them joys that
never end.
Amen.

VEXILLA REGIS

VEXILLA Regis
prodeunt :
Fulget crucis myste-
rium,
Qua vita mortem per-
tulit,

FORTH comes the
Standard of the
King :
All hail, thou Mystery
ador'd !
Hail, Cross ! on which

Et morte vitam pro-
tulit.

the Life himself
Died, and by death
our life restor'd !

Quæ vulnerata lanceæ
Mucrone diro, crimi-
num
Ut nos lavaret sordi-
bus
Manavit unda et san-
guine.

On which our Saviour's
holy side,
Rent open with a cruel
spear,
Of blood and water
pour'd a stream,
To wash us from de-
filement clear.

Impleta sunt, quæ
concinit
David fideli carmine,
Dicendo nationibus :
Regnavit a ligno
Deus.

O sacred Wood ! in
thee fulfill'd
Was holy David's
truthful lay !
Which told the world
that from a Tree
The Lord should all
the nations sway.

Arbor decora et ful-
gida,
Ornata regis purpura,
Electa digno stipite
Tam sancta membra
tangere.

Most royally empur-
pled o'er,
How beauteously thy
stem doth shine !
How glorious was its
lot to touch
Those limbs so holy
and divine !

Beata, cujus brachiis
Pretium pependit sæ-
culi,

Thrice blest, upon
whose arms out-
stretch'd

Statera facta corporis,
Tulitque prædam tartari.

The Saviour of the
world reclined;
'Balance sublime! upon whose beam
Was weigh'd the ransom of mankind.

O Crux ave, spes
unica,
Hoc Passionis tempore
Piis adauge gratiam,
Reisque dele crimina.

Hail, Cross! thou only
hope of man,
Hail on this holy Passion-day!
To saints increase the
grace they have;
From sinners purge
their guilt away.

Te, fons salutis, Trinitas,
Collaudet omnis spiritus:
Quibus crucis victoriam
Largiris, adde præmium.

Amen.

Salvation's spring,
blest Trinity,
Be praise to thee
through earth and
skies:
Thou through the
Cross the victory
Dost give; oh, also
give the prize!

Amen.

AVE MARIS STELLA

AVE maris stella,
  Dei Mater alma,
Atque semper virgo,
Felix cœli porta.

HAIL, thou star of
  ocean,
Portal of the sky !
Ever-virgin Mother
Of the Lord most
  high.

Sumens illud Ave
Gabrielis ore,
Funda nos in pace,
Mutans Hevæ nomen.

Oh ! by Gabriel's Ave,
Utter'd long ago,
Eva's name reversing,
Stablish peace below.

Solve vincla reis,
Profer lumen cæcis,
Mala nostra pelle,
Bona cuncta posce.

Break the captive's
  fetters,
Light on blindness
  pour ;
All our ills expelling,
Every bliss implore.

Monstra te esse ma-
  trem,
Sumat per te preces,
Qui pro nobis natus,
Tulit esse tuus.

Show thyself a
  mother ;
Offer him our sighs,
Who for us incarnate
Did not thee despise.

Virgo singularis,
Inter omnes mitis,
Nos culpis solutos,
Mites fac et castos.

Virgin of all virgins !
To thy shelter take us:
Gentlest of the gentle!
Chaste and gentle
  make us.

Vitam præsta puram,
Iter para tutum,
Ut videntes Jesum,
Semper collætemur.

Still as on we journey,
Help our weak en-
deavour :
Till with thee and
Jesus
We rejoice for ever.

Sit laus Deo Patri,
Summo Christus
   decus,
Spiritui Sancto,
Tribus honor unus.
         Amen.

Through the highest
   heaven,
To the Almighty
   Three.
Father, Son, and
   Spirit,
One same glory be.
         Amen.

GRACE BEFORE MEALS

BLESS us, O Lord, and these Thy gifts, which of Thy bounty we are about to receive, through Christ our Lord. *Amen.*

GRACE AFTER MEALS

WE give Thee thanks, Almighty God, for all Thy benefits, Who livest and reignest, world without end. *Amen.*

FEASTS AND FASTS THROUGHOUT THE YEAR

Festivals that are observed by the Catholics of England, with an Obligation of hearing Mass and resting from servile Works.

ALL Sundays in the year.

January 1. The Circumcision of our Lord, or New Year's Day.

January 6. The Epiphany.

June 29. SS. Peter and Paul.

August 15. The Assumption of the Blessed Virgin Mary.

November 1. All Saints'.

December 25. Christmas Day.

Ascension Day (40 days after Easter).

Corpus Christi (Thursday after Trinity Sunday).

In Ireland besides the above :

March 17. St. Patrick.
December 8. The Immaculate Conception.

In Scotland :

March 19.   Joseph.
December 8. The Immaculate Conception.

Fasting Days

All the week-days of Lent, beginning on Ash Wednesday.
Ember-days, four times a year, viz.: Wednesdays, Fridays, and Saturdays:
(1) Next after the first Sunday in Lent;
(2) in Whitsun week;   (3) next after September 14;   (4) next after the third Sunday of Advent.

Should, however, any one of the above days coincide with a Holy Day of Obligation, the law of fasting is abrogated for that day.

Days of Abstinence from Flesh Meat

All Fridays, except Fridays on which a Holy Day of Obligation (or, in England, December 26) falls.
The Wednesdays in Lent.
Ember Saturday in Lent.
The Ember Wednesdays.
The Vigils mentioned below (unless their feasts fall on Sunday or Monday).

Vigils, with Fasts of Obligation annexed to them

1. The Vigil of the Assumption, August 14.
2. The Vigil of All Saints, October 31.
3. The Vigil of the Nativity of our Lord, December 24.
4. The Vigil of Pentecost.

The Six Precepts of the Church

1. TO hear Mass on Sundays, and all holidays of obligation.
2. To fast and abstain on the days commanded.
3. To confess our sins at least once a year.
4. To receive the Blessed Eucharist at Easter.
5. To contribute to the support of our pastors.
6. Not to solemnize marriage at the forbidden times ; nor to marry persons within the forbidden degrees of kindred, or otherwise prohibited by the Church ; nor clandestinely.

INDULGENCES

1. *What an Indulgence is*

BY an Indulgence is meant the remission of the *temporal punishment* due to us on account of our sins. Every sin, however grievous, is remitted through the Sacrament of Penance, or by an act of perfect contrition, as regards its *guilt* and the *eternal punishment* due to it. But the debt of *temporal punishment* is not always remitted at the same time. This latter is done away with by deep penitence, or by works of satisfaction—*e.g.*, prayers, alms, fasting, &c.; or by the patient endurance of troubles and adversities sent us by God, &c.; or by the satisfaction of our Lord Jesus Christ and the Saints, applied to us through Indulgences by those who have the power to apply them. And although, in order to escape this temporal punishment, we must not rely on Indulgences alone, to the neglect of good works; yet because, at the best, our own good works are very imperfect, and the debt of punishment due by us very great, we ought to endeavour, as frequently as possible, to avail ourselves of the benefits of Indulgences.

Indulgences are of two kinds: 1st, a *plenary* Indulgence, when duly gained, is a full and entire remission of all the temporal punishment due to sin. The eight Indulgences granted to the faithful in England at the principal festivals in the year are plenary Indulgences. A jubilee is also a plenary Indulgence occasionally granted by the Pope to the whole Church, in the most ample manner, and with the greatest solemnity. There are many other plenary Indulgences granted to various good works.

2nd, a *partial*, or limited Indulgence, as of ten years or a hundred days, etc., remits as much of the temporal punishment as would have been remitted by ten years, or a hundred days, etc., of the canonical penances formerly imposed on public penitents.

2. *What is required for obtaining an Indulgence*

1. *A Plenary Indulgence.*—To approach to the Sacraments of Penance and the Holy Eucharist; to perform the special work to which the Indulgence is attached. Most plenary Indulgences have attached to them as a condition that we are to pray for the intention of the Holy Father. For this purpose we may say a litany, a portion of the rosary, Jesus psalter, or five *Paters* and five *Aves*. One Communion suffices for several Indulgences, if they can be gained on the same day.

2. *Partial Indulgence.*—To be in a state of grace; to perform the work to which the Indulgence is attached.

EPISTLES AND GOSPELS

FOR ALL THE SUNDAYS AND DAYS OF OBLIGATION OF THE YEAR

FIRST SUNDAY OF ADVENT

EPISTLE. *Romans* xiii, 11–14. *Brethren:* Know that it is now the hour for us to rise from sleep. For now our salvation is nearer than when we believed. The night is past and the day is at hand. Let us therefore cast off the works of darkness, and put on the armour of light. Let us walk honestly, as in the day: not in rioting and drunkenness, not in chambering and impurities, not in contention and envy; but put ye on the Lord Jesus Christ.

GOSPEL. *Luke* xxi, 25–33. *At that time:* Jesus said to His disciples: There shall be signs in the sun, and in the moon, and in the stars; and upon the earth distress of nations, by reason of the confusion of the roaring of the sea and of the waves; men withering away for fear, and expectation of what shall come upon the whole world. For the powers of the heavens shall be moved; and then they shall see the Son of man coming in a cloud with great power and majesty. But when these things begin to come to pass, look up, and lift up your heads, because your redemption is at hand. And He spoke to them a similitude. See the fig-tree, and all the trees: when they now shoot forth their fruit, you know that summer is nigh; so you also, when you shall see these things come to pass, know that the kingdom of God is at hand. Amen, I say to you, this generation shall not pass away, till all things be fulfilled. Heaven and earth shall pass away, but My words shall not pass away.

SECOND SUNDAY OF ADVENT

EPISTLE. *Romans* **xv, 4-13.** *Brethren :* What things soever were written, were written for our learning : that through patience and the comfort of the scriptures, we might have hope. Now the God of patience and of comfort grant you to be of one mind one towards another, according to Jesus Christ ; that with one mind, and with one mouth, you may glorify God and the Father of our Lord Jesus Christ. Wherefore receive one another, as Christ also hath received you unto the honour of God. For I say that Christ Jesus was minister of the circumcision for the truth of God, to confirm the promises made unto the fathers. But that the Gentiles are to glorify God for His mercy, as it is written : *Therefore will I confess to thee, O Lord, among the Gentiles, and will sing to Thy name.* And again he saith : *Rejoice, ye Gentiles, with His people.* And again : *Praise the*

Lord, all ye Gentiles ; and magnify Him, all ye people. And again, Isaiah saith : *There shall be a root of Jesse ; and He that shall rise up to rule the Gentiles, in Him the Gentiles shall hope.* Now the God of Hope fill you with all joy and peace in believing, that you may abound in hope, and in the power of the Holy Ghost.

GOSPEL. *Matthew* xi, 2–10. *At that time :* When John had heard in prison the works of Christ : sending two of his disciples he said to Him : Art thou He that art to come, or look we for another ? And Jesus making answer said to them : Go and relate to John what you have heard and seen. The blind see, the lame walk, the lepers are cleansed, the deaf hear, the dead rise again, the poor have the gospel preached to them. And blessed is he that shall not be scandalized in Me. And when they went their way, Jesus began to say to the multitudes, concerning John : What went you out into the desert to see ? a reed shaken with the wind ? But what went you out to see ? a man clothed in soft garments ? Behold they that are clothed in soft garments, are in the houses of kings. But what went you out to see ? a prophet ? yea I tell you, and more than a prophet. For this is he of whom it is written : *Behold, I send my angel before Thy face, who shall prepare Thy way before Thee.*

THIRD SUNDAY OF ADVENT

EPISTLE. *Philippians* iv, 4–7. *Brethren :*
Rejoice in the Lord always ; again, I say,
rejoice. Let your modesty be known to all
men. The Lord is nigh. Be nothing solicitous ; but in everything, by prayer and
supplication, with thanksgiving, let your
petitions be made known to God. And the
peace of God, which surpasseth all understanding, keep your hearts and minds in
Christ Jesus our Lord.

GOSPEL. *John* i, 19–28. *At that time :*
The Jews sent from Jerusalem priests and
Levites to John, to ask him : Who art
thou ? And he confessed, and did not deny :
and he confessed : I am not the Christ.
And they asked him : What then ? Art
thou Elias ? And he said : I am not. Art
thou the prophet ? And he answered : No.
They said therefore unto him : Who art
thou, that we may give an answer to them
that sent us ? What sayest thou of thyself ?
He said : *I am the voice of one crying in the
wilderness, make straight the way of the
Lord,* as said the prophet Isaias. And they
that were sent, were of the Pharisees.
And they asked him, and said to him :
Why then dost thou baptize, if thou be not
Christ, nor Elias, nor the prophet ? John
answered them, saying : I baptize with
water ; but there hath stood one in the

midst of you, whom you know not. The
same is He that shall come after me, who
is preferred before me ; the latchet of whose
shoe I am not worthy to loose. These things
were done in Bethania beyond the Jordan,
where John was baptizing.

FOURTH SUNDAY OF ADVENT

EPISTLE. I *Corinthians* iv, 1–5. *Brethren :*
Let a man so account of us as of the ministers of Christ, and the dispensers of the
mysteries of God. Here now it is required
amongst the dispensers, that a man be found
faithful. But to me it is a very small thing
to be judged by you, or by man's day ;
but neither do I judge my own self. For I
am not conscious to myself of anything,
yet I am not hereby justified ; but he that
judgeth me, is the Lord. Therefore judge
not before the time ; until the Lord come,
who both will bring to light the hidden
things of darkness, and will make manifest
the counsel of the hearts : and then shall
every man have praise from God.

GOSPEL. *Luke* iii, 1–6. Now in the fifteenth
year of the reign of Tiberius Cæsar, Pontius
Pilate being governor of Judea, and Herod
being Tetrarch of Galilee, and Philip his
brother Tetrarch of Iturea, and the country
of Trachonitis, and Lysanias Tetrarch of
Abilina ; under the high priests Annas and
Caiphas ; the word of the Lord came to

John, the son of Zachary, in the desert.
And he came into all the country about the
Jordan, preaching the baptism of penance
for the remission of sins ; as it was written
in the book of the sayings of Isaias the
prophet : *A voice of one crying in the wilderness : Prepare ye the way of the Lord, make
straight His paths. Every valley shall be filled ;
and every mountain and hill shall be brought
low ; and the crooked shall be made straight ;
and the rough ways plain ; and all flesh shall
see the salvation of God.*

CHRISTMAS DAY

FIRST MASS.   AT MIDNIGHT

EPISTLE. *Titus* ii, 11–15. *Dearly Beloved :*
The grace of God our Saviour hath appeared
to all men ; instructing us, that, denying
ungodliness and worldly desires, we should
live soberly, and justly, and godly in this
world, looking for the blessed hope and
coming of the glory of the great God and
our Saviour Jesus Christ, who gave Himself
for us, that He might redeem us from all
iniquity, and might cleanse to Himself a
people acceptable, a pursuer of good works.
These things speak, and exhort : in Christ
Jesus our Lord.

GOSPEL. *Luke* ii, 1–14. *At that time :*
There went out a decree from Cæsar
Augustus, that the whole world should be
enrolled. This enrolling was first made by

Cyrinus, the Governor of Syria. And all went to be enrolled, every one into his own city. And Joseph also went up from Galilee, out of the city of Nazareth into Judea, to the city of David, which is called Bethlehem : because he was of the house and family of David, to be enrolled with Mary, his espoused wife, who was with child. And it came to pass, that when they were there, her days were accomplished, that she should be delivered. And she brought forth her firstborn Son, and wrapped Him up in swaddling clothes, and laid Him in a manger because there was no room for them in the inn. And there were in the same country shepherds watching, and keeping the night watches over their flock. And behold an angel of the Lord stood by them, and the brightness of God shone round about them ; and they feared with a great fear. And the angel said to them : Fear not ; for, behold, I bring you good tidings of great joy, that shall be to all the people : for this day is born to you a SAVIOUR, who is Christ the Lord, in the city of David. And this shall be a sign unto you. You shall find the infant wrapped in swaddling clothes, and laid in a manger. And suddenly there was with the angel a multitude of the heavenly army, praising God, and saying : Glory to God in the highest ; and on earth peace to men of good will.

SECOND MASS.   AT BREAK OF DAY

EPISTLE. *Titus* iii, 4–7. *Dearly beloved :* The goodness and kindness of God our Saviour appeared ; not by the works of justice, which we have done, but according to His mercy, He saved us, by the laver of regeneration, and renovation of the Holy Ghost ; whom He hath poured forth upon us abundantly, through Jesus Christ our Saviour : that, being justified by His grace, we may be heirs, according to hope of life everlasting ; in Christ Jesus our Lord.

GOSPEL. *Luke* ii, 15–20. *At that time :* The shepherds said one to another : Let us go over to Bethlehem, and let us see this word that is come to pass, which the Lord hath shewed to us. And they came with haste ; and they found Mary and Joseph, and the Infant lying in a manger. And seeing, they understood of the word that had been spoken to them concerning this Child. And all that heard, wondered ; and at those things that were told them by the shepherds. But Mary kept all these words, pondering *them* in her heart. And the shepherds returned, glorifying and praising God, for all the things they had heard and seen, as it was told unto them.

THIRD MASS.   IN THE DAY-TIME

EPISTLE. *Hebrews* i, 1–12. God, Who, at sundry times and in divers manners, spoke in times past to the fathers by the prophets, last of all, in these days, hath spoken to us by His Son, Whom He hath appointed heir of all things, by Whom also He made the world. Who being the brightness of His glory, and the figure of His substance, and upholding all things by the word of His power, making purgation of sins, sitteth on the right hand of the majesty on high. Being made so much better than the angels, as He hath inherited a more excellent name than they. For to which of the angels hath He said at any time. *Thou art My son, to-day have I begotten Thee?* And again, *I will be to Him a Father, and He shall be to Me a Son?* And again, when He bringeth in the first begotten into the world, He saith : *And let all the angels of God adore Him.* And to the angels indeed He saith : *He that maketh His angels spirits, and His ministers a flame of fire.* But to the Son : *Thy throne, O God, is for ever and ever : a sceptre of justice is the sceptre of Thy kingdom. Thou hast loved justice, and hated iniquity : therefore God, Thy God, hath anointed Thee with the oil of gladness above Thy fellows.* And : *Thou in the beginning, O Lord, didst found the earth : and the works of Thy hands are the heavens. They shall perish, but Thou shalt continue : and they shall all grow old as a garment. And as a vesture shalt Thou change them, and they shall be changed : but Thou art the selfsame, and Thy years shall not fail.*

GOSPEL. *John* i, 1–14. In the beginning was the Word, and the Word was with God, and the Word was God. The same was in the beginning with God. All things were made by Him : and without Him was made nothing that was made. In Him was life, and the life was the light of men. And the light shineth in darkness, and the darkness did not comprehend it. There was a man sent from God, whose name was John. This man came for a witness, to give testimony of the light, that all men might believe through Him. He was not the light, but was to give testimony of the light. That was the true light, which enlighteneth every man that cometh into this world. He was in the world, and the world was made by Him, and the world knew Him not. He came unto His own, and His own received him not. But as many as received Him, He gave them power to be made the sons of God, to them that believe in His name. Who are born, not of blood, nor of the will of the flesh, nor of the will of man, but of God. *And *the Word was made flesh*, and dwelt among us, and we saw His glory, the glory as it were of the only begotten of the Father, full of grace and truth.   * *Here all kneel.*

SUNDAY WITHIN THE OCTAVE OF CHRISTMAS

EPISTLE. *Galatians* iv, 1–7. *Brethren :* As long as the heir is a child, he differeth nothing from a servant, though he be lord of all ; but is under tutors and governors until the time appointed by the father : so we also, when we were children, were serving under the elements of the world. But when the fulness of the time was come, God sent His Son, made of a woman, made under the law : that He might redeem them who were under the law : that we might receive the adoption of sons. And because you are sons, God hath sent the Spirit of His Son into your hearts, crying : *Abba*, Father. Therefore now he is not a servant, but a son. And if a son, an heir also through God.

GOSPEL. *Luke* ii, 33–40. *At that time :* Joseph and Mary the mother of Jesus, were wondering at those things which were spoken concerning Him. And Simeon blessed them, and said to Mary His mother : Behold, this Child is set for the fall, and for the resurrection of many in Israel, and for a sign which shall be contradicted ; and thy own soul a sword shall pierce, that, out of many hearts, thoughts may be revealed. And there was one Anna, a prophetess, the daughter of Phanuel, of

the tribe of Aser ; she was far advanced
in years, and had lived with her husband
seven years from her virginity. And she
was a widow until fourscore and four years ;
who departed not from the temple, by
fastings and prayers serving day and night.
Now she, at the same hour, coming in,
confessed to the Lord, and spoke of Him
to all that looked for the redemption of
Israel. And after they had performed all
things according to the law of the Lord,
they returned into Galilee, to their city
Nazareth. And the Child grew, and waxed
strong, full of wisdom ; and the grace of
God was in Him.

THE CIRCUMCISION

EPISTLE. *Titus* ii. 11–15. *Dearly beloved :*
The grace of God our Saviour hath appeared
to all men ; instructing us, that, denying
ungodliness and worldly desires, we should
live soberly, and justly, and godly in this
world, looking for the blessed hope and
coming of the glory of the great God and our
Saviour Jesus Christ, who gave Himself
for us, that He might redeem us from all
iniquity, and might cleanse to Himself a
people acceptable, a pursuer of good works.
These things speak, and exhort : in Christ
Jesus our Lord.

GOSPEL. *Luke* ii, 21. *At that time :* After
eight days were accomplished, that the

Child should be circumcised, His name was
called Jesus, which was called by the angel,
before He was conceived in the womb.

FEAST OF THE HOLY NAME OF JESUS

(Sunday after the Circumcision)

LESSON. *Acts* iv, 8–12. *In those days :*
Peter, being filled with the Holy Ghost,
said to them : Ye princes of the people,
and ancients, hear : If we this day are examined concerning the good deeds done to
the infirm man, by what means he hath been
made whole : be it known to you all, and to
all the people of Israel, that by the name of
our Lord Jesus Christ of Nazareth, whom
you crucified, whom God hath raised from
the dead, even by Him this man standeth
here before you whole. This is *the stone which
was rejected by you the builders, which is
become the head of the corner.* Neither is there
salvation in any other. For there is no other
name under heaven given to men, whereby
we must be saved.

GOSPEL. *Luke* ii, 21. *At that time :* After
eight days were accomplished, that the
Child should be circumcised, His name was
called Jesus, which was called by the angel,
before He was conceived in the womb.

THE EPIPHANY

LESSON. *Isaias* lx, 1–6. Arise, be enlightened, O Jerusalem : for thy light is come, and the glory of the Lord is risen upon thee. For behold darkness shall cover the earth, and a mist the people : but the Lord shall arise upon thee, and His glory shall be seen upon thee. And the Gentiles shall walk in thy light, and kings in the brightness of thy rising. Lift up thy eyes round about, and see : all these are gathered together, they are come to thee : thy sons shall come from afar, and thy daughters shall rise up at thy side. Then shalt thou see, and abound, and thy heart shall wonder and be enlarged, when the multitude of the sea shall be converted to thee, the strength of the Gentiles shall come to thee. The multitude of camels shall cover thee, the dromedaries of Madian and Epha : all they from Saba shall come, bringing gold and frankincense : and showing forth praise to the Lord.

GOSPEL : *Matthew* ii, 1–12. When Jesus therefore was born in Bethlehem of Juda, in the days of king Herod, behold, there came wise men from the east to Jerusalem, saying, Where is He that is born King of the Jews ? For we have seen His star in the east, and are come to adore Him. And king Herod hearing this, was troubled, and all Jerusalem with him. And assembling together all the chief priests and the scribes of the people, he inquired of them where Christ should be born. But they said to him : In Bethlehem of Juda. For so it is written by the prophet : *And thou Bethlehem the land of Juda are. not the least among the princes of Juda ! for out of thee shall come forth the captain that shall rule my people Israel.* Then Herod privately calling the wise men learned diligently of them the time of the star which appeared to them ; and sending them into Bethlehem, said : Go and diligently inquire after the Child, and when you have found Him, bring me word again that I also may come and adore Him. Who having heard the king, went their way ; and behold the star which they had seen in the east, went before them, until it came and stood over where the Child was. And seeing the star, they rejoiced with exceeding great joy. And entering into the house, they found the Child with Mary His mother, * and falling down they adored Him ; and opening their treasures, they offered Him gifts : gold, frankincense, and myrrh. And having received an answer in sleep that they should not return to Herod, they went back another way into their country.

* *Here all kneel.*

FEAST OF THE HOLY FAMILY
(SUNDAY AFTER THE EPIPHANY)

EPISTLE. *Col. iii*, 12-17, *as on p. 298.*
GOSPEL. *Luke ii*, 42-52, *as on p. 292.*

FIRST SUNDAY AFTER EPIPHANY

EPISTLE. *Rom.* xii, 1-5. *Brethren :* I
beseech you by the mercy of God, that you
present your bodies a living sacrifice, holy,
pleasing unto God, your reasonable service.
And be not conformed to this world ; but
be reformed in the newness of your mind,
that you may prove what is the good, and
the acceptable, and the perfect will of God.
For I say, by the grace that is given me, to
all that are among you, not to be more
wise than it behoveth to be wise, but to
be wise unto sobriety, and according as God
hath divided to every one the measure of
faith. For as in one body we have many
members, but all the members have not the
same office : so we being many, are one body
in Christ, and every one members one of
another : in Christ Jesus our Lord.

GOSPEL. *Luke* ii, 42-52. When Jesus was
twelve years old, they went up to Jerusalem
according to the custom of the feast, and
having fulfilled the days, when they returned, the Child Jesus remained in Jerusalem ; and His parents knew it not. And
thinking that He was in the company, they
came a day's journey, and sought Him
among their kinsfolk and acquaintance. And
not finding Him, they returned into Jerusalem, seeking Him. And it came to pass,
that after three days, they found Him in the

temple, sitting in the midst of the doctors, hearing them, and asking them questions. And all that heard Him were astonished at His wisdom and His answers. And seeing Him, they wondered. And His mother said to Him : Son, why hast Thou done so to us ? Behold Thy father and I have sought Thee sorrowing. And He said to them : How is it that you sought Me ? Did you not know that I must be about My Father's business ? And they understood not the word that He spoke unto them. And He went down with them and came to Nazareth, and was subject to them. And His mother kept all these words in her heart. And Jesus advanced in wisdom, and age, and grace with God and men.

SECOND SUNDAY AFTER EPIPHANY

EPISTLE. *Romans* xii, *6–16. Brethren :* Having different gifts, according to the grace that is given us, either prophecy, to be used according to the rule of faith ; or ministry, in ministering ; or he that teacheth, in doctrine ; he that exhorteth, in exhorting ; he that giveth, with simplicity ; he that ruleth, with carefulness ; he that sheweth mercy, with cheerfulness. Let love be without dissimulation. Hating that which is evil, cleaving to that which is good. Loving one another with the charity of brotherhood, with honour preventing one another. In carefulness not slothful : In spirit fervent : Serving the Lord ; Rejoicing in hope : Patient in tribulation : Instant in prayer : Communicating to the necessities of the saints : Pursuing hospitality. Bless them that persecute you : bless, and curse not. Rejoice with them that rejoice ; weep with them that weep. Being of one mind one towards the other ; not minding high things, but consenting to the humble.

GOSPEL. *John* ii, 1–11. *At that time :* There was a marriage in Cana of Galilee ; and the mother of Jesus was there. And Jesus also was invited, and His disciples, to the marriage. And the wine failing, the mother of Jesus saith to Him : They have no wine. And Jesus saith to her : Woman, what is it to Me and to thee ? My hour is not yet come. His mother said to the waiters: Whatsoever He shall say to you do ye. Now there were set there six waterpots of stone, according to the manner of the purifying of the Jews, containing two or three measures apiece. Jesus saith to them : Fill the waterpots with water. And they filled them up to the brim. And Jesus saith to them : Draw out now, and carry to the chief steward of the feast. And they carried it. And when the chief steward had tasted the water made wine, and knew not whence it was, but the waiters knew who had drawn the water ;

the chief steward called the bridegroom, and saith to him : Every man at first setteth forth good wine, and when men have well drunk, then that which is worse. But thou hast kept the good wine until now. This beginning of miracles did Jesus in Cana of Galilee ; and manifested His glory, and His disciples believed in Him.

THIRD SUNDAY AFTER EPIPHANY

EPISTLE. *Romans* xii, 16–21. *Brethren :* Be not wise in your own conceits. To no man rendering evil for evil ; providing good things, not only in the sight of God, but also in the sight of all men. If it be possible, as much as is in you, have peace with all men. Revenge not yourselves, my dearly beloved ; but give place unto wrath, for it is written : *Revenge is mine, I will repay*, saith the Lord. But *if thy enemy be hungry, give him to eat ; if he thirst, give him to drink. For, doing this, thou shalt heap coals of fire upon his head.* Be not overcome by evil, but overcome evil by good.

GOSPEL. *Matthew* viii, 1–13. *At that time :* When Jesus was come down from the mountain, great multitudes followed Him : and behold a leper came and adored Him, saying : Lord, if Thou wilt, Thou canst make me clean. And Jesus stretching forth His hand, touched him, saying : I will, be thou made clean. And forthwith his leprosy was cleansed. And Jesus saith to him : See thou tell no man : but go, show thyself to the priest, and offer the gift which Moses commanded for a testimony unto them. And when He had entered into Capharnaum, there came to Him a centurion, beseeching Him, and saying, Lord, my servant lieth at home sick of the palsy, and is grievously tormented. And Jesus saith to him : I will come and heal him. And the centurion making answer, said : Lord, I am not worthy that Thou shouldst enter under my roof ; but only say the word, and my servant shall be healed. For I also am a man subject to authority, having under me soldiers ; and I say to this, Go, and he goeth, and to another, Come, and he cometh, and to my servant, Do this, and he doeth it. And Jesus hearing this marvelled ; and said to them that followed Him : Amen I say to you, I have not found so great faith in Israel. And I say unto you that many shall come from the east and the west, and shall sit down with Abraham, and Isaac, and Jacob in the kingdom of heaven : but the children of the kingdom shall be cast out into the exterior darkness : there shall be weeping and gnashing of teeth. And Jesus said to the centurion : Go, and as thou hast believed, so be it done to thee. And the servant was healed at the same hour.

FOURTH SUNDAY AFTER
EPIPHANY

EPISTLE. *Romans* xiii, 8–10. *Brethren :*
Owe no man anything, but to love one
another. For he that loveth his neighbour,
hath fulfilled the law. For *Thou shalt not
commit adultery : Thou shalt not kill :
Thou shalt not steal : Thou shalt not bear
false witness : Thou shalt not covet :* and if
there be any other commandment, it is
comprised in this word, *Thou shalt love
thy neighbour as thyself.* The love of our
neighbour worketh no evil. Love therefore
is the fulfilling of the law.

GOSPEL. *Matthew* viii 23–27. *At that time :*
When Jesus entered into the boat His
disciples followed Him : and behold a great
tempest arose in the sea, so that the boat
was covered with waves, but He was asleep.
And His disciples came to Him, and awaked
Him, saying : Lord, save us, we perish.
And Jesus saith to them : Why are you
fearful, O ye of little faith ? Then rising up,
He commanded the winds, and the sea, and
there came a great calm. But the men
wondered, saying : What manner of man
is this, for the winds and the sea obey
Him ?

FIFTH SUNDAY AFTER EPIPHANY

EPISTLE. *Colossians* iii, 12-17. *Brethren :*
Put ye on therefore, as the elect of God,
holy, and beloved, the bowels of mercy,
benignity, humility, modesty, patience :
bearing with one another, and forgiving
one another, if any have a complaint against
another : even as the Lord hath forgiven
you, so do you also. But above all these
things have charity, which is the bond of
perfection : and let the peace of Christ
rejoice in your hearts, wherein also you are
called in one body : and be ye thankful.
Let the word of Christ dwell in you abundantly, in all wisdom : teaching and ad-
monishing one another in psalms, hymns,
and spiritual canticles, singing in grace
in your hearts to God. All whatsoever you
do in word or in work, do all in the name
of the Lord Jesus Christ, giving thanks to
God and the Father through Jesus Christ
our Lord.

GOSPEL. *Matthew* xiii, 24-30. *At that
time :* Jesus spoke this parable to the
multitude, saying : The kingdom of heaven
is likened to a man that sowed good seed
in his field. But while men were asleep,
his enemy came and oversowed cockle
among the wheat and went his way. And
when the blade was sprung up, and had

brought forth fruit, then appeared also the cockle. And the servants of the good man of the house coming said to him : Sir, didst thou not sow good seed in thy field ? whence then hath it cockle ? And he said to them : An enemy hath done this. And the servants said to him : Wilt thou that we go and gather it up ? And he said : No, lest perhaps gathering up the cockle, you root up the wheat also together with it. Suffer both to grow until the harvest, and in the time of the harvest I will say to the reapers : Gather up first the cockle and bind it into bundles to burn, but the wheat gather ye into my barn.

SIXTH SUNDAY AFTER EPIPHANY

EPISTLE. I *Thessalonians* i, 2–10. *Brethren:* We give thanks to God always. for you all ; making a remembrance of you in our prayers without ceasing, being mindful of the work of your faith, and labour, and charity, and of the enduring of the hope of our Lord Jesus Christ before God and our Father : knowing, brethren beloved of God, your election : for our gospel hath not been unto you in word only, but in power also, and in the Holy Ghost, and in much fulness, as you know what manner of men we have been among you for your sakes. And you became followers of us, and of the Lord ; receiving the word in much tribulation, with joy of the Holy Ghost: so that you were made a pattern to all that believe in Macedonia, and in Achaia. For from you was spread abroad the word of the Lord, not only in Macedonia, and in Achaia, but also in every place your faith, which is towards God, is gone forth, so that we need not to speak anything. For they themselves relate of us, what manner of entering in we had unto you; and how you turned to God from idols, to serve the living and true God. And to wait for His Son from heaven (whom He raised up from the dead) Jesus, Who hath delivered us from the wrath to come.

GOSPEL. *Matthew* xiii, 31–35. *At that time:* Jesus spoke to the multitude this parable: The kingdom of heaven is like to a grain of mustard seed, which a man took and sowed in his field. Which is the least indeed of all seeds; but when it is grown up, it is greater than all herbs, and becometh a tree, so that the birds of the air come, and dwell in the branches thereof. Another parable He spoke to them: The kingdom of heaven is like to leaven, which a woman took and hid in three measures of meal, until the whole was leavened. All these things Jesus spoke in parables to the multitudes: and without parables He did not speak to them. That it might be fulfilled which was spoken by the prophet, saying:

I will open My mouth in parables, I will utter things hidden from the foundation of the world.

If there be not six Sundays between the Epiphany and Septuagesima, what remains are omitted, and taken in between the twenty-third and the last Sunday after Pentecost.

SEPTUAGESIMA SUNDAY

EPISTLE. 1 *Corinthians* ix, 24, *to* x, 5. *Brethren :* Know you not that they that run in the race, all run indeed, but one receiveth the prize ? So run that you may obtain. And every one that striveth for the mastery, refraineth himself from all things : and they indeed that they may receive a corruptible crown, but we an incorruptible one. I therefore so run, not as at an uncertainty : I so fight, not as one beating the air : but I chastise my body, and bring it into subjection : lest perhaps, when I have preached to others, I myself should become a castaway. For I would not have you ignorant, brethren, that our fathers were all under the cloud, and all passed through the sea, and all in Moses were baptized, in the cloud, and in the sea: and did all eat the same spiritual food, and all drank the same spiritual drink ; (and they drank of the spiritual Rock that followed them, and the Rock was Christ). But with most of them God was not well pleased.

Gospel. *Matthew* xx, 1-16. *At that
time :* Jesus spoke to His disciples this
parable : The kingdom of heaven is like to
an householder, who went out early in the
morning to hire labourers into his vineyard. And having agreed with the labourers
for a penny a day, he sent them into his
vineyard. And going out about the third
hour, he saw others standing in the market-
place idle. And he said to them : Go you
also into my vineyard, and I will give you
what shall be just. And they went their
way. And again he went out about the sixth
and the ninth hour, and did in like manner.
But about the eleventh hour he went out
and found others standing, and he saith
to them : Why stand you here all the day
idle ? They say to him : Because no man
hath hired us. He saith to them : Go you
also into my vineyard. And when evening
was come, the lord of the vineyard saith
to his steward : Call the labourers and pay
them their hire, beginning from the last
even to the first. When therefore they were
come, that came about the eleventh hour,
they received every man a penny. But when
the first also came, they thought that they
should receive more : and they also received
every man a penny. And receiving it they
murmured against the master of the house,
saying : These last have worked but one
hour, and thou hast made them equal to
us, that have borne the burden of the day

and the heats. But he answering said to one of them : Friend, I do thee no wrong : didst thou not agree with me for a penny ? Take what is thine, and go thy way : I will also give to this last even as to thee. Or, is it not lawful for me to do what I will ? Is thy eye evil because I am good ? So shall the last be first, and the first last. For many are called, but few chosen.

SEXAGESIMA SUNDAY

EPISTLE. 2 *Corinthians* xi, 19, *to* xii, 9

Brethren : You gladly suffer the foolish ; whereas yourselves are wise. For you suffer if a man bring you into bondage, if a man devour you, if a man take from you, if a man be lifted up, if a man strike you on the face. I speak according to dishonour, as if we had been weak in this part. Wherein if any man dare (I speak foolishly), I dare also. They are Hebrews : so am I. They are Israelites : so am I. They are the seed of Abraham : so am I. They are the ministers of Christ (I speak as one less wise) : I am more : in many more labours, in prisons more frequently, in stripes above measure, in deaths often. Of the Jews five times did I receive forty stripes, save one. Thrice was I beaten with rods, once I was stoned, thrice I suffered shipwreck, a night and a day I was in the depth of the sea. In journeying often in perils of waters, in

perils of robbers, in perils from my own
nation, in perils from the Gentiles, in perils
in the city, in perils in the wilderness, in
perils in the sea, in perils from false brethren.
In labour and painfulness, in much watchings, in hunger and thirst, in fastings often,
in cold and nakedness. Besides those things
which are without : my daily instance, the
solicitude for all the churches. Who is
weak, and I am not weak ? Who is scandalized, and I am not on fire ? If I must
needs glory, I will glory of the things that
concern my infirmity. The God and Father
of our Lord Jesus Christ, who is blessed
for ever, knoweth that I lie not. At Damas-
cus, the governor of the nation under
Aretas the king, guarded the city of the
Damascenes, to apprehend me. And through
a window in a basket was I let down by
the wall, and so escaped his hands. If I must
glory (it is not expedient indeed) : but I will
come to the visions and revelations of the
Lord. I know a man in Christ above fourteen
years ago (whether in the body, I know not,
or out of the body, I know not ; God knoweth), such a one caught up to the third
heaven. And I know such a man (whether in
the body or out of the body, I know not : God
knoweth) : that he was caught up into paradise, and heard secret words, which it is not
granted to man to utter. For such an one I
will glory ; but for myself I will glory nothing, but in my infirmities. For though I

should have a mind to glory, I shall not be foolish ; for I will say the truth. But I forbear, lest any man should think of me above that which he seeth in me, or anything he heareth from me. And lest the greatness of the revelations should exalt me, there was given me a sting of my flesh, an angel of Satan, to buffet me. For which thing thrice I besought the Lord, that it might depart from me. And He said to me : My grace is sufficient for thee : for power is made perfect in infirmity. Gladly therefore will I glory in my infirmities, that the power of Christ may dwell in me.

GOSPEL. *Luke* viii, 4–15. *At that time :* When a very great multitude was gathered together, and hastened out of the cities unto Jesus, He spoke by a similitude. The sower went out to sow his seed. And as he sowed, some fell by the wayside, and it was trodden down, and the fowls of the air devoured it. And other some fell upon a rock : and as soon as it was sprung up, it withered away, because it had no moisture. And other some fell among thorns, and the thorns growing up with it, choked it. And other some fell upon good ground, and being sprung up, yielded fruit a hundredfold. Saying these things, He cried out : He that hath ears to hear, let him hear. And His disciples asked Him what this parable might be. To whom He said : To you it is given to know the mystery of the kingdom of God : but to the rest in parables, that seeing they may not see, and hearing may not understand. Now the parable is this : The seed is the word of God. And they by the wayside, are they that hear ; then the devil cometh, and taketh the word out of their heart, lest believing they should be saved. Now they upon the rock, are they who when they hear, receive the word with joy : and these have no roots ; for they believe for awhile, and in time of temptation, they fall away. And that which fell among thorns, are they who have heard, and going their way, are choked with the cares and riches and pleasures of this life, and yield no fruit. But that on the good ground, are they who in a good and perfect heart, hearing the word, keep it, and bring forth fruit in patience.

QUINQUAGESIMA SUNDAY

EPISTLE. I *Corinthians* xiii, 1–13. *Brethren :* If I speak with the tongues of men, and of angels, and have not charity, I am become as sounding brass, or a tinkling cymbal. And if I should have prophecy and should know all mysteries, and all knowledge, and if I should have all faith, so that I could remove mountains, and have not charity, I am nothing. And if I should distribute all my goods to feed the poor, and if I should deliver my body to be burned, and have not charity, it profiteth me nothing. Charity is patient, is kind: charity envieth not, dealeth not perversely ; is not puffed up ; is not ambitious, seeketh not her own, is not provoked to anger, thinketh no evil : rejoiceth not in iniquity, but rejoiceth with the truth ; beareth all things, believeth all things, hopeth all things, endureth all things. Charity never falleth away : whether prophecies shall be made void, or tongues shall cease, or knowledge shall be destroyed. For we know in part, and we prophesy in part. But when that which is perfect is come, that which is in part shall be done away. When I was a child, I spoke as a child, I understood as a child, I thought as a child, But when I became a man, I put away the things of a child. We see now through a glass in a dark manner ; but then face to face. Now I know in part ; but then I shall know even as I am known. And now there remain faith, hope, and charity, these three : but the greatest of these is charity.

GOSPEL. *Luke* xviii, 31–43. *At that time :* Jesus took unto Him the twelve, and said to them : Behold, we go up to Jerusalem, and all things shall be accomplished which were written by the prophets concerning the Son of man. For He shall be delivered to the Gentiles, and shall be mocked, and scourged, and spit upon : and after they have scourged Him, they will put Him to death ; and the third day He shall rise again. And they understood none of these things, and this word was hid from them, and they understood not the things that were said. Now it came to pass when He drew nigh to Jericho that a certain blind man sat by the wayside begging. And when he heard the multitude passing by, he asked what this meant. And they told him, that Jesus of Nazareth was passing by. And he cried out, saying : Jesus, Son of David, have mercy on me. And they that went before, rebuked him, that he should hold his peace : but he cried out much more : Son of David have mercy on me. And Jesus standing, commanded him to be brought unto Him. And when he was come near, He asked him, saying : What wilt thou that I do to thee ? But he said : Lord, that I may see. And Jesus said to him : Receive thy sight : thy faith hath made thee whole. And immediately he saw, and followed Him, glorifying God. And all the people, when they saw it, gave praise to God.

ASH WEDNESDAY

LESSON. *Joel* ii, 12–19. Thus saith the Lord : Be converted to Me with all your heart, in fasting, in weeping, and in mourning. And rend your hearts, and not your garments, and turn to the Lord your God : for He is gracious and merciful, patient and rich in mercy, and ready to repent of the evil. Who knoweth but He will return, and forgive, and leave a blessing behind Him, sacrifice and libation to the Lord your God ? Blow the trumpet in Sion, sanctify a fast, call a solemn assembly, gather together the people, sanctify the Church, assemble the ancients, gather together the little ones, and them that suck at the breasts : let the bridegroom go forth from his bed, and the bride out of her bridechamber. Between the porch and the altar the priests the Lord's ministers shall weep, and shall say : Spare, O Lord, spare Thy people : and give not Thy inheritance to reproach, that the heathens should rule over them. Why should they say among the nations : Where is their God ? The Lord hath been zealous for His land, and hath spared His people : And the Lord answered and said to His people : Behold I will send you corn, and wine, and oil, and you shall be filled with them : and I will no more make you a reproach among the nations : said the Lord Almighty.

GOSPEL. *Matthew* vi, 16–21. *At that time :* Jesus said to His disciples : When you fast be not as the hypocrites, sad. For they disfigure their faces, that they may

11

appear unto men to fast. Amen I say to
you, they have received their reward.
But thou, when thou fastest, anoint thy
head, and wash thy face ; that thou appear
not to men to fast, but to Thy Father who
is in secret : and Thy Father who seeth
in secret, will repay thee. Lay not up to
yourselves treasures on earth : where the
rust, and moth consume, and where thieves
break through and steal. But lay up to
yourselves treasures in heaven : where
neither the rust nor moth doth consume,
and where thieves do not break through,
nor steal. For where thy treasure is, there
is thy heart also.

FIRST SUNDAY IN LENT

EPISTLE. 2 *Corinthians* vi, 1–10. *Brethren :* We exhort you, that you receive not
the grace of God in vain. For He saith :
*In an accepted time have I heard thee ; and
in the day of salvation have I helped thee.*
Behold, now is the accepted time ; behold
now is the day of salvation. Giving no
offence to any man, that our ministry be
not blamed : but in all things let us exhibit
ourselves as the ministers of God, in much
patience, in tribulation, in necessities, in
distresses, in stripes, in prisons, in seditions,
in labours, in watchings, in fastings, in
chastity, in knowledge, in long-suffering,
in sweetness, in the Holy Ghost, in charity

unfeigned, in the word of truth, in the power of God; by the armour of justice on the right hand and on the left; by honour and dishonour, by evil report and good report; as deceivers, and yet true; as unknown, and yet known; as dying, and behold we live; as chastised, and not killed; as sorrowful, yet always rejoicing; as needy, yet enriching many; as having nothing, and possessing all things.

GOSPEL. *Matthew* iv, 1–11. *At that time :* Jesus was led by the spirit into the desert to be tempted by the devil. And when He had fasted forty days and forty nights, afterwards He was hungry. And the tempter coming said to Him : If Thou be the Son of God, command that these stones be made bread. Who answered and said : It is written, *Not in bread alone doth man live, but in every word that proceedeth from the mouth of God.* Then the devil took Him up into the holy city, and set Him upon the pinnacle of the temple, and said to Him : If Thou be the Son of God, cast Thyself down, for it is written : *That He hath given His angels charge over Thee, and in their hands shall they bear Thee up, lest perhaps Thou dash Thy foot against a stone.* Jesus said to him : It is written again : *Thou shalt not tempt the Lord thy God.* Again the devil took Him up into a very high mountain, and showed Him all

the kingdoms of the world, and the glory
of them, and said to Him : All these will
I give Thee, if falling down Thou wilt adore
me. Then Jesus saith to him : Begone,
Satan : for it is written, *The Lord thy God
shalt thou adore, and Him only shalt thou
serve.* Then the devil left Him ; and behold
angels came and ministered to Him.

SECOND SUNDAY IN LENT

EPISTLE. 1 *Thessalonians* iv, 1–7. *Brethren :* We pray and beseech you in the
Lord Jesus, that as you have received of
us, how you ought to walk, and to please
God, so also you would walk, that you may
abound the more. For you know what precepts I have given to you by the Lord
Jesus. For this is the will of God, your
sanctification ; that you should abstain
from fornication ; that every one of you
should know how to possess his vessel in
sanctification and honour ; not in the
passion of lust, like the Gentiles that know
not God : and that no man overreach, nor
circumvent his brother in business : because
the Lord is the Avenger of all these things,
as we have told you before, and have
testified. For God hath not called us unto
uncleanness but unto sanctification in
Christ Jesus our Lord.

GOSPEL. *Matthew* xvii, 1–9. *At that
time :* Jesus taketh unto Him Peter and

James, and John his brother, and bringeth them up into a high mountain apart : and He was transfigured before them. And His face did shine as the sun ; and His garments became white as snow. And behold there appeared to them Moses and Elias talking with Him. And Peter answering, said to Jesus : Lord, it is good for us to be here : if Thou wilt, let us make here three tabernacles, one for Thee, and one for Moses, and one for Elias. And as he was yet speaking, behold a bright cloud overshadowed them. And lo, a voice out of the cloud, saying : This is my beloved Son, in whom I am well pleased : hear ye Him. And the disciples hearing, fell upon their face, and were very much afraid. And Jesus came and touched them and said unto them : Arise, and fear not. And they lifting up their eyes saw no one but only Jesus. And as they came down from the mountain, Jesus charged them, saying : Tell the vision to no man, till the Son of man be risen from the dead.

THIRD SUNDAY IN LENT

EPISTLE. *Ephesians* v, 1–9. *Brethren :* Be ye therefore followers of God, as most dear children ; and walk in love, as Christ also hath loved us, and hath delivered Himself for us, an oblation and a sacrifice to God for an odour of sweetness. But

fornication, and all uncleanness, or covet-
ousness, let it not so much as be named
among you, as becometh saints : or obsce-
nity, or foolish talking, or scurrility, which
is to no purpose ; but rather giving of
thanks. For know you this and understand,
that no fornicator, or unclean, or covetous
person (which is a serving of idols), hath
inheritance in the kingdom of Christ and
of God. Let no man deceive you with vain
words. For because of these things cometh
the anger of God upon the children of
unbelief. Be ye not therefore partakers
with them. For you were heretofore darkness, but now light in the Lord. Walk then
as children of the light. For the fruit of
the light is in all goodness, and justice and
truth.

GOSPEL. *Luke* xi, 14–28. *At that time :*
Jesus was casting out a devil, and the same
was dumb : and when He had cast out the
devil, the dumb spoke : and the multitudes
were in admiration at it : but some of
them said : He casteth out devils by
Beelzebub, the prince of devils. And others
tempting, asked of Him a sign from heaven.
But He seeing their thoughts, said to them :
Every kingdom divided against itself, shall
be brought to desolation, and house upon
house shall fall. And if Satan also be divided
against himself, how shall his kingdom
stand ? because you say, that through

Beelzebub I cast out devils. Now if I cast out devils by Beelzebub ; by whom do your children cast them out ? Therefore they shall be your judges. But if I by the finger of God cast out devils ; doubtless the kingdom of God is come upon you. When a strong man armed keepeth his court, those things are in peace which he possesseth. But if a stronger than he come upon him, and overcome him ; he will take away all his armour wherein he trusted, and will distribute his spoils. He that is not with Me, is against Me : and he that gathereth not with Me, scattereth. When the unclean spirit is gone out of a man, he walketh through places without water, seeking rest ; and not finding, he saith : I will return into my house whence I came out. And when he is come, he findeth it swept and garnished. Then he goeth and taketh with him seven other spirits more wicked than himself, and entering in they dwell there. And the last state of that man becomes worse than the first. And it came to pass, as He spoke these things, a certain woman from the crowd, lifting up her voice, said to him : Blessed is the womb that bore Thee, and the paps that gave thee suck. But He said : Yea rather, blessed are they who hear the word of God, and keep it.

FOURTH SUNDAY IN LENT

EPISTLE. *Galatians* iv, 22–31. *Brethren* : It is written that Abraham had two sons : the one by a bondwoman, and the other by a freewoman. But he who *was* of the bondwoman, was born according to the flesh : but he of the freewoman, *was* by promise. Which things are said by an allegory. For these are the two testaments. The one from Mount Sina, engendering unto bondage : which is Agar : for Sina is a mountain in Arabia, which hath affinity to that Jerusalem which now is, and is in bondage with her children. But that Jerusalem, which is above, is free : which is our mother. For it is written : *Rejoice thou barren, that bearest not : break forth and cry, thou that travailest not : for many are the children of the desolate, more than of her that hath a husband.* Now we, brethren, as Isaac was, are the children of promise. But as then he, that was born according to the flesh, persecuted him that was after the spirit : so also is it now. But what saith the Scripture ? *Cast out the bondwoman and her son ; for the son of the bondwoman shall not be heir with the son of the freewoman.* So then, brethren, we are not the children of the bondwoman, but of the free : by the freedom wherewith Christ hath made us free.

GOSPEL. *John* vi, 1–15. *At that time :* Jesus went over the sea of Galilee, which is that of Tiberias. And a great multitude followed Him because they saw the miracles which He did on them that were diseased. Jesus therefore went up into a mountain, and there He sat with His disciples. Now the Pasch, the festival day of the Jews, was at hand. When Jesus therefore had lifted up His eyes, and seen that a very great multitude cometh to Him, He said to Philip : Whence shall we buy bread, that these may eat ? And this He said to try him, for He Himself knew what He would do. Philip answered Him : Two hundred pennyworth of bread is not sufficient for them, that every one may take a little. One of His disciples, Andrew, the brother of Simon Peter, saith to Him : There is a boy here that hath five barley loaves, and two fishes ; but what are these among so many ? Then Jesus said : Make the men sit down. Now there was much grass in the place. The men therefore sat down, in number about five thousand. And Jesus took the loaves : and when He had given thanks, He distributed to them that were set down. In like manner also of the fishes, as much as they would. And when they were filled, He said to His disciples : Gather up the fragments that remain, lest they be lost. They gathered up therefore, and filled twelve baskets with the fragments of the five barley loaves, which remained over and above to them that had eaten. Now those men, when they had seen what a miracle Jesus had done, said : This is of a truth the prophet, that is to come into the world. Jesus, therefore, when He knew that they would come to take Him by force, and make Him king, fled again into the mountain Himself alone.

PASSION SUNDAY

EPISTLE. *Hebrews* ix, 11–15. *Brethren :* Christ, being come an high priest of the good things to come, by a greater and more perfect tabernacle not made with hand, that is, not of this creation : neither by the blood of goats, or of calves, but by His own blood, entered once into the holies, having obtained eternal redemption. For if the blood of goats and of oxen, and the ashes of an heifer being sprinkled, sanctify such as are defiled, to the cleansing of the flesh : how much more shall the blood of Christ, who by the Holy Ghost offered himself unspotted unto God, cleanse our conscience from dead works, to serve the living God ? And therefore He is the mediator of the New Testament : that by means of His death, for the redemption of those transgressions, which were under the former testament, they that are called may receive the promise of eternal inheritance in Christ Jesus our Lord.

GOSPEL. *John* viii, 46–59. *At that time :* Jesus said to the multitude of the Jews : Which of you shall convince Me of sin ? If I say the truth to you, why do you not believe Me ? He that is of God, heareth the words of God. Therefore you hear them not, because you are not of God. The Jews therefore answered, and said to Him : Do not we say well that Thou art a Samaritan, and hast a devil ? Jesus answered : I have not a devil : but I honour My Father, and you have dishonoured Me. But I seek not Mine own glory : there is One that seeketh and judgeth. Amen, amen I say to you : if any man keep My word, he shall not see death for ever. The Jews therefore said : Now we know that Thou hast a devil. Abraham is dead, and the prophets ; and Thou sayest : If any man keep My word, he shall not taste death for ever. Art Thou greater than our father Abraham, who is dead ? And the prophets are dead. Who dost Thou make Thyself ? Jesus answered : If I glorify Myself, My glory is nothing. It is My Father that glorifieth Me, of whom you say that He is your God. And you have not known Him, but I know Him. And if I shall say that I know Him not, I shall be like to you, a liar. But I do know Him, and do keep His word. Abraham your father rejoiced that he might see My day : he saw it, and was glad. The Jews therefore said to Him : Thou art not yet fifty years

old, and hast Thou seen Abraham ? Jesus
said to them : Amen, amen, I say to you,
before Abraham was made, I am. They
took up stones therefore to cast at Him.
But Jesus hid Himself, and went out of the
temple.

PALM SUNDAY

Lesson. *Exodus* xv, 27 *to* xvi 7. In
those days, the children of Israel came
into Elim, where there were twelve fountains of water, and seventy palm-trees :
and they encamped by the waters. And
they set forward from Elim, and all the
multitude of the children of Israel came
into the desert of Sin, which is between
Elim and Sinai, the fifteenth day of the
second month, after they came out of the
land of Egypt. And all the congregation
of the children of Israel murmured against
Moses and Aaron in the wilderness. And
the children of Israel said to them : Would
to God we had died by the hand of the
Lord in the land of Egypt, when we sat
over the fleshpots, and ate bread to the
full. Why have you brought us into this
desert, that you might destroy all the
multitude with famine ? And the Lord
said to Moses : Behold I will rain bread
from heaven for you : let the people go
forth, and gather what is sufficient for every
day : that I may prove them whether

they will walk in My law, or no. But the sixth day let them provide for to bring in : and let it be double to that they were wont to gather every day. And Moses and Aaron said to the children of Israel : In the evening you shall know that the Lord hath brought you forth out of the land of Egypt : and in the morning you shall see the glory of the Lord.

GOSPEL. *Matthew* xxi, 1–9. *At that time :* When Jesus drew nigh to Jerusalem, and was come to Bethphage, unto Mount Olivet, He sent two disciples, saying to them : Go ye into the village that is over against you, and immediately you shall find an ass tied, and a colt with her : loose them, and bring them to Me. And if any man shall say anything to you, say ye, that the Lord hath need of them : and forthwith he will let them go. Now all this was done that it might be fulfilled which was spoken by the prophet, saying : *Tell ye the daughter of Sion : Behold thy King cometh to thee, meek, and sitting upon an ass, and a colt the foal of her that is used to the yoke.* And the disciples going did as Jesus commanded them. And they brought the ass and the colt, and laid their garments upon them, and made Him sit thereon. And a very great multitude spread their garments in the way : and others cut boughs from the trees, and strewed them in the way : and the multitudes that went before and that followed, cried, saying : *Hosanna to the Son of David ! blessed is He that cometh in the name of the Lord.*

EPISTLE. *Philippians ii, 5–11. Brethren :* Let this mind be in you which was also in Christ Jesus : Who being in the form of God, thought it not robbery to be equal with God : but emptied Himself, taking the form of a servant, being made in the likeness of men, and in habit found as a man. He humbled Himself, becoming obedient unto death, even to the death of the cross. For which cause God also hath exalted Him, and hath given Him a name which is above all names : * that in the name of Jesus every knee should bow, of those that are in heaven, on earth, and under the earth : and that every tongue should confess that the Lord Jesus Christ is in the glory of God the Father.
* Here all kneel.

THE PASSION OF OUR LORD
ACCORDING TO ST. MATTHEW
(xxvi and xxvii)

At that time : Jesus said to His disciples : You know that after two days shall be the Pasch, and the Son of Man shall be delivered up to be crucified : then were gathered together the chief priests and ancients of the

people into the court of the high priest, who
was called Caiphas : and they consulted to-
gather, that by subtilty they might apprehend Jesus, and put Him to death. But they
said : Not on the festival day, lest perhaps
there should be a tumult among the people.
And when Jesus was in Bethania, in the
house of Simon the leper, there came to Him
a woman having an alabaster box of precious
ointment, and poured it on His head as He
sat at table. And the disciples seeing it, had
indignation, saying : To what purpose is this
waste ? For this might have been sold for
much, and given to the poor. And Jesus
knowing it, said to them : Why do you
trouble this woman ? for she hath wrought a
good work upon me. For the poor you have
always with you : but Me you have not
always. For she in pouring this ointment
upon My body, hath done it for My burial.
Amen I say to you, wheresoever this Gospel
shall be preached in the whole world, that
also which she hath done, shall be told for a
memory of her. Then went one of the twelve,
who was called Judas Iscariot, to the chief
priests, and said to them : What will you
give me, and I will deliver Him unto you ?
But they appointed him thirty pieces of
silver. And from thenceforth he sought op-
portunity to betray Him. And on the first
day of the azymes, the disciples came to
Jesus, saying : Wherefore wilt Thou that we
prepare for Thee to eat the Pasch ? But Jesus

said : Go ye into the city to a certain man, and say to him, The Master saith : My time is near at hand, with thee I make the Pasch with my disciples. And the disciples did as Jesus appointed to them, and they prepared the Pasch. But when it was evening, He sat down with His twelve disciples. And whilst they were eating, He said : Amen I say to you, that one of you is about to betray Me. And they being very much troubled, began every one to say : Is it I, Lord ? But He answering, said : He that dippeth his hand with Me in the dish, he shall betray Me. The Son of Man indeed goeth, as it is written of Him : but woe to that man by whom the Son of Man shall be betrayed : it were better for him if that man had not been born. And Judas that betrayed Him, answering, said : Is it I, Rabbi ? He saith to Him : Thou hast said *it*. And whilst they were at supper, Jesus took bread and blessed, and broke : and gave to His disciples, and said : Take ye, and eat. This is My body. And taking the chalice, He gave thanks, and gave to them, saying : Drink ye all of this. For this is My blood of the New Testament which shall be shed for many unto remission of sins. And I say to you, I will not drink from henceforth of this fruit of the wine, until that day when I shall drink it with you new in the kingdom of My Father. And a hymn being said, they went out unto Mount Olivet. Then Jesus said to them : All you shall be scandalized in Me this night. For it is written : *I will strike the shepherd and the sheep of the flock shall be dispersed.* But after I shall be risen again, I will go before you into Galilee. And Peter answering, said to Him : Although all shall be scandalized in Thee, I will never be scandalized. Jesus said to him : Amen I say to thee, that in this night before the cock crow, thou wilt deny Me thrice. Peter saith to Him : Yea, though I should die with Thee, I will not deny Thee. And in like manner said all the disciples. Then Jesus came with them into a country place which is called Gethsemani ; and He said to His disciples : Sit you here, till I go yonder and pray. And taking with Him Peter and the two sons of Zebedee, He began to grow sorrowful and to be sad. Then He saith to them : My soul is sorrowful even unto death : stay you here, and watch with Me. And going a little further, He fell upon His face, praying, and saying : My Father, if it be possible, let this chalice pass from Me. Nevertheless, not as I will, but as Thou wilt. And He cometh to His disciples and findeth them asleep, and He saith to Peter : What ? Could you not watch one hour with Me ? Watch ye, and pray that ye enter not into temptation. The spirit indeed is willing, but the flesh is weak. Again the second time, He went and prayed, saying : My Father, if this chalice

may not pass away, but I must drink it,
Thy will be done. And He cometh again,
and findeth them sleeping : for their eyes
were heavy. And leaving them, He went
again : and He prayed the third time,
saying the selfsame word. Then He cometh
to His disciples, and saith to them : Sleep
ye now, and take your rest ; behold the
hour is at hand, and the Son of Man shall
be betrayed into the hands of sinners.
Rise, let us go : behold, he is at hand that
will betray Me. As He yet spoke, behold
Judas, one of the twelve, came, and with
him a great multitude with swords and
clubs, sent from the chief priests and the
ancients of the people. And he that betrayed Him, gave them a sign, saying :
Whomsoever I shall kiss, that is He, hold
Him fast. And forthwith coming to Jesus,
he said : Hail, Rabbi. And he kissed Him.
And Jesus said to him : Friend, whereto
art thou come ? Then they came up, and
laid hands on Jesus, and held him. And
behold one of them that were with Jesus,
stretching forth his hand, drew out his
sword : and striking the servant of the
high priest, cut off his ear. Then Jesus saith
to him : Put up again thy sword into its
place : for all that take the sword shall
perish with the sword. Thinkest thou that
I cannot ask My Father, and He will give
Me presently more than twelve legions of
angels ? How then shall the scriptures be

fulfilled, that so it must be done ? In that same hour Jesus said to the multitude : You are come out, as it were to a robber, with swords and clubs to apprehend me. I sat daily with you, teaching in the temple, and you laid not hands on Me. Now all this was done, that the scriptures of the prophets might be fulfilled. Then the disciples all leaving Him, fled. But they holding Jesus led Him to Caiphas the high priest, where the scribes and the ancients were assembled. And Peter followed Him afar off, even to the court of the high priest. And going in, he sat with the servants, that he might see the end. And the chief priests and the whole council sought false witness against Jesus, that they might put Him to death : and they found not, whereas many false witnesses had come in. And last of all there came two false witnesses : and they said : This man said, I am able to destroy the temple of God, and after three days to rebuild it. And the high priest rising up, said to Him : Answerest Thou nothing to the things which these witness against Thee ? But Jesus held His peace. And the high priest said to Him : I adjure Thee by the living God, that Thou tell us if Thou be the Christ the Son of God. Jesus saith to him : Thou hast said *it*. Nevertheless I say to you, hereafter you shall see the Son of man sitting on the right hand of the power of God, and coming in the clouds of heaven. Then the high priest rent his

garments, saying : He hath blasphemed ;
what further need have we of witnesses ?
Behold, now you have heard the blasphemy : what think you ? But they answering, said : He is guilty of death. Then did
they spit in His face, and buffeted Him :
and others struck His face with the palms
of their hands, saying : Prophesy unto us,
O Christ, who is he that struck Thee ?
But Peter sat without in the court ; and
there came to him a servant maid, saying:
Thou also wast with Jesus the Galilean.
But he denied before them all, saying :
I know not what thou sayest. And as he
went out of the gate, another maid saw him,
and she saith to them that were there : This
man also was with Jesus of Nazareth.
And again he denied with an oath : I know
not the man. And after a little while they
came that stood by, and said to Peter :
Surely thou also art one of them ; for even
thy speech doth discover thee. Then he
began to curse and to swear that he knew
not the Man. And immediately the cock
crew. And Peter remembered the word of
Jesus which He had said : Before the
cock crow, thou wilt deny Me thrice. And
going forth, he wept bitterly. And when
morning was come, all the chief priests and
ancients of the people took council against
Jesus, that they might put Him to death.
And they brought Him bound, and delivered Him to Pontius Pilate the governor.

Then Judas, who betrayed Him, seeing that He was condemned, repenting himself, brought back the thirty pieces of silver to the chief priests and ancients, saying : I have sinned in betraying innocent blood. But they said : What is that to us ? look thou to it. And casting down the pieces of silver in the temple, he departed : and went and hanged himself with an halter. But the chief priests having taken the pieces of silver, said : It is not lawful to put them into the corbona, because it is the price of blood. And after they had consulted together, they bought with them the potter's field, to be a burying-place for strangers. For this cause that field was called Haceldama, that is, The field of blood, even to this day. Then was fulfilled that which was spoken by Jeremias the prophet, saying : *And they took the thirty pieces of silver, the price of Him that was prized, whom they prized of the children of Israel. And they gave them unto the potter's field, as the Lord appointed to me.* And Jesus stood before the governor, and the governor asked Him, saying : Art Thou the King of the Jews ? Jesus saith to him : Thou sayest it. And when He was accused by the chief priests and ancients, He answered nothing. Then Pilate saith to Him : Dost not Thou hear how great testimonies they allege against Thee ? And He answered Him to never a word ; so that the governor wondered exceedingly. Now upon the solemn day the governor was accustomed to release to the people one prisoner, whom they would. And he had then a notorious prisoner, that was called Barabbas. They therefore being gathered together, Pilate said : Whom will you that I release to you, Barabbas, or Jesus that is called Christ ? For he knew that for envy they had delivered Him. And as he was sitting in the place of judgment, his wife sent to him, saying : Have thou nothing to do with that just Man ; for I have suffered many things this day in a dream because of Him. But the chief priests and ancients persuaded the people, that they should ask Barabbas, and make Jesus away. And the governor answering, said to them : Whether will you of the two to be released unto you ? But they said, Barabbas. Pilate saith to them : What shall I do then with Jesus that is called Christ ? They say all : Let Him be crucified. The governor said to them : Why, what evil hath He done ? but they cried out the more, saying : Let Him be crucified. And Pilate seeing that he prevailed nothing, but that rather a tumult was made ; taking water washed his hands before the people, saying : I am innocent of the blood of this just Man ; look you to it. And the whole people answering said : His blood be upon us, and upon our children. Then he released to them Barabbas, and having scourged Jesus, delivered Him unto them to be crucified. Then the soldiers of the governor taking Jesus into the hall, gathered together unto Him the whole band; and stripping Him, they put a scarlet cloak about Him. And platting a crown of thorns, they put it upon His head, and a reed in His right hand. And bowing the knee before Him, they mocked Him, saying: Hail, King of the Jews. And spitting upon Him, they took the reed and struck His head. And after they had mocked Him, they took off the cloak from Him, and put on Him His own garments, and led Him away to crucify Him. And going out, they found a man of Cyrene, named Simon: him they forced to take up His cross. And they came to the place that is called Golgotha, which is the place of Calvary. And they gave Him wine to drink mingled with gall. And when He had tasted, He would not drink. And after they had crucified Him they divided His garments, casting lots; that it might be fulfilled which was spoken by the prophet, saying: *They divided My garments among them; and upon My vesture they cast lots.* And they sat and watched Him. And they put over His head his cause written: THIS IS JESUS THE KING OF THE JEWS. Then were crucified with Him two thieves: one on the right hand, and one on the left. And they that passed by, blasphemed Him, wagging their heads, and saying: Vah, Thou that destroyest the temple of

God, and in three days dost rebuild it: save Thy own self: if Thou be the Son of God, come down from the cross. In like manner also the chief priests, with the scribes and ancients, mocking, said: He saved others; Himself He cannot save. If He be the King of Israel, let Him now come down from the cross, and we will believe Him. He trusted in God; let Him now deliver Him if He will have Him; for He said: I am the Son of God. And the selfsame thing the thieves also, that were crucified with Him reproached Him with. Now from the sixth hour there was darkness over the whole earth, until the ninth hour. And about the ninth hour Jesus cried with a loud voice, saying: Eli, Eli, lamma sabacthani? that is, My God, my God, why hast Thou forsaken Me? And some that stood there and heard, said: This Man calleth Elias. And immediately one of them running took a sponge, and filled it with vinegar; and put it on a reed, and gave Him to drink. And the others said: Let be, let us see whether Elias will come to deliver Him. And Jesus again crying with a loud voice, yielded up the ghost. (*Here all kneel and pause.*) And behold the veil of the temple was rent in two from the top even to the bottom, and the earth quaked, and the rocks were rent. And the graves were opened: and many bodies of the saints that had slept arose, and coming

out of the tombs after His resurrection,
came into the holy city, and appeared to
many. Now the centurion and they that
were with him watching Jesus, having seen
the earthquake, and the things that were
done, were sore afraid, saying : Indeed, this
was the Son of God. And there were there
many women afar off who had followed
Jesus from Galilee, ministering unto Him :
among whom was Mary Magdalen, and
Mary the mother of James and Joseph,
and the mother of the sons of Zebedee.
And when it was evening, there came a
certain rich man of Arimathea, named
Joseph, who also himself was a disciple of
Jesus. He went to Pilate, and asked the
body of Jesus. Then Pilate commanded
that the body should be delivered. And
Joseph taking the body, wrapped it up in a
clean linen cloth. And laid it in his own new
monument, which he had hewed out in a
rock. And he rolled a great stone to the
door of the monument, and went his way.
And there was there Mary Magdalen, and
the other Mary sitting over against the
sepulchre. (*Here is said the Munda cor
meum.*) And the next day, which followed
the day of preparation, the chief priests and
the Pharisees came together to Pilate,
saying : Sir, we have remembered, that
that Seducer said, while He was yet alive :
After three days I will rise again. Command
therefore the sepulchre to be guarded until

the third day : lest perhaps His disciples come and steal Him away, and say to the people : He is risen from the dead ; and the last error shall be worse than the first. Pilate saith to them : You have a guard ; go, guard it as you know. And they departing, made the sepulchre sure, sealing the stone, and setting guards.

GOOD FRIDAY

LESSON. *Osee* vi, 1–6. Thus saith the Lord : In their affliction they will rise early to Me. Come, and let us return to the Lord : for He hath taken us, and He will heal us : He will strike, and He will cure us. He will revive us after two days : on the third day He will raise us up, and we shall live in His sight. We shall know, and we shall follow on, that we may know the Lord. His going forth is prepared as the morning light, and He will come to us as the early and the latter rain to the earth. What shall I do to thee, O Ephraim ? what shall I do to thee, O Juda ? your mercy *is* as a morning cloud, and as the dew that goeth away in the morning. For this reason have I hewed *them* by the prophets, I have slain them by the words of My mouth ; and Thy Judgments shall go forth as the light. For I desired mercy, and not sacrifice : and the knowledge of God more than holocausts.

LESSON. *Exodus* xii, 1–11. In *those days :*
The Lord said to Moses and Aaron in the
land of Egypt : This month shall be to you
the beginning of months : it shall be the
first in the months of the year. Speak ye
to the whole assembly of the children of
Israel, and say to them : On the tenth day
of this month let every man take a lamb
by their families and houses. But if the
number be less than may suffice to eat the
lamb, he shall take unto him his neighbour
that joineth to his house, according to the
number of souls which may be enough to
eat the lamb. And it shall be a lamb without
blemish, a male, of one year : according
to which rite also you shall take a kid.
And you shall keep it until the fourteenth
day of this month : and the whole multitude
of the children of Israel shall sacrifice it in
the evening. And they shall take of the
blood thereof, and put it upon both the
sideposts, and on the upper doorposts of
the houses, wherein they shall eat it. And
they shall eat the flesh that night roasted
at the fire, and unleavened bread with wild
lettuce. You shall not eat thereof anything
raw, nor boiled in water, but only roasted
at the fire : you shall eat the head with the
feet and the entrails thereof. Neither shall
there remain anything of it until morning.
If there be anything left, you shall burn it
with fire. And thus you shall eat it : You
shall gird your reins, and you shall have

shoes on your feet, holding staves in your hands, and you shall eat in haste ; for it is the Phase (that is the Passage) of the Lord.

THE PASSION OF OUR LORD JESUS CHRIST ACCORDING TO ST. JOHN—
(xviii and xix)

At that time : Jesus went forth with his disciples over the brook Cedron, where there was a garden, into which He entered with His disciples. And Judas also, who betrayed Him, knew the place ; because Jesus had often resorted thither together with His disciples. Judas therefore having received a band of soldiers and servants from the chief priests and the Pharisees, cometh thither with lanterns and torches and weapons. Jesus therefore, knowing all things that should come upon Him, went forth and said to them : Whom seek ye ? They answered Him : Jesus of Nazareth. Jesus saith to them : I am He. And Judas also, who betrayed Him, stood with them. As soon therefore as He had said to them : I am He ; they went backward, and fell to the ground. Again therefore He asked them : Whom seek ye ? And they said, Jesus of Nazareth. Jesus answered, I have told you that I am He. If therefore you seek Me, let these go their way, that the word might be fulfilled which He said : Of them whom Thou hast give me, I have not lost any one. Then Simon Peter, having a sword, drew it, and struck the servant of the high priest, and cut off his right ear. And the name of the servant was Malchus. Jesus therefore said to Peter : Put up thy sword into the scabbard. The chalice which My Father hath given Me, shall I not drink it ? Then the band and the tribune, and the servants of the Jews, took Jesus and bound Him : and they led Him away to Annas first, for he was father-in-law to Caiphas, who was the high priest of that year. Now Caiphas was he who had given the counsel to the Jews : That it was expedient that one man should die for the people. And Simon Peter followed Jesus, and so did another disciple. And that disciple was known to the high priest, and went in with Jesus into the court of the high priest. But Peter stood at the door without. The other disciple therefore, who was known to the priest, went out and spoke to the portress, and brought in Peter. The maid therefore that was portress, saith to Peter : Art not thou also one of this Man's disciples ? He saith : I am not. Now the servants and ministers stood at a fire of coals, because it was cold, and warmed themselves. And with them was Peter also, standing, and warming himself. The high priest therefore asked Jesus of His disciples, and of His doctrine. Jesus answered him : I have spoken openly to the world : I have always taught in the synagogue, and in the temple whither all the Jews resort; and in secret I have spoken nothing. Why askest thou Me ? ask them who have heard what I have spoken unto them : behold they know what things I have said. And when He had said these things, one of the servants standing by, gave Jesus a blow, saying : Answerest Thou the high priest so ? Jesus answered him : If I have spoken evil, give testimony of the evil; but if well, why strikest thou Me ? And Annas sent Him bound to Caiphas the high priest. And Simon Peter was standing, and warming himself. They said therefore to him : Art not thou also one of His disciples ? He denied it, and said : I am not. One of the servants of the high priest (a kinsman to him whose ear Peter cut off) saith to him : Did not I see thee in the garden with Him ? Again therefore Peter denied; and immediately the cock crew. Then they led Jesus from Caiphas to the governor's hall. And it was morning; and they went not into the hall, that they might not be defiled, but that they might eat the Pasch. Pilate therefore went out to them, and said : What accusation bring you against this Man ? They answered, and said to him : If He were not a malefactor, we would not have delivered Him up to thee. Pilate therefore said to them : Take Him you, and judge Him according to your law. The Jews therefore said to him : It is not lawful for us to put any man to death. That the word of Jesus might be fulfilled, which He said, signifying what death He should die. Pilate therefore went into the hall again, and called Jesus, and said to Him : Art Thou the King of the Jews ? Jesus answered : Sayest thou this thing of thyself, or have others told it thee of Me ? Pilate answered : Am I a Jew ? Thy own nation, and the chief priests, have delivered Thee up to me : what hast Thou done ? Jesus answered : My kingdom is not of this world. If My kingdom were of this world, My servants would certainly strive that I should not be delivered to the Jews : but now My kingdom is not from hence. Pilate therefore said to Him : Art Thou a king then ? Jesus answered : Thou sayest that I am a king. For this was I born, and for this came I into the world ; that I should give testimony to the truth. Every one that is of the truth, heareth My voice. Pilate saith to Him : What is truth ? And when he said this, he went out again to the Jews, and saith to them : I find no cause in Him. But you have a custom that I should release one unto you at the Pasch : will you, therefore, that I release unto you the King of the Jews ? Then cried they all again, saying : Not this Man, but Barabbas. Now Barabbas was a robber. Then therefore, Pilate took Jesus and

scourged Him. And the soldiers platting a
crown of thorns, put it upon His head ; and
they put on Him a purple garment. And
they came to Him, and said : Hail, King
of the Jews ; and they gave Him blows.
Pilate therefore went forth again, and
saith to them : Behold I bring Him forth
unto you, that you may know that I find
no cause in Him. (Jesus therefore came
· forth, bearing the crown of thorns and the
purple garment.) And he saith to them :
Behold the Man. When the chief priests,
therefore, and the servants, had seen Him,
they cried out, saying : Crucify Him,
crucify Him, Pilate saith to them : Take
Him you, and crucify Him : for I find no
cause in Him. The Jews answered him :
We have a law ; and according to the law
He ought to die, because He made Himself
the Son of God. When Pilate therefore had
heard this saying, he feared the more. And
he entered into the hall again, and he said
to Jesus : Whence art Thou ? But Jesus
gave him no answer. Pilate therefore saith
to Him : Speakest Thou not to me ? knowest Thou not that I have power to crucify
Thee, and I have power to release Thee ?
Jesus answered : Thou shouldst not have
any power against me, unless it were given
thee from above. Therefore, he that hath
delivered Me to thee, hath the greater
sin. And from thenceforth Pilate sought
to release Him. But the Jews cried out,

saying : If thou release this Man, thou art not Cæsar's friend. For whosoever maketh himself a king, speaketh against Cæsar. Now when Pilate had heard these words, he brought Jesus forth, and sat down in the judgment seat, in the place that is called Lithostrotos, and in Hebrew, Gabbatha. And it was the parasceve of the Pasch, about the sixth hour, and he saith to the Jews : Behold your King. But they cried out : Away with Him ; away with Him ; crucify Him. Pilate saith to them : Shall I crucify your King ? The chief priests answered : We have no king but Cæsar. Then therefore he delivered Him to them to be crucified. And they took Jesus and led Him forth. And bearing His own cross, He went forth to that place which is called Calvary, but in Hebrew Golgotha. Where they crucified Him, and with Him two others, one on each side, and Jesus in the midst. And Pilate wrote a title also, and he put it upon the cross. And the writing was : JESUS OF NAZARETH, THE KING OF THE JEWS. This title therefore many of the Jews did read : because the place where Jesus was crucified was nigh to the city : and it was written in Hebrew, in Greek, and in Latin. Then the chief priests of the Jews said to Pilate : Write not, The King of the Jews : but that He said, I am the King of the Jews. Pilate answered : What I have written, I have written. The soldiers therefore when

they had crucified Him, took His garments
(and they made four parts, to every soldier a
part) and also His coat. Now the coat was
without seam, woven from the top throughout. They said then one to another : let us
not cut it, but let us cast lots for it, whose it
shall be ; that the Scripture might be
fulfilled, saying : *They have parted my
garments among them, and upon my vesture
they have cast lots.* And the soldiers indeed
did these things. Now there stood by the
cross of Jesus, His mother, and His mother's
sister, Mary of Cleophas, and Mary Magdalen. When Jesus therefore had seen His
mother and the disciple standing whom He
loved, He saith to His mother : Woman,
behold thy son. After that, He saith to the
disciple : Behold thy mother. And from
that hour, the disciple took her to his own.
Afterwards, Jesus knowing that all things
were now accomplished, that the Scripture
might be fulfilled, said : I thirst. Now there
was a vessel set there full of vinegar. And
they, putting a sponge full of vinegar about
hyssop, put it to His mouth. Jesus therefore,
when He had taken the vinegar, said : It
is consummated. And bowing His head, He
gave up the ghost. (*Here all kneel and
pause.*) Then the Jews (because it was the
parasceve) that the bodies might not
remain upon the cross on the Sabbath day
(for that was a great Sabbath day), besought
Pilate that their legs might be broken, and

that they might be taken away. The soldiers therefore came; and they broke the legs of the first, and of the other that was crucified with Him. But after they were come to Jesus, when they saw that He was already dead, they did not break His legs. But one of the soldiers with a spear opened His side, and immediately there came out blood and water. And he that saw it, hath given testimony; and his testimony is true. And he knoweth that he saith true; that you also may believe. For these things were done, that the Scripture might be fulfilled: *You shall not break a bone of Him.* And again another Scripture saith: *They shall look on Him whom they pierced. (Here is said the Munda Cor meum.)* And after these things, Joseph of Arimathea (because he was a disciple of Jesus, but secretly for fear of the Jews) besought Pilate that he might take away the body of Jesus. And Pilate gave leave. He came therefore, and took away the body of Jesus. And Nicodemus also came (he who at the first came to Jesus by night), bringing a mixture of myrrh, and aloes, about an hundred pound weight. They took therefore the body of Jesus, and bound it in linen cloths, with the spices, as the manner of the Jews is to bury. Now there was where He was crucified, a garden in the place, and in the garden a new sepulchre, wherein no man yet had been laid. There, therefore, because of the parasceve of the Jews, they laid Jesus, because the sepulchre was nigh at hand.

EASTER SUNDAY

EPISTLE. I *Corinthians* v, **7–8.** *Brethren :* Purge out the old leaven, that you may be a new paste, as you are unleavened. For Christ our Pasch is sacrificed. Therefore let us feast, not with the old leaven, nor with the leaven of malice and wickedness ; but with the unleavened bread of sincerity and truth.

GOSPEL. *Mark* xvi. **1–7.** *At that time :* Mary Magdalen, and Mary the mother of James, and Salome, brought sweet spices, that coming, they might anoint Jesus. And very early in the morning, the first day of the week, they come to the sepulchre, the sun being now risen. And they said one to another : Who shall roll us back the stone from the door of the sepulchre ? And looking, they saw the stone rolled back. For it was very great. And entering into the sepulchre, they saw a young man sitting on the right side, clothed with a white robe : and they were astonished. Who saith to them : Be not affrighted ; you seek Jesus of Nazareth, who was crucified : He is risen, He is not here, behold the place where they laid Him. But go, tell his disciples and Peter that He goeth before you into Galilee ; there you shall see Him, as He told you.

QUASIMODO, OR LOW SUNDAY

EPISTLE. 1 *John* v, 4–10. *Dearly beloved :* Whatsoever is born of God, overcometh the world : and this is the victory which overcometh the world, our faith. Who is he that overcometh the world, but he that believeth that Jesus is the Son of God ? This is He that came by water and blood, Jesus Christ : not by water only, but by water and blood. And it is the Spirit which testifieth, that Christ is the truth. And there are three who give testimony in heaven, the Father, the Word, and the Holy Ghost. And these three are one. And there are three that give testimony on earth : the Spirit, and the water, and the blood : and these three are one. If we receive the testimony of men, the testimony of God is greater. For this is the testimony of God, which is greater, because He hath testified of His Son. He that believeth in the Son of God, hath the testimony of God in himself.

GOSPEL. *John* xx, 19–31. *At that time :* When it was late that same day, the first day of the week, and the doors were shut, where the disciples were gathered together, for fear of the Jews, Jesus came and stood in the midst, and said to them : Peace be to you. And when He had said this, He showed them His hands and His side. The

disciples therefore were glad, when they
saw the Lord. He said therefore to them
again : Peace be to you. As the Father hath
sent Me I also send you. When He had said
this, He breathed on them ; and He said
to them : Receive ye the Holy Ghost.
Whose sins you shall forgive, they are
forgiven them ; and whose *sins* you shall
retain, they are retained. Now Thomas,
one of the twelve, who is called Didymus,
was not with them when Jesus came. The
other disciples therefore said to him : We
have seen the Lord. But he said to them :
Except I shall see in His hands the print of
the nails, and put my fingers into the
place of the nails, and put my hand into
His side, I will not believe. And after eight
days again His disciples were within, and
Thomas with them. Jesus cometh, the
doors being shut, and stood in the midst,
and said : Peace be to you. Then He saith
to Thomas : Put in thy finger hither, and
see My hands : and bring hither thy hand,
and put it into My side ; and be not faithless, but believing. Thomas answered, and
said to Him : My Lord, and My God. Jesus
saith to him : Because thou hast seen Me,
Thomas, thou hast believed : blessed are
they that have not seen, and have believed.
Many other signs also did Jesus in the sight
of His disciples, which are not written in
this book. But these are written, that you
may believe that Jesus is the Christ, the

Son of God : and that, believing, you may have life in His name.

SECOND SUNDAY AFTER EASTER

EPISTLE. 1 *Peter* ii, 21-25. *Dearly beloved :* Christ also suffered for us, leaving you an example that you should follow His steps. *Who did no sin, neither was guile found in His mouth.* Who, when He was reviled, did not revile : when He suffered, He threatened not : but delivered Himself to him that judged Him unjustly. Who His own self bore our sins in His body upon the tree : that we, being dead to sins, should live to justice : by whose stripes you were healed. For you were as sheep going astray : but you are now converted to the Shepherd and Bishop of your souls.

GOSPEL. *John* x, 11-16. *At that time :* Jesus said to the Pharisees : I am the Good Shepherd. The good shepherd giveth his life for his sheep. But the hireling and he that is not the shepherd, whose own the sheep are not, seeth the wolf coming, and leaveth the sheep, and flieth : and the wolf catcheth, and scattereth the sheep : and the hireling flieth, because he is a hireling : and he hath no care for the sheep. I am the Good Shepherd ; and I know Mine, and Mine know Me. As the Father knoweth Me, and I know the Father : and I lay down my life for My sheep. And other sheep I have that are not of this fold : them also I must bring, and they shall hear My voice, and there shall be one fold and one Shepherd.

THIRD WEDNESDAY AFTER EASTER

(SOLEMNITY OF ST. JOSEPH)

LESSON. *Genesis* xlix, 22–26. Joseph is a growing son, a growing son and comely to behold ; the daughters run to and fro upon the wall. But they that held darts provoked him, and quarelled with him, and envied him. His bow rested upon the strong, and the bands of his arms and his hands were loosed, by the hands of the Mighty One of Jacob : thence he came forth a pastor, the stone of Israel. The God of thy father shall be thy helper, and the Almighty shall bless thee with the blessings of heaven above, with the blessings of the deep that lieth beneath, with the blessings of the breasts and of the womb. The blessings of thy father are strengthened with the blessings of his fathers : until the desire of the everlasting hills shall come ; may they be upon the head of Joseph, and upon the crown of the Nazarite among his brethren.

GOSPEL. *Luke* iii, 21–23. *At that time :* It came to pass, when all the people were baptized, that Jesus also being baptized and praying, heaven was opened ; and the

Holy Ghost descended in a bodily shape, as a dove upon Him: and a voice came from heaven: Thou art My beloved Son; in Thee I am well pleased. And Jesus Himself was beginning about the age of thirty years; being (as it was supposed) the Son of Joseph.

THIRD SUNDAY AFTER EASTER

EPISTLE. 1 *Peter* ii, 11–19. *Dearly beloved :* I beseech you as strangers and pilgrims to refrain yourselves from carnal desires which war against the soul, having your conversation good among the Gentiles: that whereas they speak against you as evildoers, they may, by the good works which they shall behold in you, glorify God in the day of visitation. Be ye subject therefore to every human creature for God's sake: whether it be to the king as excelling; or to governors as sent by him for the punishment of evildoers, and for the praise of the good : for so is the will of God, that by doing well you may put to silence the ignorance of foolish men : as free, and not as making liberty a cloak for malice, but as the servants of God. Honour all men. Love the brotherhood. Fear God. Honour the King. Servants, be subject to your masters with all fear, not only to the good and gentle, but also to the froward. For this is thankworthy in Christ Jesus our Lord.

GOSPEL. *John* xvi, 16–22. *At that time :* Jesus said to His disciples : A little while, and now you shall not see Me ; and again a little while, and you shall see me : because I go to the Father. Then some of His disciples said one to another : What is this that He saith to us : A little while, and you shall not see Me ; and again a little while, and you shall see Me, and, because I go to the Father ? They said therefore : What is this that He saith : A little while ? We know not what He speaketh. And Jesus knew that they had a mind to ask Him : and He said to them : Of this do you inquire among yourselves, because I said : A little while, and you shall not see Me ; and again a little while, and you shall see me ? Amen, amen I say to you, that you shall lament and weep, but the world shall rejoice ; and you shall be made sorrowful, but your sorrow shall be turned into joy. A woman, when she is in labour, hath sorrow, because her hour is come ; but when she hath brought forth the child, she remembereth no more the anguish, for joy that a man is born into the world. So also you now indeed have sorrow ; but I will see you again, and your heart shall rejoice : and your joy no man shall take from you.

FOURTH SUNDAY AFTER EASTER

EPISTLE. *James* i, 17–21. *Dearly beloved :* Every best gift, and every perfect gift, is

from above, coming down from the Father
of lights, with whom there is no change,
nor shadow of alteration. For of His own
will hath He begotten us by the word of
truth, that we might be some beginning
of His creature. You know, my dearest
brethren ; and let every man be swift to
hear, but slow to speak, and slow to anger.
For the anger of man worketh not the
justice of God. Wherefore casting away all
uncleanness, and abundance of naughtiness,
with meekness receive the ingrafted word,
which is able to save your souls.

GOSPEL. *John* xvi, 5-14. *At that time :*
Jesus said to His disciples : I go to Him
that sent Me, and none of you asketh Me :
Whither goest Thou ? But because I have
spoken these things to you, sorrow hath
filled your heart. But I tell you the truth :
it is expedient to you that I go : for if I
go not, the Paraclete will not come to you ;
but if I go, I will send Him to you. And
when He is come, He will convince the
world of sin, and of justice, and of judgment. Of sin : because they believed not
in Me. And of justice : because I go to the
Father ; and you shall see Me no longer.
And of judgment : because the prince of
this world is already judged. I have yet
many things to say to you : but you cannot
bear them now. But when He, the Spirit
of Truth, is come, He will teach you all

truth. For He shall not speak of Himself; but what things soever He shall hear, He shall speak; and the things that are to come, He shall show you. He shall glorify Me; because He shall receive of Mine, and shall show *it* to you.

FIFTH SUNDAY AFTER EASTER

EPISTLE. *James* i, 22–27 *Dearly beloved:* Be ye doers of the word, and not hearers only, deceiving your own selves. For if a man be a hearer of the word, and not a doer, he shall be compared to a man beholding his own countenance in a glass. For he beheld himself, and went his way, and presently forgot what manner of man he was. But he that hath looked into the perfect law of liberty, and hath continued therein, not becoming a forgetful hearer, but a doer of the work; this man shall be blessed in his deed. And if any man think himself to be religious, not bridling his tongue, but deceiving his own heart, this man's religion is vain. Religion clean and undefiled before God and the Father, is this: to visit the fatherless and widows in their tribulation: and to keep one's self unspotted from the world.

GOSPEL. *John* xvi, 23–30. *At that time:* Jesus said to His disciples: Amen, amen I say to you: if you ask the Father any thing in My name, He will give it you.

Hitherto you have not asked any thing in My name. Ask, and you shall receive; that your joy may be full. These things I have spoken to you in proverbs. The hour cometh, when I will no more speak to you in proverbs, but will show you plainly of the Father. In that day you shall ask in My name; and I say not to you, that I will ask the Father for you: for the Father Himself loveth you, because you have loved Me, and have believed that I came out from God. I came forth from the Father, and am come into the world: again I leave the world, and I go to the Father. His disciples say to Him: Behold, now Thou speakest plainly, and speakest no proverb. Now we know that Thou knowest all things, and Thou needest not that any man should ask Thee. By this we believe that Thou camest forth from God.

ASCENSION DAY

LESSON. *Acts* i, 1–11. The former treatise I made, O Theophilus, of all things which Jesus began to do and to teach, until the day on which, giving commandments by the Holy Ghost to the Apostles whom He had chosen, He was taken up. To whom also He showed Himself alive after His Passion, by many proofs, for forty days appearing to them, and speaking of the kingdom of God. And eating together with them, He commanded them, that they should not depart from Jerusalem, but should wait for the promise of the Father, which you have heard (saith He) by My mouth. For John indeed baptized with water, but you shall be baptized with the Holy Ghost, not many days hence. They therefore who were come together, asked Him, saying: Lord, wilt Thou at this time restore again the kingdom to Israel? But He said to them: It is not for you to know the times or moments, which the Father hath put in His own power: but you shall receive the power of the Holy Ghost coming upon you, and you shall be witnesses unto Me in Jerusalem, and in all Judea, and Samaria, and even to the uttermost part of the earth. And when He had said these things, while they looked on, He was raised up: and a cloud received Him out of their sight. And while they were beholding Him going up to heaven, behold two men stood by them in white garments. Who also said: Ye men of Galilee, why stand you looking up to heaven? This Jesus who is taken up from you into heaven, shall so come, as you have seen Him going into heaven.

GOSPEL. *Mark* xvi, 14-20. *At that time:* Jesus appeared to the eleven as they were at table: and He upbraided them with their incredulity and hardness of heart,

because they did not believe them who
had seen Him after He was risen again.
And He said to them : Go ye into the
whole world, and preach the Gospel to every
creature. He that believeth and is baptized,
shall be saved : but he that believeth not
shall be condemned. And these signs shall
follow them that believe : In My name they
shall cast out devils : they shall speak with
new tongues. They shall take up serpents ;
and if they shall drink any deadly thing,
it shall not hurt them : they shall lay
hands upon the sick, and they shall recover.
And the Lord Jesus, after He had spoken
to them, was taken up into heaven, and
sitteth on the right hand of God. But they
going forth preached every where : the
Lord working withal, and confirming the
word with signs that followed.

SUNDAY WITHIN THE OCTAVE OF THE ASCENSION

EPISTLE. I *Peter* iv, 7–11. *Most dearly
beloved :* Be prudent therefore and watch
in prayers. But before all things have a
constant mutual charity among yourselves :
for charity covereth a multitude of sins.
Using hospitality one towards another,
without murmuring, as every man hath
received grace, ministering the same one to
another : as good stewards of the manifold
grace of God. If any man speak, *let him*

speak as the words of God. If any man minister, *let him do it* as of the power which God administereth : that in all things God may be honoured through Jesus Christ our Lord.

GOSPEL. *John* xv, 26, xvi 4. *At that time :* Jesus said to His disciples : When the Paraclete cometh, whom I will send you from the Father, the Spirit of truth, who proceedeth from the Father, He shall give testimony of Me. And you shall give testimony, because you are with Me from the beginning. These things have I spoken to you, that you may not be scandalized. They will put you out of the synagogues : yea, the hour cometh, that whosoever killeth you, will think that he doth a service to God. And these things will they do to you ; because they have not known the Father, nor Me. But these things I have told you, that when the hour shall come, you may remember that I told you.

WHIT SUNDAY

LESSON. *Acts* ii, 1-11. When the days of the Pentecost were accomplished, they were all together in one place : and suddenly there came a sound from heaven, as of a mighty wind coming, and it filled the whole house where they were sitting. And there appeared to them parted tongues as it were of fire, and it sat upon every one of them; and they were all filled with the Holy Ghost, and they began to speak with divers tongues, according as the Holy Ghost gave them to speak. Now there were dwelling at Jerusalem, Jews, devout men, out of every nation under heaven. And when this was noised abroad, the multitude came together, and were confounded in mind, because that every man heard them speak in his own tongue. And they were all amazed, and wondered, saying: Behold, are not all these that speak, Galileans? and how have we heard, every man our tongue wherein we were born? Parthians, and Medes, and Elamites, and inhabitants of Mesopotamia, Judea, and Cappadocia, Pontus and Asia, Phrygia, and Pamphilia, Egypt, and the parts of Lybia about Cyrene, and strangers of Rome, Jews also, and proselytes, Cretes, and Arabians: we have heard them speak in our own tongues the wonderful works of God.

GOSPEL. *John* xiv, 23–31.*At that time:* Jesus said to His disciples: If any one love Me, he will keep My word, and My Father will love him, and we will come to him, and will make our abode with him. He that loveth Me not, keepeth not My words. And the word which you have heard is not Mine, but the Father's who sent Me. These things have I spoken to you, abiding with you. But the Paraclete, the Holy Ghost, whom the Father will send in My name, He will teach you all things, and bring all things to your mind, whatsoever I shall have said to you. Peace I leave with you. My peace I give unto you : not as the world giveth, do I give unto you. Let not your heart be troubled, nor let it be afraid. You have heard that I said to you : I go away, and I come unto you. If you loved Me, you would indeed be glad, because I go to the Father : for the Father is greater than I. And now I have told you before it come to pass : that when it shall come to pass, you may believe. I will not now speak many things with you. For the prince of this world cometh, and in Me he hath not anything. But that the world may know, that I love the Father : and as the Father hath given Me commandment, so do I.

TRINITY SUNDAY

EPISTLE. *Romans* xi, 33–36. O the depth of the riches of the wisdom and of the knowledge of God ! How incomprehensible are His judgments, and how unsearchable His ways ! For who hath known the mind of the Lord ? Or who hath been His counsellor ? Or who hath first given to Him, and recompense shall be made him ? For of Him, and by Him, and in Him, are all things : to Him be glory for ever. Amen.

GOSPEL. *Matthew* xxviii, 18–20. *At that time :* Jesus said to His disciples : All power is given to Me in heaven and in earth. Going, therefore, teach ye all nations ; baptizing them in the name of the Father, and of the Son, and of the Holy Ghost. Teaching them to observe all things whatsoever I have commanded you : and behold I am with you all days, even to the consummation of the world.

EPISTLE *of the* First Sunday *after* Pentecost. I *John* iv, 8–21. *Dearly beloved :* God is charity. By this hath the charity of God appeared towards us, because God hath sent His only begotten Son into the world, that we may live by Him. In this is charity : not as though we had loved God, but because He hath first loved us, and sent His Son to be a propitiation for our sins. My dearest, if God hath so loved us ; we also ought to love one another. No man hath seen God at any time. If we love one another, God abideth in us, and His charity is perfected in us. In this we know that we abide in Him, and He in us : because He hath given us of His Spirit. And we have seen, and do testify, that the Father hath sent His Son *to be* the Saviour of the world. Whosoever shall confess that Jesus is the Son of God, God abideth in him, and he in God. And we have known, and have believed the charity, which God hath to us. God is charity : and he that abideth in charity, abideth in God, and God in him. In this is the charity of God perfected with us, that we may have confidence in the day of judgment : because as He is, we also are in this world. Fear is not in charity : but perfect charity casteth out fear, because fear hath pain. And he that feareth, is not perfected in charity. Let us therefore love God, because God first hath loved us. If any man say, I love God, and hateth his brother ; he is a liar. For he that loveth not his brother, whom he seeth, how can he love God, whom he seeth not ? And this commandment we have from God, that he, who loveth God, love also his brother.

GOSPEL *of the* First Sunday *after* Pentecost. *Luke* vi, 36–42. *At that time :* Jesus said to His disciples : Be ye therefore merciful, as your Father also is merciful. Judge not, and you shall not be judged. Condemn not, and you shall not be condemned. Forgive, and you shall be forgiven. Give and it shall be given to you : good measure and pressed down and shaken together and running over shall be given into your bosom. For with the same measure that you shall mete withal, it shall be measured to you again. And He spoke also to them a similitude : Can the blind lead the blind ? Do they not both fall into the ditch ? The disciple is not

above His Master : but every one shall be
perfect, if he be as His Master. And why
seest thou the mote in thy brother's eye ;
but the beam that is in thy own eye thou
considerest not ? Or how canst thou say
to thy brother : Brother, let me pull the
mote out of thy eye, when thou thyself
seest not the beam in thy own eye? Hypo-
crite, cast first the beam out of thy own
eye ; and then thou shalt see clearly to take
out the mote from thy brother's eye.

CORPUS CHRISTI

EPISTLE. 1 *Corinthians* xi, 23–29. *Brethren :* I have received of the Lord that
which also I delivered to you, that the
Lord Jesus, the same night in which He was
betrayed, took bread, and giving thanks,
broke, and said : Take ye and eat : this is
My body, which shall be delivered for you :
this do for the commemoration of Me.
In like manner also the chalice, after He
had supped, saying : This chalice is the new
testament in My blood : this do ye, as often
as you shall drink, for the commemoration of Me. For as often as you shall eat
this bread, and drink the chalice, you shall
show the death of the Lord until He come.
Therefore whosoever shall eat this bread,
or drink the chalice of the Lord unworthily,
shall be guilty of the body and of the
blood of the Lord. But let a man prove him-

self : and so let him eat of that bread, and drink of the chalice. For he that eateth and drinketh unworthily, eateth and drinketh judgment to himself, not discerning the body of the Lord.

GOSPEL. *John* vi, 56–59. *At that time :* Jesus said to the multitude of the Jews : My flesh is meat indeed : and My blood is drink indeed. He that eateth My flesh, and drinketh My blood, abideth in Me, and I in him. As the living Father hath sent Me, and I live by the Father ; so he that eateth Me, the same also shall live by Me. This is the bread that came down from heaven. Not as your fathers did eat manna, and are dead. He that eateth this bread shall live for ever.

SECOND SUNDAY AFTER PENTECOST

EPISTLE. I *John* iii, 13–18. *Dearly beloved :* Wonder not if the world hate you. We know that we have passed from death to life, because we love the brethren. He that loveth not, abideth in death. Whosoever hateth his brother is a murderer. And you know that no murderer hath eternal life abiding in himself. In this we have known the charity of God, because He hath laid down His life for us : and we ought to lay down our lives for the brethren. He that hath the substance of this world, and shall see his brother in need, and shall shut up his bowels from him : how doth the charity of God abide in him ? My little children, let us not love in word, nor in tongue, but in deed, and in truth.

GOSPEL. *Luke* xiv, 16–24. *At that time :* Jesus spoke this parable to the Pharisees : A certain man made a great supper, and invited many. And he sent his servant at the hour of supper to say to them that were invited, that they should come, for now all things are ready. And they began all at once to make excuse. The first said to him : I have bought a farm and I must needs go out and see it ; I pray thee, hold me excused. And another said : I have bought five yoke of oxen, and I go to try them ; I pray thee, hold me excused. And another said : I have married a wife, and therefore I cannot come. And the servant returning, told these things to his lord. Then the master of the house, being angry, said to his servant : Go out quickly into the streets and lanes of the city, and bring in hither the poor, and the feeble, and the blind, and the lame. And the servant said : Lord, it is done as thou hast commanded, and yet there is room. And the Lord said to the servant : Go out into the highways and hedges, and compel them to come in, that my house may be filled. But I say unto you, that none of those men that were invited, shall taste of my supper.

FEAST OF THE SACRED HEART

(Friday after Octave of Corpus Christi)

EPISTLE. *Eph.* iii, 8–19. Brethren, unto me, the least of all the saints, is given this grace, to preach among the Gentiles the unsearchable riches of Christ, and to enlighten all men, that they may see what is the dispensation of the mystery which hath been hidden from eternity in God, who created all things. For this cause I bow my knees to the Father of our Lord Jesus Christ, of whom all paternity in heaven and on earth is named, that He would grant you, according to the riches of His glory, to be strengthened by His spirit with might unto the inward man; that Christ may dwell by faith in your hearts; that, being rooted and founded in charity, you may be able to comprehend, with all the saints, what is the breadth, and length, and height, and depth; to know also the charity of Christ, which surpasseth all knowledge; that you may be filled unto all the fulness of God.

GOSPEL. *John* xix, 31–37. *At that time:* The Jews, because it was the Parasceve, that the bodies might not remain upon the cross on the sabbath-day (for that was a great sabbath-day), besought Pilate that their legs might be broken, and that they might be taken away. The soldiers, therefore, came ; and they broke the legs of the first, and of the other that was crucified with him. But when they came to Jesus, and saw that He was already dead, they did not break His legs ; but one of the soldiers opened His side with a spear ; and immediately there came out blood and water. And he that saw it, gave testimony ; and his testimony is true. And he knoweth that he saith true, that you also may believe. For these things were done that the scripture might be fulfilled, You shall not break a bone of Him. And again another scripture saith, They shall look on Him whom they pierced.

THIRD SUNDAY AFTER PENTECOST

EPISTLE. 1 *Peter* v, 6–11. *Dearly beloved :* Be you humbled under the mighty hand of God, that He may exalt you in the time of visitation ; casting all your care upon Him, for He hath care of you. Be sober and watch, because your adversary the devil, as a roaring lion, goeth about seeking whom he may devour. Whom resist ye, strong in faith ; knowing that the same affliction befalls your brethren who are in the world. But the God of all grace, who hath called us unto His eternal glory in

Christ Jesus, after you have suffered a little, will Himself perfect you, and confirm you, and establish you. To Him be glory and empire for ever and ever. Amen.

GOSPEL. *Luke* xv, 1-10. *At that time :* The publicans and sinners drew near unto Jesus to hear Him. And the Pharisees and the scribes murmured, saying : This man receiveth sinners, and eateth with them. And He spoke to them this parable, saying : What man of you that hath an hundred sheep, and if he shall lose one of them, doth he not leave the ninety-nine in the desert, and go after that which was lost, until he find it ? And when he hath found it, lay it upon his shoulders, rejoicing, and coming home, call together his friends and neighbours, saying to them : Rejoice with me, because I have found my sheep that was lost ? I say to you, that even so there shall be joy in heaven upon one sinner that doth penance, more than upon ninety-nine just who need not penance. Or what woman having ten groats, if she lose one groat, doth not light a candle, and sweep the house and seek diligently until she find it ? And when she hath found it, call together her friends and neighbours, saying : Rejoice with me, because I have found the groat which I had lost. So I say to you, there shall be joy before the angels of God upon one sinner doing penance.

FOURTH SUNDAY AFTER PENTECOST

EPISTLE. *Romans* viii. 18–23. *Brethren :*
I reckon that the sufferings of this time
are not worthy to be compared with the
glory to come that shall be revealed in us.
For the expectation of the creature waiteth
for the revelation of the sons of God. For
the creature was made subject to vanity,
not willingly, but by reason of him that
made it subject, in hope : because the
creature also itself shall be delivered from
the servitude of corruption, into the liberty
of the glory of the children of God. For
we know that every creature groaneth
and travaileth in pain, even till now. And
not only it, but ourselves also, who have
the first fruits of the Spirit, even we ourselves groan within ourselves, waiting for
the adoption of the sons of God, the redemption of our body : in Christ Jesus our
Lord.

GOSPEL. *Luke* v, 1–11. *At that time :*
When the multitude pressed upon Jesus
to hear the word of God, He stood by the
lake of Genesareth. And He saw two ships
standing by the lake ; but the fishermen
were gone out of them, and were washing
their nets. And going up into one of the
ships that was Simon's, He desired him
to draw back a little from the land. And

sitting, He taught the multitude out of the ship. Now when He had ceased to speak, He said to Simon : Launch out into the deep, and let down your nets for a draught. And Simon, answering, said to Him : Master, we have laboured all the night, and have taken nothing, but at Thy word I will let down the net. And when they had done this, they enclosed a very great multitude of fishes, and their net broke. And they beckoned to their partners that were in the other ship, that they should come and help them. And they came, and filled both the ships, so that they were almost sinking. Which when Simon Peter saw, he fell down at Jesus' knees, saying : Depart from me, for I am a sinful man, O Lord. For he was wholly astonished, and all that were with him, at the draught of fishes which they had taken. And so were also James and John, the sons of Zebedee, who were Simon's partners. And Jesus saith to Simon : Fear not : from henceforth thou shalt catch men. And having brought their ships to land, leaving all things, they followed Him.

FIFTH SUNDAY AFTER
PENTECOST

EPISTLE. 1 *Peter* iii, 8–15. *Dearly beloved :* Be ye all of one mind, having compassion one of another, being lovers of the brotherhood, merciful, modest, humble ; not rendering evil for evil, nor railing for railing, but contrariwise, blessing : for unto this are you called, that you may inherit a blessing. *For he that will love life, and see good days, let him refrain his tongue from evil, and his lips that they speak no guile. Let hi t decline from evil, and do good : let him seek after peace and pursue it ; because the eyes of the Lord are upon the just, and H`s ears unto their prayers ; but the countenance of the Lord is upon them that do evil things.* And who is he that can hurt you, if you be zealous of good ? But if also you suffer any thing for justice's sake, blessed are ye. And be not afraid of their fear, and be not troubled. But sanctify the Lord Christ in your hearts.

GOSPEL. *Matthew* v, 20–24. *At that time :* Jesus said to His disciples : Unless your justice abound more than that of the scribes and Pharisees, you shall not enter into the kingdom of heaven. You have heard that it was said to them of old : Thou shalt not kill. And whosoever shall kill shall be in danger of the judgment. But I say to you, that whosoever is angry with his brother, shall be in danger of the judgment. And whosoever shall say to his brother, Raca, shall be in danger of the Council. And whosoever shall say, Thou fool, shall be in danger of hell fire. If therefore thou offer thy gift at the altar, and there remember that thy brother hath any thing against thee, leave there thy offering before the altar, and go first to be reconciled to thy brother ; and then coming, thou shalt offer thy gift.

SIXTH SUNDAY AFTER PENTECOST

EPISTLE. *Romans* vi, 3–11. *Brethren :* All we who are baptized in Christ Jesus, are baptized in His death. For we are buried together with Him by baptism into death ; that as Christ is risen from the dead by the glory of the Father, so we also may walk in newness of life. For if we have been planted together in the likeness of His death, we shall be also in the likeness of His resurrection. Knowing this, that our old man is crucified with Him, that the body of sin may be destroyed, to the end that we may serve sin no longer. For he that is dead is justified from sin. Now if we be dead with Christ, we believe that we shall live also together with Christ : knowing that Christ rising again from the dead, dieth now no more, death shall no more have dominion over Him. For in that He died to sin, He died once ; but in that He liveth, He liveth unto God : so do you also reckon, that you are dead to sin, but alive unto God : in Christ Jesus our Lord.

GOSPEL. *Mark* viii, 1–9. *At that time :* When there was a great multitude with Jesus, and they had nothing to eat, calling His disciples together, He saith to them : I have compassion on the multitude, for behold they have now been with Me three days, and have nothing to eat. And if I shall send them away fasting to their own home, they will faint in the way ; for some of them came from afar off. And His disciples answered Him : From whence can any one fill them here with bread in the wilderness ? And He asked them : How many loaves have ye ? Who said : Seven. And He commanded the people to sit down on the ground. And taking the seven loaves, giving thanks, He broke and gave to His disciples for to set before them ; and they set them before the people. And they had a few little fishes ; and He blessed them, and commanded them to be set before them. And they did eat and were filled ; and they took up that which was left of the fragments, seven baskets. And they that had eaten were about four thousand ; and He sent them away .

SEVENTH SUNDAY AFTER PENTECOST

EPISTLE. *Romans* vi, 19–23. *Brethren :* I speak a human thing, because of the infirmity of your flesh. For as you have yielded your members to serve uncleanness and iniquity, unto iniquity; so now yield your members to serve justice, unto sanctification. For when you were the servants of sin, you were free men to justice. What fruit therefore had you then in those things of which you are now ashamed ? For the end of them is death. But now being made free from sin, and become servants to God, you have your fruit unto sanctification, and the end life everlasting. For the wages of sin is death. But the grace of God, life everlasting, in Christ Jesus our Lord.

GOSPEL. *Matthew* vii, 15–21. *At that time :* Jesus said to His disciples : Beware of false prophets, who come to you in the clothing of sheep, but inwardly they are ravening wolves. By their fruits you shall know them. Do men gather grapes of thorns, or figs of thistles ? Even so every good tree bringeth forth good fruit, and the evil tree bringeth forth evil fruit. A good tree cannot bring forth evil fruit, neither can an evil tree bring forth good fruit. Every tree that bringeth not forth good fruit shall be cut down, and shall be cast into the fire. Wherefore by their fruits you shall know them. Not every one that saith to Me, Lord, Lord, shall enter into the kingdom of heaven : but he that doth the will of My Father Who is in heaven, he shall enter into the kingdom of heaven.

EIGHTH SUNDAY AFTER PENTECOST

EPISTLE. *Romans* viii, 12–17. *Brethren :* We are debtors not to the flesh, to live according to the flesh. For if you live according to the flesh, you shall die : but if by the Spirit you mortify the deeds of the flesh, you shall live. For whosoever are led by the Spirit of God, they are the sons of God. For you have not received the spirit of bondage again in fear ; but you have received the spirit of adoption of sons, whereby we cry : Abba (Father). For the Spirit himself giveth testimony to our spirit, that we are the sons of God. And if sons, heirs also ; heirs indeed of God, and joint heirs with Christ.

GOSPEL. *Luke* xvi, 1–9. *At that time :* Jesus spoke to His disciples this parable : There was a certain rich man who had a steward ; and the same was accused unto him, that he had wasted his goods. And he called him, and said to him : How is it that I hear this of thee ? Give an account of thy stewardship, for now thou canst be steward no longer. And the steward said within himself : What shall I do, because my lord taketh away from me the stewardship ? To dig I am not able ; to beg I am ashamed. I know what I will do, that when I shall be removed from the steward-

13

ship, they may receive me into their houses. Therefore calling together every one of his lord's debtors, he said to the first : How much dost thou owe my lord ? But he said : An hundred barrels of oil. And he said to him : Take thy bill and sit down quickly and write fifty. Then he said to another : And how much dost thou owe ? Who said : An hundred quarters of wheat. He said to him : Take thy bill and write eighty. And the lord commended the unjust steward, forasmuch as he had done wisely : for the children of this world are wiser in their generation than the children of light. And I say to you : Make unto you friends of the mammom of iniquity ; that when you shall fail, they may receive you into ever-lasting dwellings.

NINTH SUNDAY AFTER
PENTECOST

EPISTLE. 1 *Corinthians* x, 6–13. *Brethren :* Let us not covet evil things as they also coveted. Neither become ye idolaters, as some of them, as it is written : *The people sat down to eat and drink, and rose up to play.* Neither let us commit fornication, as some of them committed fornication, and there fell in one day three and twenty thousand. Neither let us tempt Christ : as some of them tempted, and perished by the serpents. Neither do you murmur : as some of them murmured, and were destroyed by the destroyer. Now all those things happened to them in figure : and they are written for our correction, upon whom the ends of the world are come. Wherefore he that thinketh himself to stand, let him take heed lest he fall. Let no temptation take hold on you, but such as is human. And God is faithful, who will not suffer you to be tempted above that which you are able : but will make also with temptation issue, that you may be able to bear it.

Gospel. *Luke* xix, 41–47. *At that time :* When Jesus drew near to Jerusalem, seeing the city, He wept over it, saying : If thou also hadst known, and that in this thy day, the things that are to thy peace ; but now they are hidden from thy eyes. For the days shall come upon thee : and thy enemies shall cast a trench about thee, and compass thee round, and straiten thee on every side, and beat thee flat to the ground, and thy children who are in thee ; and they shall not leave in thee a stone upon a stone, because thou hast not known the time of thy visitation. And entering into the temple, He began to cast out them that sold therein, and them that bought. Saying to them : It is written : *My house is the house of prayer.* But you have made it a den of thieves. And He was teaching daily in the temple.

TENTH SUNDAY AFTER PENTECOST

EPISTLE. 1 *Corinthians* xii, 2–11. *Brethren :* You know that when you were heathens you went to dumb idols, according as you were led. Wherefore I give you to understand, that no man, speaking by the spirit of God, saith anathema to Jesus. And no man can say the Lord Jesus, but by the Holy Ghost. Now there are diversities of graces, but the same Spirit ; and there are diversities of ministries, but the same Lord ; and there are diversities of operations, but the same God, who worketh all in all. And the manifestation of the Spirit is given to every man unto profit. To one indeed, by the Spirit, is given the word of wisdom ; and to another, the word of knowledge, according to the same Spirit ; to another, faith in the same spirit ; to another, the grace of healing in one Spirit ; to another, the working of miracles ; to another, prophecy ; to another, the discerning of spirits ; to another, *divers* kinds of tongues ; to another, interpretation of speeches. But all these things one and the same Spirit worketh, dividing to every one according as He will.

GOSPEL. *Luke* xviii, 9–14. *At that time :* Jesus spoke this parable to some who trusted in themselves as just, and despised

others : Two men went up into the temple
to pray : the one a Pharisee, and the
other a publican. The Pharisee standing,
prayed thus with himself : O God, I give
Thee thanks that I am not as the rest of
men, extortioners, unjust, adulterers, as
also is this publican. I fast twice a week :
I give tithes of all that I possess. And the
publican, standing afar off, would not so
much as lift up his eyes towards heaven,
but struck his breast, saying : O God, be
merciful to me a sinner. I say to you, this
man went down into his house justified
rather than the other : because every one
that exalteth himself shall be humbled :
and he that humbleth himself shall be
exalted.

ELEVENTH SUNDAY AFTER PENTECOST

EPISTLE. I *Corinthians* xv, 1–10. *Brethren :* I make known unto you the gospel
which I preached to you, which also you
have received, and wherein you stand ;
by which also you are saved, if you hold
fast after what manner I preached unto you,
unless you have believed in vain. For I
delivered unto you first of all, which I also
received ; how that Christ died for our
sins, according to the scriptures ; and that
He was buried, and that He rose again
the third day, according to the scriptures ;
and that He was seen by Cephas ; and after

that by the eleven. Then was He seen by
more than five hundred brethren at once,
of whom many remain until this present,
and some are fallen asleep. After that, He
was seen by James, then by all the apostles.
And last of all, He was seen also by me, as
by one born out of due time. For I am
the least of the apostles, who am not
worthy to be called an apostle, because I
persecuted the church of God. But by the
grace of God, I am what I am ; and His
grace in me hath not been void.

GOSPEL. *Mark* vii, 31–37. *At that time :*
Jesus going out of the coast of Tyre, came
by Sidon to the sea of Galilee, through the
midst of the coasts of Decapolis. And they
bring to Him one deaf and dumb, and they
besought Him that He would lay His hand
upon him. And taking him from the multitude apart, He put His fingers into his ears,
and spitting, He touched his tongue ; and
looking up to heaven, He groaned, and said
to him : Ephpheta, which is, Be thou opened.
And immediately his ears were opened, and
the string of his tongue was loosed, and he
spoke right. And He charged them that
they should tell no man. But the more He
charged them, so much the more a great
deal did they publish it. And so much the
more did they wonder, saying : He hath
done all things well : He hath made both
the deaf to hear, and the dumb to speak.

TWELFTH SUNDAY AFTER PENTECOST

EPISTLE. *2 Corinthians* iii, 4–9. *Brethren :* Such confidence we have, through Christ towards God. Not that we are sufficient to think anything of ourselves, as of ourselves ; but our sufficiency is from God. Who also hath made us fit ministers of the new testament, not in the letter, but in the spirit. For the letter killeth, but the spirit quickeneth. Now if the ministration of death, engraven with letters upon stones, was glorious, so that the children of Israel could not steadfastly behold the face of Moses, for the glory of his countenance, which is made void, how shall not the ministration of the spirit be rather in glory ? For if the ministration of condemnation be glory, much more the ministration of justice aboundeth in glory.

GOSPEL. *Luke* x, 23–27. *At that time :* Jesus said to His disciples : Blessed are the eyes that see the things which you see. For I say to you, that many prophets and kings have desired to see the things that you see, and have not seen them ; and to hear the things that you hear, and have not heard them. And behold a certain lawyer stood up, tempting Him, and saying, Master, what must I do to possess eternal life ? But He said to him : What is written in the law ? How readest thou ? He answering said : *Thou shalt love the Lord thy God with thy whole heart, and with thy whole soul, and with all thy strength, and with all thy mind : and thy neighbour as thyself.* And He said to him : Thou hast answered rightly : this do, and thou shalt live. But he, willing to justify himself, said to Jesus : And who is my neighbour ? And Jesus answering, said : A certain man went down from Jerusalem to Jericho, and fell among robbers, who also stripped him, and having wounded him went away, leaving him half dead, And it chanced that a certain priest went down the same way, and seeing him, passed by. In like manner also a Levite, when he was near the place and saw him, passed by. But a certain Samaritan being on his journey, came near him ; and seeing him, was moved with compassion. And going up to him, bound up his wounds, pouring in oil and wine ; and setting him upon his own beast, brought him to an inn, and took care of him. And the next day he took out two pence, and gave to the host, and said : Take care of him ; and whatsoever thou shalt spend over and above, I, at my return, will repay thee. Which of these three, in thy opinion, was neighbour to him that fell among the robbers ? But he said : He that showed mercy to him. And Jesus said to him : Go, and do thou in like manner.

THIRTEENTH SUNDAY AFTER PENTECOST

EPISTLE. *Galatians* iii, 16–22. *Brethren:*
To Abraham were the promises made and
to his seed. He saith not, *And to his seeds*,
as of many; but as of one, *And to thy seed*,
which is Christ. Now this I say, that the
testament which was confirmed by God,
·the law which was made after four hundred
and thirty years, doth not disannul, to
make the promise of no effect. For if the
inheritance be of the law, it is no more of
promise. But God gave it to Abraham by
promise. Why then was the law? It was set
because of transgressions, until the seed
should come, to whom He made the
promise, being ordained by angels in the
hand of a mediator. Now a mediator is not
of one: but God is one. Was the law then
against the promises of God? God forbid.
For if there had been a law given which
could give life, verily justice should have
been by the law. But the scripture hath
concluded all under sin, that the promise,
by the faith of Jesus Christ, might be
given to them that believe.

GOSPEL. *Luke* xvii, 11–19. *At that time:*
As Jesus was going to Jerusalem, He
passed through the midst of Samaria and
Galilee. And as He entered into a certain
town, there met Him ten men that were

lepers, who stood afar off ; and lifted up their voice, saying : Jesus, master, have mercy on us. Whom when He saw, He said : Go, show yourselves to the priests. And it came to pass, as they went, that they were made clean. And one of them, when he saw that he was made clean, went back, with a loud voice glorifying God. And he fell on his face before His feet, giving thanks : and this was a Samaritan. And Jesus answering, said, Were not ten made clean ? and where are the nine ? There is no one found to return and give glory to God, but this stranger. And He said to him : Arise, go thy way ; for thy faith hath made thee whole.

FOURTEENTH SUNDAY AFTER PENTECOST

EPISTLE. *Galatians* v, 16–24. *Brethren :* Walk in the spirit, and you shall not fulfil the lusts of the flesh. For the flesh lusteth against the spirit : and the spirit against the flesh ; for these are contrary to one another : so that you do not the things that you would. But if you are led by the spirit, you are not under the law. Now the works of the flesh are manifest, which are fornication, uncleanness, immodesty, luxury, idolatory, witchcrafts, enmities, contentions, emulations, wraths, quarrels, dissensions, sects, envies, murders, drunkenness, revellings, and such like. Of the which I foretell you, as I have foretold to you, that they who do such things shall not obtain the kingdom of God. But the fruit of the Spirit is, charity, joy, peace, patience, benignity, goodness, longanimity, mildness, faith, modesty, continency, chastity. Against such there is no law. And they that are Christ's, have crucified their flesh, with the vices and concupiscences.

GOSPEL. *Matthew* vi, 24–33. *At that time :* Jesus said to His disciples : no man can serve two masters. For either he will hate the one, and love the other : or he will sustain the one, and despise the other. You cannot serve God and Mammon. Therefore I say to you, be not solicitous for your life, what you shall eat, nor for your body, what you shall put on. Is not the life more than the meat : and the body more than the raiment ? Behold the birds of the air, for they neither sow, nor do they reap, nor gather into barns : and your heavenly Father feedeth them. Are not you of much more value than they ? And which of you by taking thought, can add to his stature one cubit ? And for raiment why are you solicitous ? Consider the lilies of the field, how they grow : they labour not, neither do they spin. But I say to you, that not even Solomon in all his glory was arrayed as one of these. And if the grass of the field, which is to-day, and to-morrow is cast into the oven, God doth so clothe : how much more you, O ye of little faith ? Be not solicitous therefore, saying, What shall we eat : or what shall we drink, or wherewith shall we be clothed ? For after all these things do the heathens seek. For your Father knoweth that you have need of all these things. Seek ye therefore first the kingdom of God, and His justice, and all these things shall be added unto you.

FIFTEENTH SUNDAY AFTER PENTECOST

EPISTLE. *Galatians* v, 25, vi, 10. *Brethren :* If we live in the Spirit, let us also walk in the Spirit. Let us not be made desirous of vain glory, provoking one another, envying one another. Brethren, and if a man be overtaken in any fault, you, who are spiritual, instruct such a one in the spirit of meekness, considering thyself lest thou also be tempted. Bear ye one another's burdens ; and so you shall fulfil the law of Christ. For if any man think himself to be something, whereas he is nothing, he deceiveth himself. But let every one prove his own work, and so he shall have glory in himself only, and not in another. For every one shall bear his own burden. And let him that is instructed in the word, communicate to him that instructeth him, in all good things. Be not deceived, God is not mocked. For what things a man shall sow, those also shall he reap. For he that soweth in his flesh, of the flesh also shall reap corruption. But he that soweth in the spirit, of the spirit shall reap life everlasting. And in doing good, let us not fail. For in due time we shall reap, not failing. Therefore, whilst we have time, let us work good to all men, but especially to those who are of the household of the faith.

GOSPEL. *Luke* vii, 11-16. *At that time :* Jesus went into a city called Naim ; and there went with Him His disciples, and a great multitude, And when He came nigh to the city, behold a dead man was carried out, the only son of his mother ; and she was a widow : and a great multitude of the city were with her. Whom when the Lord had seen, being moved with mercy towards her, He said to her : Weep not. And He came near and touched the bier. And they that carried it, stood still. And He said : Young man, I say to thee, arise. And he that was dead, sat up, and began to speak. And He gave him to his mother. And there came a fear on them all : and they glorified God, saying : A great prophet is risen up among us : and, God hath visited His people.

SIXTEENTH SUNDAY AFTER PENTECOST

EPISTLE. *Ephesians* iii, 13-21. *Brethren :* I pray you not to faint at my tribulations for you, which is your glory. For **this** cause I bow my knees to the Father of our Lord Jesus Christ, of whom all paternity in heaven and earth is named, that He would grant you, according to the riches of His glory, to be strengthened by His Spirit with might unto the inward man, that Christ may dwell by faith in your hearts, that being rooted and founded in charity, you may be able to comprehend, with all the saints, what is the breadth, and length, and height, and depth: to know also the charity of Christ, which surpasseth all knowledge, that you may be filled unto all the fulness of God. Now to Him who is able to do all things more abundantly than we deserve or understand, according to the power that worketh in us; to Him be glory in the church, and in Christ Jesus unto all generations, world without end. Amen.

GOSPEL. *Luke* xiv, 1–11. *At that time:* When Jesus went into the house of one of the chief of the Pharisees, on the sabbath day to eat bread, they watched Him. And behold, there was a certain man before Him that had the dropsy. And Jesus answering, spoke to the lawyers and Pharisees, saying: Is it lawful to heal on the sabbath day? But they held their peace. But He taking him, healed him, and sent him away. And answering them He said : Which of you shall have an ass or an ox fall into a pit, and will not immediately draw him out, on the sabbath day ? And they could not answer Him to these things. And He spoke a parable also to them that were invited, marking how they chose the first seats at the table, saying to them : When thou art invited to a wedding, sit not down in the first place, lest perhaps one more honourable than thou be invited by him : and he that invited thee and him, come and say to thee, Give this man place : and then thou begin with shame to take the lowest place. But when thou art invited, go, sit down in the lowest place, that when he who invited thee, cometh, he may say to thee : Friend, go up higher. Then shalt thou have glory before them that sit at table with thee. Because every one that exalteth himself, shall be humbled : and he that humbleth himself, shall be exalted.

SEVENTEENTH SUNDAY AFTER PENTECOST

EPISTLE. *Ephesians* iv, 1–6. *Brethren :* I who am a prisoner in the Lord, beseech you that you walk worthy of the vocation in which you are called, with all humility and mildness, with patience, supporting one another in charity. Careful to keep the unity of the Spirit in the bond of peace. One body and one Spirit ; as you are called in one hope of your calling. One Lord, one faith, one baptism. One God and Father of all, who is above all, and through all, and in us all. Who is blessed for evermore. Amen.

GOSPEL. *Matthew* xxii, 35-46. *At that time :* The Pharisees came to Jesus, and one of them, a doctor of the law, asked Him, tempting Him : Master, which is the great commandment in the law ? Jesus said to him : *Thou shalt love the Lord thy God with thy whole heart, and with thy whole soul and with thy whole mind.* This is the greatest and the first commandment. And the second is like to this : *Thou shalt love thy neighbour as thyself.* On these two commandments dependeth the whole law and the prophets. And the Pharisees being gathered together, Jesus asked them, saying : What think you of Christ ? Whose son is He ? They say to Him : David's. He saith to them : How then doth David in spirit call Him Lord, saying : *The Lord said to my Lord, Sit on my right hand, until I make Thy enemies Thy footstool ?* If David then call Him Lord, how is He his son ? And no man was able to answer Him a word ; neither durst any man from that day forth ask Him any more questions.

EIGHTEENTH SUNDAY AFTER PENTECOST

EPISTLE. 1 *Corinthians* i, 4–8. *Brethren :* I give thanks to my God always for you, for the grace of God that is given you in Christ Jesus, that in all things you are made rich in Him, in all utterance, and in all knowledge ; as the testimony of Christ was confirmed in you, so that nothing is wanting to you in any grace, waiting for the manifestation of our Lord Jesus Christ. Who also will confirm you unto the end without crime, in the day of the coming of our Lord Jesus Christ.

GOSPEL. *Matthew* ix, 1–8. *At that time :* Jesus entering into a boat, He passed over the water and came into His own city. And behold, they brought to Him one sick of the palsy lying in a bed. And Jesus, seeing their faith, said to the man sick of the palsy : Be of good heart, son, thy sins are forgiven thee. And behold some of the scribes said within themselves : He blasphemeth. And Jesus seeing their thoughts, said : Why do you think evil in your hearts ? Whether is easier, to say, thy sins are forgiven thee : or to say : Arise, and walk ? But that you may know that the Son of man hath power on earth to forgive sins, (then said He to the man sick of the palsy, Arise, take up thy bed, and go into thy house. And he arose, and went into his house. And the multitude seeing it, feared, and glorified God that gave such power to men.

NINETEENTH SUNDAY AFTER PENTECOST

EPISTLE. *Ephesians* iv, 23–38. *Brethren :* Be renewed in the spirit of your mind : and put on the new man, who according to God is created in justice and holiness of truth. Wherefore putting away lying, speak ye the truth every man with his neighbour ; for we are members one of another. Be angry, and sin not. Let not the sun go down upon your anger. Give not place to the devil. He that stole, let him now steal no more ; but rather let him labour, working with his hands the thing which is good, that he may have something to give to him that suffereth need.

GOSPEL. *Matthew* xxii, 2–14. *At that time :* Jesus spoke to the chief priests and Pharisees in parables, saying : The kingdom of heaven is likened to a king, who made a marriage for his son. And he sent his servants, to call them that were invited to the marriage ; and they would not come. Again he sent other servants, saying : Tell them that were invited, Behold, I have prepared my dinner ; my beeves and fatlings are killed, and all things are ready : come ye to the marriage. But they neglected, and went their ways, one to his farm, and another to his merchandise. And the rest laid hands on his servants, and having treated them contumeliously, put them to death. But when the king had heard of it, he was angry, and sending his armies, he destroyed those murderers, and burnt their city. Then he saith to his servants : The marriage indeed is ready ; but they that were invited were not worthy. Go ye therefore into the highways ; and as many as you shall find, call to the marriage. And his servants going forth into the ways, gathered together all that they found, both bad and good : and the marriage was filled with guests. And the king went in to see the guests : and he saw there a man who had not on a wedding garment. And he saith to him : Friend, how camest thou in hither not having on a wedding garment ? But he was silent. Then the king said to the waiters : Bind his hands and feet, and cast him into the exterior darkness : there shall be weeping and gnashing of teeth. For many are called, but few *are* chosen.

TWENTIETH SUNDAY AFTER PENTECOST

Epistle. *Ephesians* v, 15–21. *Brethren :* See therefore, how you walk circumspectly : not as unwise, but as wise : redeeming the time, because the days are evil. Wherefore become not unwise, but understanding what is the will of God. And be not drunk with wine, wherein is luxury : but be ye filled with the holy Spirit, speaking to yourselves in psalms and hymns, and spiritual canticles, singing and making melody in your hearts to the Lord ; giving thanks always for all things, in the name of our Lord Jesus Christ, to God and the Father : being subject one to another in the fear of Christ.

GOSPEL. *John* iv, 46–53. *At that time :* There was a certain ruler, whose son was sick at Capharnaum. He having heard that Jesus was come from Judea into Galilee, went to Him, and prayed Him to come down, and heal his son ; for he was at the point of death. Jesus therefore said unto him : Unless you see signs and wonders, you believe not. The ruler saith to him : Lord, come down before that my son die. Jesus saith to him : Go thy way ; thy son liveth. The man believed the word which Jesus said to him, and went his way. And as he was going down, his servants met him, and they brought word, saying that his son lived. He asked therefore of them the hour wherein he grew better. And they said to him : Yesterday, at the seventh hour, the fever left him. The father therefore knew, that it was at the same hour that Jesus said to him, Thy son liveth ; and himself believed, and his whole house.

TWENTY-FIRST SUNDAY AFTER PENTECOST

EPISTLE. *Ephesians,* vi, 10–17. *Brethren :* Be strengthened in the Lord, and in the might of His power. Put you on the armour of God, that you may be able to stand against the deceits of the devil. For our wrestling is not against flesh and blood ; but against principalities and powers, against the rulers of the world of this darkness, against the spirits of wickedness in the high places. Therefore take unto you the armour of God, that you may be able to resist in the evil day, and to stand in all things perfect. Stand therefore, having your loins girt about with truth, and having on the breastplate of justice, and your feet shod with the preparation of the gospel of peace : in all things taking the shield of faith, wherewith you may be able to extinguish all the fiery darts of the most wicked one. And take unto you the helmet of salvation, and the sword of the Spirit, (which is the word of God).

GOSPEL. *Matthew* xviii, 23–35. *At that time :* Jesus spoke to His disciples this parable : The kingdom of heaven is likened to a king, who would take an account of his servants. And when he had begun to take the account, one was brought to him, that owed him ten thousand talents. And

as he had not wherewith to pay it, his lord
commanded that he should be sold, and
his wife and children and all that he had,
and payment to be made. But that servant
falling down, besought him, saying : Have
patience with me, and I will pay thee all.
And the lord of that servant being moved
with pity, let him go and forgave him the
debt. But when that servant was gone out,
he found one of his fellow servants that
owed him an hundred pence : and laying
hold of him, he throttled him, saying :
Pay what thou owest. And his fellow servant falling down, besought him, saying :
Have patience with me, and I will pay thee
all. And he would not : but went and cast
him into prison, till he paid the debt. Now
his fellow servants seeing what was done,
were very much grieved, and they came and
told their lord all that was done. Then
his lord called him ; and said to him : Thou
wicked servant, I forgave thee all the debt,
because thou besoughtest me : shouldst
not thou then have had compassion also on
thy fellow servant, even as I had compassion on thee ? And his lord being angry,
delivered him to the torturers until he paid
all the debt. So also shall My heavenly
Father do to you, if you forgive not every
one his brother from your hearts.

TWENTY-SECOND SUNDAY AFTER PENTECOST

EPISTLE.. *Philippians* i, 6-11. *Brethren :* We are confident in the Lord Jesus, that He who hath begun a good work in you, will perfect it unto the day of Christ Jesus. As it is meet for me to think this for you all, for that I have you in my heart ; and that in my bands, and in the defence and confirmation of the gospel, you all are partakers of my joy. For God is my witness, how I long after you all in the bowels of Jesus Christ. And this I pray, that your charity may more and more abound in knowledge, and in all understanding : that you may approve the better things, that you may be sincere and without offence unto the day of Christ, filled with the fruit of justice, through Jesus Christ, unto the glory and praise of God.

GOSPEL. *Matthew* xxii, 15-21. *At that time :* The Pharisees going, consulted among themselves how to ensnare Jesus in *His* speech. And they sent to Him their disciples with the Herodians, saying : Master, we know that Thou art a true speaker, and teachest the way of God in truth, neither carest Thou for any man : for Thou dost not regard the person of men. Tell us therefore what dost Thou think, is it lawful to give tribute to Cæsar, or not ? But Jesus knowing their wickedness, said : Why do you tempt Me, ye hyprocrites ? Show Me the coin of the tribute. And they offered Him a penny. And Jesus saith to them : Whose image and inscription is this ? They say to Him : Cæsar's. Then He saith to them : Render therefore to Cæsar the things that are Cæsar's ; and to God, the things that are God's.

TWENTY-THIRD SUNDAY AFTER PENTECOST

Should there be but 23 Sundays after Pentecost, the Mass of the 24th is said to-day, and this on the preceding Saturday (if it be neither a double nor semi-double), in which case it is said on some vacant day before it.

EPISTLE. *Philippians* iii, 17, iv 3. *Brethren :* Be followers of me, and observe them who walk so as you have our model. For many walk, of whom I have told you often, (and now tell you weeping), that they are enemies of the cross of Christ ; whose end is destruction ; whose god is their belly ; and *whose* glory is in their shame ; who mind earthly things. But our conversation is in heaven ; from whence also we look for the Saviour, our Lord Jesus Christ, who will reform the body of our lowness, made like to the body of His glory, according to the operation whereby also He is able to subdue all things unto Himself. Therefore, my dearly beloved brethren, and most desired, my joy and my crown ; so stand fast in the Lord, my dearly beloved. I beg of Evodia, and I beseech Syntyche, to be of one mind in the Lord. And I entreat thee also, my sincere companion, help those women that have laboured with me in the Gospel, with Clement and the rest of my fellow labourers, whose names are in the book of life.

GOSPEL. *Matthew* ix, 18–26. *At that time :* As Jesus was speaking to the multitude, behold a certain ruler came up, and adored Him, saying : Lord, my daughter is even now dead ; but come, lay Thy hand upon her, and she shall live. And Jesus rising up followed him, with His disciples. And behold a woman who was troubled with an issue of blood twelve years came behind Him, and touched the hem of His garment. For she said within herself : If I shall touch only His garment, I shall be healed. But Jesus turning and seeing her, said : Be of good heart, daughter, thy faith hath made thee whole. And the woman was made whole from that hour. And when Jesus was come into the house of the ruler, and saw the minstrels and the multitude making a rout, He said : Give place, for the girl is not dead, but sleepeth. And they laughed Him to scorn. And when the multitude was put forth, He went in and took her by the hand. And the maid arose. And the fame hereof went abroad into all that country.

14

As there cannot be less than 23 nor more than 28 Sundays after Pentecost, it is to be observed, that the Mass of the 24th is always said on the Sunday which immediately precedes Advent. When, therefore, it happens that there are any intervening Sundays between the 23rd and the last, the Epistles and Gospels are taken from the Sundays which were omitted after Epiphany : for instance, if but one Sunday, the Mass is of the 6th after Epiphany : if two, of the 5th and 6th ; if three, of the 4th, 5th and 6th ; and if four, of the 3rd, 4th, 5th and 6th.

TWENTY-FOURTH, or LAST SUNDAY AFTER PENTECOST

EPISTLE. *Colossians* i, 9–14. *Brethren :* We cease not to pray for you, and to beg that you may be filled with the knowledge of the will of God, in all wisdom and spiritual understanding : that you may walk worthy of God, in all things pleasing; being fruitful in every good work, and increasing in the knowledge of God : strengthened with all might according to the power of His glory, in all patience and long-suffering with joy, giving thanks to God the Father, who hath made us worthy to be partakers of the lot of the saints in light : who hath delivered us from the power of darkness, and hath translated us into the kingdom of the Son of His love, in whom we have redemption through His blood, the remission of sins.

GOSPEL. *Matthew* xxiv, 15–35. *At that time :* Jesus said to His disciples: When, you shall see *the abomination of desolation* which was spoken of by Daniel the prophet, standing in the holy place : he that readeth let him understand. Then they that are in Judea, let them flee to the mountains, and he that is on the housetop, let him not come down to take any thing out of his house : and he that is in the field, let him not go back to take his coat. And woe to them that are with child, and that give suck in those days. But pray that your flight be not in the winter, or on the sabbath. For there shall be then great tribulation, such as hath not been from the beginning of the world until now, neither shall be. And unless those days had been shortened, no flesh should be saved : but for the sake of the elect those days shall be shortened. Then if any man shall say to you : Lo here is Christ, or there, do not believe him. For there shall arise false Christs and false prophets, and shall show great signs and wonders, insomuch as to deceive (if possible) even the elect. Behold I have told it to you, beforehand. If therefore they shall say to you : Behold He is in the desert, go ye not out : Behold *He* is in the closets, believe it not. For as lightning cometh out of the east, and appeareth even into the west : so shall also the coming of the Son of man be. Wheresoever the body shall be, there shall the eagles also be gathered together. And immediately after the tribulation of those days, the sun shall be darkened and the moon shall not give her light, and the stars shall fall from heaven, and the powers of heaven shall be moved : and then shall appear the sign of the Son of man in heaven : and then shall all tribes of the earth mourn : and they shall see the Son of man coming in the clouds of heaven with much power and majesty. And He shall send His angels with a trumpet, and a great voice : and they shall gather together His elect from the four winds, from the farthest parts of the heavens to the uttermost bounds of them. And from the fig-tree learn a parable : when the branch thereof is now tender, and the leaves come forth, you know that summer is nigh. So you also, when you shall see all these things, know ye that it is nigh, *even* at the doors. Amen I say to you, that this generation shall not pass, till all these things be done. Heaven and earth shall pass, but My words shall not pass.

PROPER OF SAINTS

THE IMMACULATE CONCEPTION
December 8

LESSON. *Prov.* viii, 22-35. The Lord possessed me in the beginning of His ways, before He made anything, from the beginning. I was set up from eternity, and of old, before the earth was made. The depths were not as yet, and I was already conceived ; neither had the fountains of water as yet sprung out : the mountains with their huge bulk had not as yet been established : before the hills I was brought forth : He had not yet made the earth, nor the rivers, nor the poles of the world. When He prepared the heavens, I was present : when with a certain law and compass He enclosed the depths : when He established the sky above, and poised the fountains of waters : when He compassed the sea with its bounds and set a law to the waters, that they should not pass their limits : when He balanced the foundations of the earth, I was with Him, forming all things, and was delighted every day, playing before Him at all times, playing in the world : and my delights were to be with the children of men. Now, therefore, ye children, hear me : Blessed are they that keep my ways. Hear instruction and be wise, and refuse it not. Blessed is the man that heareth me, and that watcheth daily at my gates and waiteth at the posts of my doors. He that shall find me shall find life, and shall draw salvation from the Lord.

GOSPEL. *Luke* i, 26–28. *At that time :* The Angel Gabriel was sent from God, into a city of Galilee, called Nazareth, to a virgin espoused to a man whose name was Joseph, of the house of David : and the name of the virgin was Mary. And the Angel being come in, said to her : Hail, full of grace, the Lord is with thee ; blessed art thou among women.

ST. PATRICK, AP. AND PATRON OF IRELAND

March 17

LESSON. *Ecclesiasticus* xliv, xlv. Behold a great priest who in his time pleased God, and was found just, and in the time of wrath became an atonement. There were none found like him in observing the law of the Most High. Therefore by an oath did the Lord make him great amongst His people. He gave him the blessing of all nations, and established His covenant on his head. He acknowledged him in His blessings : He stored up His mercy for him ; and He found favour in the eyes of

the Lord. (xlv) He exalted him in the sight
of kings ; and gave him a crown of glory.
He made with him an eternal covenant :
and bestowed on him a great priesthood :
and rendered him blessed in glory. To perform the priestly office, to sing praises to
the name of God ; and to offer Him precious
incense for an odour of sweetness.

GOSPEL. *Matthew* xxv, 14–23. *At that
time :* Jesus spoke this parable to His
disciples : A man going into a far country,
called his servants, and delivered to them
his goods ; and to one he gave five talents,
and to another two, and to another one, to
every one according to his proper ability :
and immediately he took his journey. And
he that had received the five talents, went
his way, and traded with the same, and
gained other five. And in like manner he
that had received the two, gained other
two. But he that had received the one,
going his way, digged into the earth and hid
his lord's money. But after a long time the
lord of those servants came, and reckoned
with them. And he that had received the
five talents coming, brought other five
talents, saying : Lord, thou didst deliver
to me five talents, behold I have gained
other five over and above. His lord said to
him : Well done, good and faithful servant,
because thou hast been faithful over a few
things, I will place thee over many things :

enter thou into the joy of thy lord. And
he also that had received the two talents
came and said : Lord, thou deliverest two
talents to me : behold I have gained other
two. His lord said to him : Well done, good
and faithful servant : because thou hast
been faithful over a few things, I will
place thee over many things : enter thou
into the joy of thy lord.

ST. JOSEPH

March 19

LESSON. *Ecclus.* xlv, 1–6. He was beloved
of God and men, whose memory is in
benediction ; he made him like the saints
in glory, and magnified him in the fear of
his enemies ; and with his words he made
prodigies to cease ; he glorified him in the
sight of kings, and gave him commandments in the sight of his people, and shewed
him his glory ; he sanctified him in his
faith and meekness, and chose him out of
all flesh ; for he heard him and his voice,
and brought him into a cloud ; and he gave
him commandments before his face, and a
law of life and instruction.

GOSPEL. *Matthew* i, 18–21. When Mary
the Mother of Jesus was espoused to Joseph,
she was found with child of the Holy Ghost.
Whereupon Joseph her husband, being a
just man, and not willing publicly to

expose her, was minded to put her away privately. But while he thought on these things, behold the Angel of the Lord appeared to him in his sleep, saying, Joseph, Son of David, fear not to take unto thee Mary thy wife, for that which is conceived in her is of the Holy Ghost. And she shall bring forth a son, and thou shalt call his name Jesus. For he shall save his people from their sins.

SS. PETER AND PAUL
June 29

LESSON. *Acts* xii, 1–11. *In those days :* Herod the king stretched forth his hands to afflict some of the church. And he killed James, the brother of John, with the sword. And seeing that it pleased the Jews, he proceeded to take up Peter also. Now it was the days of azymes. And when he had apprehended him, he cast him into prison, delivering him to four files of soldiers to be kept, intending, after the pasch, to bring him forth to the people. Peter therefore was kept in prison. But prayer was made without ceasing by the church unto God for him. And when Herod would have brought him forth, the same night Peter was sleeping between two soldiers, bound with two chains : and the keepers before the door kept the prison. And behold an angel of the Lord stood by him : and a light shined in the room : and he striking Peter on the side, raised him up, saying : Arise quickly. And the chains fell off from his hands. And the angel said to him : Gird thyself, and put on thy sandals. And he did so. And he said to him : Cast thy garment about thee, and follow me. And going out, he followed him, and he knew not that it was true which was done by the angel : but thought he saw a vision. And passing through the first and the second ward, they came to the iron gate that leadeth to the city, which of itself opened to them. And going out, they passed on through one street : and immediately the angel departed from him. And Peter coming to himself, said : Now I know in very deed, that the Lord hath sent His angel, and hath delivered me out of the hand of Herod, and from all the expectation of the people of the Jews.

GOSPEL. *Matthew* xvi, 13–19. *At that time :* Jesus came into the quarters of Cesarea Philippi : and He asked His disciples, saying : Whom do men say that the Son of man is ? But they said : Some John the Baptist, and other some Elias, and others Jeremias, or one of the prophets. He saith to them : But whom do you say that I am ? Simon Peter answered and said : Thou art Christ, the Son of the living God. And Jesus answering, said to him :

Blessed art thou, Simon Bar-jona : because
flesh and blood hath not revealed it to thee,
but My Father who is in heaven. And I
say to thee : That thou art Peter, and
upon this rock I will build My church, and
the gates of hell shall not prevail against
it. And I will give to thee the keys of the
kingdom of heaven. And whatsoever thou
shalt bind upon earth, it shall be bound
also in heaven : and whatsoever thou shalt
loose on earth, it shall be loosed also in
heaven.

ASSUMPTION OF THE B. V. MARY
August 15

LESSON. *Ecclesiasticus* xxiv, 11–20. I
sought rest everywhere, and I shall abide
in the inheritance of the Lord. Then the
Creator of all things commanded, and said
to me : and He that made Me, rested in
my tabernacle, and He said to me : Let thy
dwelling be in Jacob, and thy inheritance
in Israel, and take root in My elect. From
the beginning, and before the world,
was I created, and unto the world to come
I shall not cease to be, and in the holy
dwelling place I have ministered before
him. And so was I established in Sion, and
in the holy city likewise I rested, and my
power was in Jerusalem. And I took root
in an honourable people, and in the portion
of my God His inheritance, and my abode

is in the full assembly of saints. I was exalted like a cedar in Libanus, and as a cypress tree on Mount Sion. I was exalted like a palm tree in Cades, and as a rose plant in Jericho : as a fair olive tree in the plains, and as a plane tree by the water in the streets, was I exalted. I gave a sweet smell like cinnamon, and aromatical balm : I yielded a sweet odour like the best myrrh.

GOSPEL. *Luke* x, 38–42. *At that time :* Jesus entered into a certain town : and a certain woman named Martha, received Him into her house. And she had a sister called Mary, who sitting also at the Lord's feet, heard His word. But Martha was busy about much serving. Who stood and said : Lord, hast Thou no care that my sister hath left me alone to serve ? Speak to her therefore, that she help me. And the Lord answering, said to her : Martha, Martha, thou art careful, and art troubled about many things : but one thing is necessary. Mary hath chosen the best part, which shall not be taken away from her.

THE KINGSHIP OF OUR LORD
Last Sunday in October

LESSON. *Colossians* i, 12–20. *Brethren :* We give thanks unto God the Father, who hath made us worthy to be partakers of the lot of the Saints in light, who hath delivered us from the power of darkness, and hath translated us into the Kingdom of the Son of His love, in whom we have redemption through His blood, the remission of sins ; who is the image of the invisible God, the first-born of every creature ; for in Him were all things created in heaven, and on earth, visible and invisible, whether thrones, or dominations, or principalities, or powers, all things were created by Him and in Him, and He is before all, and in Him all things consist. And He is the head of the body, the Church, who is the beginning, the first-born from the dead ; that in all things He may hold the primacy ; because in Him it hath well pleased the Father that all fulness should dwell ; and through Him to reconcile all things unto Himself, making peace through the blood of His cross, both as to the things on earth, and the things that are in heaven, in Christ Jesus our Lord.

GOSPEL. *John* xviii, 33–37. *At that time :* Pilate said unto Jesus, Art Thou the King of the Jews ; Jesus answered : Sayest thou this of thyself, or did others tell it thee of Me ? Pilate answered : Am I a Jew ? Thine own nation and the chief priests have delivered Thee unto me ; what hast Thou done ? Jesus answered : My kingdom is not of this world. If My kingdom were of this world, My servants would indeed fight, that I might not be delivered to the Jews ; but now is My kingdom not from hence. Therefore Pilate said unto Him : Art Thou a King then ? Jesus answered : Thou sayest, because I am a King. For this was I born, and for this cause came I into the world, that I might bear witness to the truth. Every one that is of the truth heareth My voice.

FEAST OF ALL SAINTS
November 1

LESSON. *Apocalypse* vii, 2–12. *In those days :* Behold I, John, saw another angel ascending from the rising of the sun, having the sign of the living God ; and he cried with a loud voice to the four angels, to whom it was given to hurt the earth and the sea, saying : Hurt not the earth, nor the sea, nor the trees, till we sign the servants of our God in their foreheads. And I heard the number of them that were signed, an hundred forty-four thousand were signed, of every tribe of the children of Israel. Of the tribe of Judah, *were* twelve thousand signed : Of the tribe of Reuben, twelve thousand signed : Of the tribe of Gad, twelve thousand signed : Of the tribe of Aser, twelve thousand signed : Of the tribe of Nepthali, twelve thousand signed : Of the tribe of Manasses, twelve thousand signed : Of the tribe of Simeon, twelve thousand signed : Of the tribe of Levi, twelve thousand signed : Of the tribe of Issachar, twelve thousand signed : Of the tribe of Zabulon, twelve thousand signed : Of the tribe of Joseph, twelve thousand signed : Of the tribe of Benjamin, twelve thousand signed. After this I saw a great multitude, which no man could number, of all nations, and tribes ; and peoples, and tongues, standing before the throne, and in sight of the Lamb, clothed with white robes, and palms in their hands : and they cried with a loud voice, saying : Salvation to our God, who sitteth upon the throne, and to the Lamb. And all the angels stood round about the throne, and the ancients, and the four living creatures ; and they fell down before the throne upon their faces, and adored God, saying : Amen. Benediction, and glory, and wisdom, and thanksgiving, honour, and power, and strength to our God for ever and ever. Amen.

GOSPEL. *Matthew* v, 1-12. *At that time :* Jesus seeing the multitude, went up into a mountain, and when He was set down, His disciples came unto Him. And opening His mouth, He taught them, saying : Blessed are the poor in spirit : for theirs is the kingdom of heaven. Blessed are the meek : for they shall possess the land. Blessed are they that mourn : for they shall be comforted. Blessed are they that hunger and thirst after justice : for they shall have their fill. Blessed are the merciful : for they shall obtain mercy. Blessed are the clean of heart : for they shall see God. Blessed are the peacemakers : for they shall be called the children of God. Blessed are they that suffer persecution for justice' sake : for theirs is the kingdom of heaven. Blessed are ye when they shall revile you, and persecute you, and speak all that is evil against you, untruly, for My sake : Be glad and rejoice, for your reward is very great in heaven.

THE END

ALPHABETICAL INDEX

¶ HERE ENDS THIS
NEW EDITION OF BISHOP
CHALLONER'S
GARDEN OF THE SOUL

LAUS DEO

AH MISER EST SAPIENS
QUI SAPIT ABSQUE
DEO

CPSIA information can be obtained
at www.ICGtesting.com
Printed in the USA
BVHW041520140222
628969BV00011B/377